Visio Professional 2007: Basic

Student Manual

Visio Professional 2007: Basic

Series Product Managers:	Charles G. Blum and Adam A. Wilcox
Writer:	Dave Fink
Developmental Editor:	Steve English
Copyeditor:	Catherine Oliver
Keytester:	Cliff Coryea
Series Designer:	Adam A. Wilcox

For more information, go to www.axzopress.com.

Trademarks

Disclaimer

Student Manual
ISBN-10: 1-4239-5146-8
ISBN-13: 978-1-4239-5146-9

Student Manual with data CD
ISBN-10: 1-4239-5148-4
ISBN-13: 978-1-4239-5148-3

Printed in the United States of America

1 2 3 4 5 6 7 8 9 10 GL 09 08 07

Contents

Introduction

After reading this introduction, you will know how to:

A Use ILT Series manuals in general.

B Use prerequisites, a target student description, course objectives, and a skills inventory to properly set your expectations for the course.

C Re-key this course after class.

Topic A: About the manual

ILT Series philosophy

Our manuals facilitate your learning by providing structured interaction with the software itself. While we provide text to explain difficult concepts, the hands-on activities are the focus of our courses. By paying close attention as your instructor leads you through these activities, you will learn the skills and concepts effectively.

We believe strongly in the instructor-led class. During class, focus on your instructor. Our manuals are designed and written to facilitate your interaction with your instructor, and not to call attention to manuals themselves.

We believe in the basic approach of setting expectations, delivering instruction, and providing summary and review afterwards. For this reason, lessons begin with objectives and end with summaries. We also provide overall course objectives and a course summary to provide both an introduction to and closure on the entire course.

Manual components

The manuals contain these major components:

- Table of contents
- Introduction
- Units
- Course summary
- Quick reference
- Glossary
- Index

Each element is described below.

Table of contents

The table of contents acts as a learning roadmap.

Introduction

The introduction contains information about our training philosophy and our manual components, features, and conventions. It contains target student, prerequisite, objective, and setup information for the specific course.

Units

Units are the largest structural component of the course content. A unit begins with a title page that lists objectives for each major subdivision, or topic, within the unit. Within each topic, conceptual and explanatory information alternates with hands-on activities. Units conclude with a summary comprising one paragraph for each topic, and an independent practice activity that gives you an opportunity to practice the skills you've learned.

The conceptual information takes the form of text paragraphs, exhibits, lists, and tables. The activities are structured in two columns, one telling you what to do, the other providing explanations, descriptions, and graphics.

Course summary

This section provides a text summary of the entire course. It is useful for providing closure at the end of the course. The course summary also indicates the next course in this series, if there is one, and lists additional resources you might find useful as you continue to learn about the software.

Quick reference

The quick reference is an at-a-glance job aid summarizing some of the more common features of the software.

Glossary

The glossary provides definitions for all of the key terms used in this course.

Index

The index at the end of this manual makes it easy for you to find information about a particular software component, feature, or concept.

Manual conventions

We've tried to keep the number of elements and the types of formatting to a minimum in the manuals. This aids in clarity and makes the manuals more classically elegant looking. But there are some conventions and icons you should know about.

Item	Description
Italic text	In conceptual text, indicates a new term or feature.
Bold text	In unit summaries, indicates a key term or concept. In an independent practice activity, indicates an explicit item that you select, choose, or type.
`Code font`	Indicates code or syntax.

`Longer strings of ►`
`code will look ►`
`like this.`
	In the hands-on activities, any code that's too long to fit on a single line is divided into segments by one or more continuation characters (►). This code should be entered as a continuous string of text.

Select **bold item**	In the left column of hands-on activities, bold sans-serif text indicates an explicit item that you select, choose, or type.
Keycaps like ↵ ENTER	Indicate a key on the keyboard you must press.

Hands-on activities

The hands-on activities are the most important parts of our manuals. They are divided into two primary columns. The "Here's how" column gives short instructions to you about what to do. The "Here's why" column provides explanations, graphics, and clarifications. Here's a sample:

Do it!

A-1: Creating a commission formula

Here's how	Here's why
1 Open Sales	This is an oversimplified sales compensation worksheet. It shows sales totals, commissions, and incentives for five sales reps.
2 Observe the contents of cell F4	F4 = =E4*C Rate The commission rate formulas use the name "C_Rate" instead of a value for the commission rate.

For these activities, we have provided a collection of data files designed to help you learn each skill in a real-world business context. As you work through the activities, you will modify and update these files. Of course, you might make a mistake and therefore want to re-key the activity starting from scratch. To make it easy to start over, you will rename each data file at the end of the first activity in which the file is modified. Our convention for renaming files is to add the word "My" to the beginning of the file name. In the above activity, for example, a file called "Sales" is being used for the first time. At the end of this activity, you would save the file as "My sales," thus leaving the "Sales" file unchanged. If you make a mistake, you can start over using the original "Sales" file.

In some activities, however, it might not be practical to rename the data file. If you want to retry one of these activities, ask your instructor for a fresh copy of the original data file.

Topic B: Setting your expectations

Properly setting your expectations is essential to your success. This topic will help you do that by providing:

- Prerequisites for this course
- A description of the target student
- A list of the objectives for the course
- A skills assessment for the course

Course prerequisites

Before taking this course, you should be familiar with personal computers and the use of a keyboard and a mouse. Furthermore, this course assumes that you've completed the following courses or have equivalent experience:

- *Windows XP: Basic* or *Windows Vista: Basic*

Target student

This course is for students who have little or no Visio experience. You will get the most out of the course if your goal is to become proficient in creating flow diagrams, basic organization charts, and network diagrams.

Course objectives

These overall course objectives will give you an idea about what to expect from the course. It is also possible that they will help you see that this course is not the right one for you. If you think you either lack the prerequisite knowledge or already know most of the subject matter to be covered, you should let your instructor know that you think you are misplaced in the class.

After completing this course, you will know how to:

- Create and navigate in a file; use Visio Help; manipulate windows and stencils; and select, scale, and resize objects.
- Draw and reshape objects; work with compound lines; duplicate objects; and align, distribute, group, and rotate objects.
- Plan a flowchart; use master shapes; connect shapes in a diagram; use basic text features; and create a simple organization chart.
- Use various text formatting options; format text blocks; and format shapes and lines.
- Set file properties for a new drawing; create background pages; work with detail pages and links; use Print Preview mode; and print a diagram.
- Create network, rack, and brainstorming diagrams.
- Use advanced connection and layout techniques; set custom properties for shapes; and create and modify property reports.

Skills inventory

Use the following form to gauge your skill level entering the class. For each skill listed, rate your familiarity from 1 to 5, with five being the most familiar. *This is not a test*. Rather, it is intended to provide you with an idea of where you're starting from at the beginning of class. If you're wholly unfamiliar with all the skills, you might not be ready for the class. If you think you already understand all of the skills, you might need to move on to the next course in the series. In either case, you should let your instructor know as soon as possible.

Skill	1	2	3	4	5
Creating a new file					
Using Visio Help					
Navigating in a Visio file					
Modifying stencils					
Selecting, scaling, and resizing objects					
Drawing objects and changing their size					
Working with compound lines					
Duplicating objects					
Aligning, distributing, grouping, and rotating objects					
Planning a flowchart					
Using master shapes					
Connecting shapes in a diagram					
Using basic text features					
Creating an organization chart					
Using various text formatting options					
Formatting text blocks					
Formatting shapes and lines					
Setting file properties for a new drawing					
Creating background pages					
Working with detail pages and links					
Using Print Preview mode					
Printing a diagram					

Skill	1	2	3	4	5
Creating network diagrams					
Creating rack and directory service diagrams					
Creating brainstorming diagrams					
Using advanced connection and layout techniques					
Setting custom properties for shapes					
Creating and modifying property reports					

Topic C: Re-keying the course

If you have the proper hardware and software, you can re-key this course after class. This section explains what you'll need in order to do so, and how to do it.

Hardware requirements

Your personal computer should have:

- A keyboard and a mouse
- 500 MHz processor (or higher)
- At least 256 MB RAM
- At least 1.5 GB of available hard disk space
- CD-ROM or DVD drive
- SVGA monitor (1024×768 or higher resolution)

Software requirements

- Windows XP, Windows Vista, or Windows Server 2003, updated with the most recent service packs
- Microsoft Visio Professional 2007
- Microsoft Excel 2000 or later (If this is not installed, you will not be able to complete activity C-4 in the unit titled "Working with pages.")
- A printer driver (An actual printer is not required, but if a printer driver is not installed, you will not be able to complete activities A-2, D-1, or D-2 in the unit titled "Working with pages.")

Network requirements

The following network components and connectivity are also required for rekeying this course:

- Internet access, for the following purposes:
  - Downloading the latest critical updates and service packs from www.windowsupdate.com
  - Downloading the Student Data files from www.courseilt.com (if necessary)

Setup instructions to re-key the course

Before you re-key the course, you will need to perform the following steps.

1 If necessary, download the latest critical updates and service packs from www.windowsupdate.com.

2 From the Control Panel, open the Display Properties dialog box and apply the following settings:

- Theme — Windows XP
- Screen resolution — 1024 by 768 pixels
- Color quality — High (24 bit) or higher

If you choose not to apply these display settings, your screens might not match the screen shots in this manual.

3 If necessary, reset any Visio Professional 2007 defaults that you have changed. To do this, insert the Visio installation CD, select Repair in the Startup window, and click Continue. If you do not wish to reset the defaults, you can still re-key the course, but some activities might not work exactly as documented.

4 Verify that you have a copy of Microsoft Excel installed on your machine.

5 Create a folder named Student Data at the root of the hard drive. For a standard hard drive setup, this will be C:\Student Data.

6 Download the Student Data files for the course. (If you do not have an Internet connection, you can ask your instructor for a copy of the data files on a disk.)

a Connect to www.courseilt.com/instructor_tools.html.

b Click the link for Visio 2007 to display a page of course listings, and then click the link for Visio Professional 2007: Basic.

c Click the link for downloading the Student Data files, and follow the instructions that appear on your screen.

7 Copy the data files to the Student Data folder.

CertBlaster software

CertBlaster pre- and post-assessment software is available for this course. To download and install this free software, complete the following steps:

1 Go to www.courseilt.com/certblaster.

2 Click the link for Visio 2007.

3 Save the .EXE file to a folder on your hard drive. (Note: If you skip this step, the CertBlaster software will not install correctly.)

4 Click Start and choose Run.

5 Click Browse and then navigate to the folder that contains the .EXE file.

6 Select the .EXE file and click Open.

7 Click OK and follow the on-screen instructions. When prompted for the password, enter **c_vis07**.

Unit 1
The Visio environment

Unit time: 50 minutes

Complete this unit, and you'll know how to:

A Create a drawing and use interactive Help.

B Navigate in a Visio drawing.

C Manipulate windows and stencils.

D Select, scale, and resize objects.

Topic A: Visio basics

Explanation

Visio is an application used to create business graphics. While Visio is best known for being used to create flowcharts, you can use it for a variety of diagramming tasks. You can create organization charts, floor plans, circuit diagrams, network diagrams, and Web site maps, to name just a few. After creating diagrams in Visio, you can view them in any Web browser running Microsoft Visio Viewer, or you can use them in other Office applications, such as Word, Excel, and PowerPoint.

Visio overview

Visio is a *vector-based* illustration tool. This means that drawings are composed of mathematically computed lines. The result is sharp images that are not resolution-dependent (as bitmap images are).

Bitmap images are composed of dots that are created with pixels. A *pixel* (picture element) is the smallest unit of display of a color on a monitor. The number of pixels per square inch determines the *resolution*, or fineness of detail. The more pixels per inch an image has, the greater its resolution. High-resolution images are sharp but can result in large files. Although Visio is a vector-based application, you can include bitmap images, such as photographs, in your illustrations.

The basic drawing object in a Visio drawing is a shape. Shapes are grouped together on *stencils*. Stencils hold the basic *master shapes*, or building blocks, used for specific types of drawings. Stencils are designated by the type of drawing they're best suited for. For example, for flow diagramming, you use the flowchart stencil.

In addition, you can use drawing tools to create basic objects such as lines and boxes. By drawing and editing basic shapes, you can create different elements, which you can combine with other objects to create complex drawings.

Object attributes, known as *styles*, are used to produce special effects and add character to a drawing. Styles include colors, fill patterns, line properties, and other formats.

The Getting Started window

When you start Visio, the Getting Started window appears, as shown in Exhibit 1-1. The window is divided into three sections. The left section shows a list of template categories, the middle section shows thumbnails of the templates within a category, and the right section provides some basic information about a selected template. (The Getting Started window will not appear again during the current work session unless you choose File, New, Getting Started.)

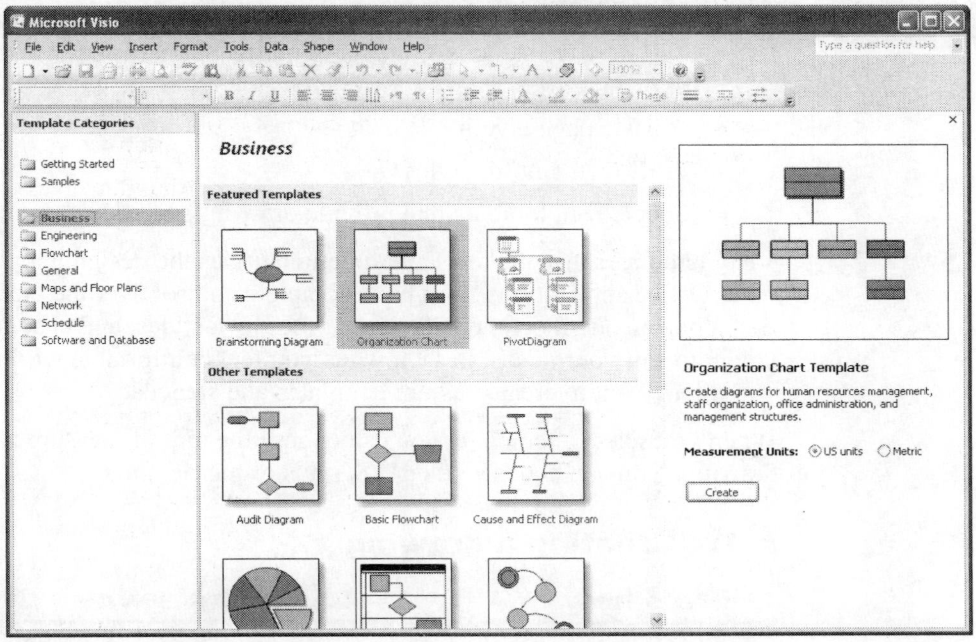

Exhibit 1-1: The Getting Started window

Template overview

Typically, a new drawing is based on a template, which provides a starting point. A template contains the basic elements needed to create certain types of diagrams or charts, as shown in Exhibit 1-2.

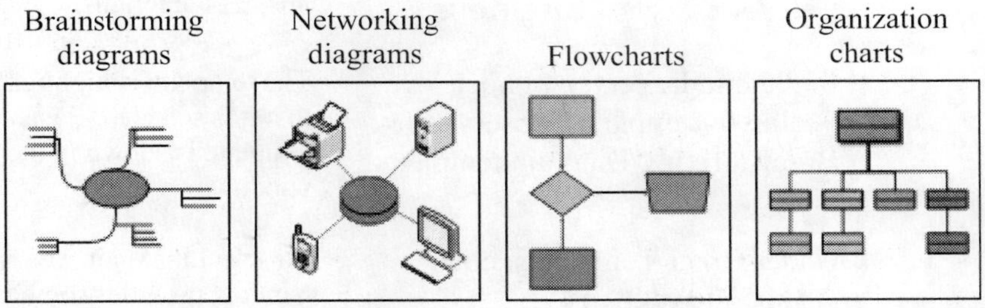

Exhibit 1-2: Sample templates in the Getting Started window

Templates typically include:

- One or more stencils, containing master shapes used in a specific type of drawing
- A basic page layout
- Line, text, and fill styles
- Specialized toolbars that provide drawing-specific commands

Visio templates provide the same functionality as the design templates provided with other Office applications. You have complete control over the elements in a template file. You can add more stencils, create your own styles, and change the starting-page layout to suit your needs. In fact, when you feel comfortable working with templates, you might want to create custom templates and stencils.

When you select a template, you can choose the unit of measure to be used in the drawing. You can choose either U.S. units or metric units.

Do it!

A-1: Creating a drawing

	Here's how	Here's why
1	Click **Start**	
	Choose **All Programs**, **Microsoft Office**, **Microsoft Office Visio 2007**	To start Microsoft Visio. The Getting Started window appears.
	Maximize the window	If necessary.
2	In the left section, under Template Categories, select **Business**	To display the various templates used to create business diagrams.
3	In the middle section, under Featured Templates, observe the Brainstorming Diagram template	The template is highlighted in orange, indicating that it is selected. Basic information about the template is shown in the right section of the window.
4	Under Other Templates, click **Basic Flowchart**	To select it. Again, the right section of the window provides some basic information about the selected template.
	In the right section, verify that US units is selected	
	Click **Create**	To create a new drawing based on the Basic Flowchart template.

The work area

Explanation

The *work area* is divided into two main sections, as shown in Exhibit 1-3. The section on the left is the *Shapes window*, which contains the stencils associated with a selected template. You can move this window. The other section is the *drawing page*, named Page-1 by default. The elements of the work area are listed in the following table:

Element	Description
Toolbars	Display buttons representing various commands and features. Each toolbar contains buttons with related functions.
Shapes window	Displays the stencils associated with the selected template. Each stencil is specialized for a specific type of drawing. You can open multiple stencils with each drawing.
Status bar	Displays statistical information (such as a shape's size and position) about objects and shapes as they are selected and placed in the drawing. The display is interactive and is based on the current operation.
Page tabs	Used to switch between pages in a multi-page drawing. To switch to a different page, click one of the tabs. You can also use the navigation buttons to the left to scroll page tabs.
Rulers	Display measurement units to help you precisely position objects in a drawing. Rulers also provide access to guides that help you align objects and shapes while drawing.
Grid	Acts as an extension of the ruler and divides the page into small squares based on the ruler divisions. Use the grid to align shapes and objects as you place them on the drawing page.

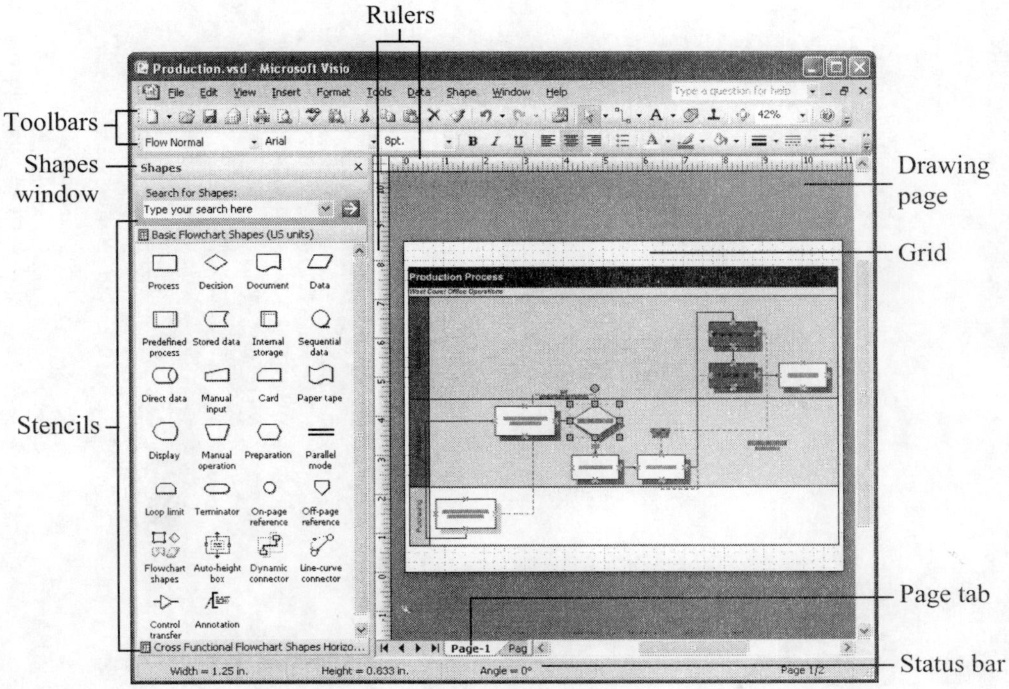

Exhibit 1-3: The work area

Do it!

A-2: Examining the work area

Here's how	Here's why
1 Observe the drawing page	By default, the grid is visible. You can use the grid to position drawing objects.
2 Observe the page tab	(At the bottom of the drawing page.) It displays Page-1, the default name of the active page.
3 Observe the toolbars	By default, the Standard and Formatting toolbars appear when you start Visio.
4 Observe the rulers	They also help you position drawing objects accurately.

Visio Help

Explanation

As you begin to work with Visio on your own, you'll likely encounter windows or stencil objects that you aren't familiar with. There are several ways you can get information about Visio components and techniques.

One way to get more information about components of the Visio environment is to use interactive ScreenTips, which appear when you point to toolbar buttons or stencil shapes, as shown in Exhibit 1-4. In addition, the status bar often provides information about shapes as you position and manipulate them.

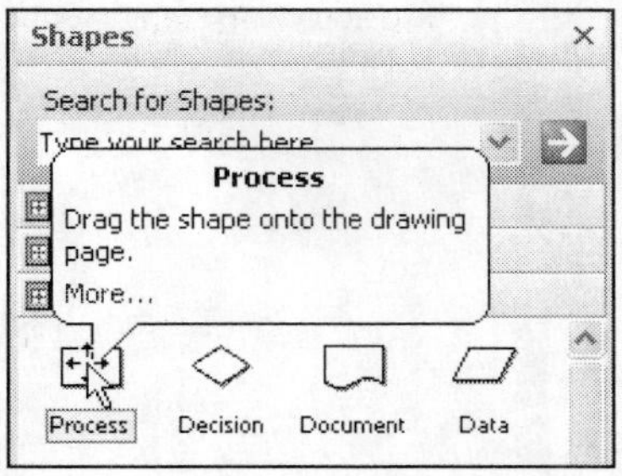

Exhibit 1-4: An example of a ScreenTip

Another way to get more information about Visio is to use Visio's Help system, which is an interactive HTML window that blends traditional Help dialog boxes and the look of an HTML browser, as shown in Exhibit 1-5. You can open the Visio Help window by choosing Help, Microsoft Office Visio Help or by clicking the "More" links in ScreenTips.

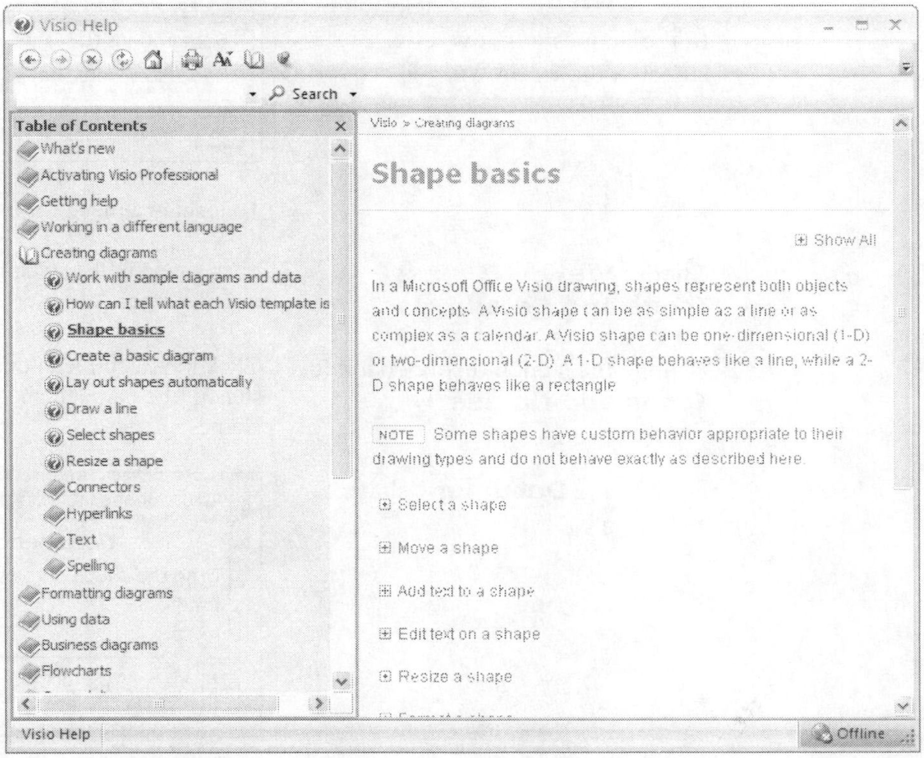

Exhibit 1-5: The Visio Help window

Changing the stencil display

For stencil shapes, you can view additional information by changing the way the shapes are displayed. You can click the small stencil icon on the left side of a stencil's title bar and choose an option from the View submenu, as shown in Exhibit 1-6. You can also change views by displaying the Stencil toolbar and clicking one of the view buttons.

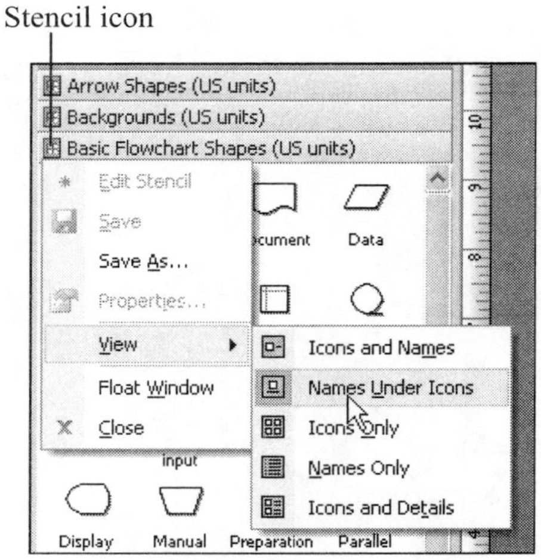

Exhibit 1-6: Changing the stencil display

Do it!

A-3: Using Visio Help

Here's how	Here's why
1 In the Shapes window, click the stencil icon, as shown	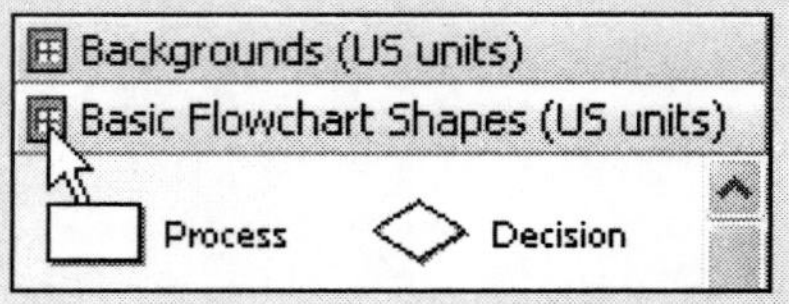 To display a menu for that stencil.
Choose **View, Icons and Details**	Each shape in the stencil now shows some basic instructions.
2 Change the stencil display back to **Icons and Names**	Click the stencil icon on the left side of the stencil title bar, and choose View, Icons and Names.
3 Point to the **Document** shape, as shown	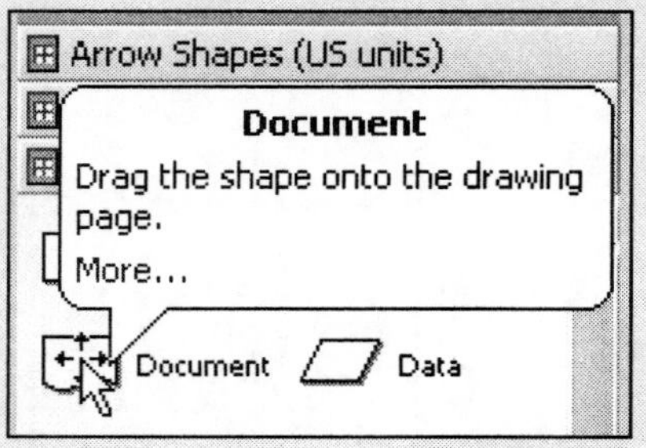 A ScreenTip for the selected shape appears, showing the same basic instructions.

4 In the ScreenTip, click **More**	To open the Visio Help window.
5 Maximize the window	If necessary.
6 On the toolbar, click 	(The Show Table of Contents button.) To show the contents of the Help system, organized by topics.
7 Under Table of Contents, click **Creating diagrams**	To display subtopics and documents for shapes and text.
8 Click **Shape basics**	The information appears in the new Help window.
9 Read the information	The Help system provides detailed information about shapes.
10 Expand the **Select a shape** category	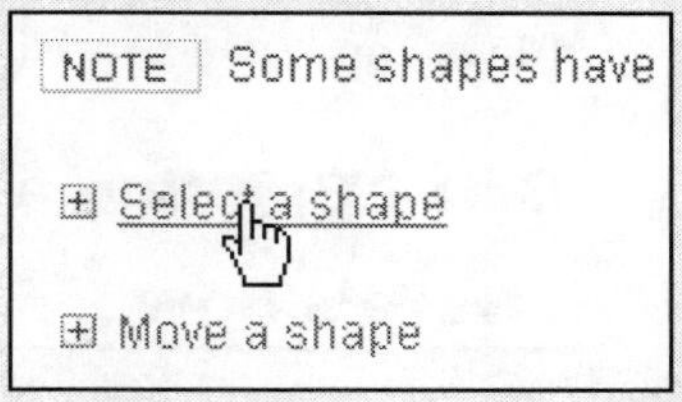 Click the text to expand it, or click the small plus sign to the left of the text.
11 Close the Visio Help window	Click the Close button in the upper-right corner of the window.

Topic B: Navigating in Visio

Explanation

Visio provides a number of tools that you can use to navigate through a drawing. To move between pages in a drawing, you can use the Go To command. You can also customize the view settings to suit your needs.

Visio file types

There are three types of Visio files: drawings (.vsd), stencils (.vss), and templates (.vst). Templates contain the associated stencils, page layout, and styles used to format shapes, text, and other drawing objects. You can use one of Visio's built-in templates, or you can create your own.

By default, the Open dialog box displays only Visio drawing files. To select a different file type, use the File types list, which includes all Visio file types as well as file types from some other applications. When you import a drawing from another application, the file is converted to Visio format.

Do it!

B-1: Opening a Visio drawing

Here's how	Here's why
1 On the Standard toolbar, click 	To open the Open dialog box. (You can also choose File, Open or press Ctrl+O.)
2 Navigate to the current unit folder	To view a list of Visio files.
3 In the upper-right corner of the Open window, click as shown	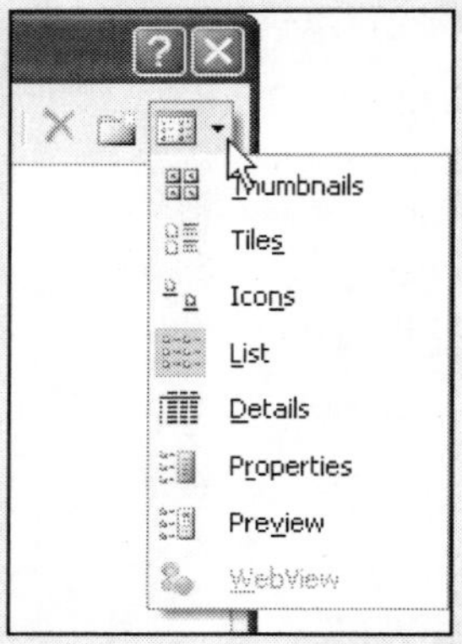 To display a menu of file viewing options.
Choose **Preview**	
4 In the document list, select **Overview.vsd**	From the list of files.
Observe the Preview area	A preview of the selected file is displayed.
5 Click **Open**	To open the file.

View settings

Explanation

As you work, you'll likely need to open or close certain windows, or zoom in and out of portions of a drawing to see things more clearly. You can perform these tasks by using toolbars and keyboard commands.

The View toolbar

One way to quickly change view settings is to use the View toolbar, shown in Exhibit 1-7. Toolbars, in general, provide a quick way to perform certain tasks more efficiently. Instead of choosing commands from menus in the menu bar, you can simply click buttons on the toolbars. By default, only the Standard and Formatting toolbars are shown, but you can open and close other toolbars by right-clicking any visible toolbar and choosing the toolbar you want from the list.

The View toolbar provides some quick ways to show or hide different aspects of the work area, as well as drawing aids. For example, you can use the toolbar to show and hide rulers and guides and to open certain windows, such as the Pan & Zoom window.

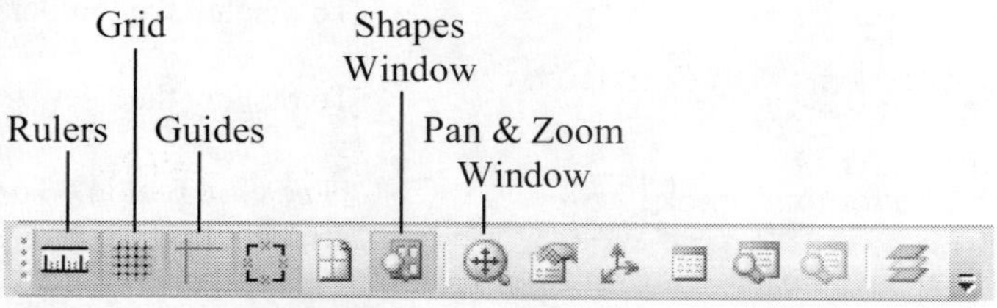

Exhibit 1-7: The View toolbar

Zooming

While working on a drawing, you'll often want to zoom in to see specific portions more clearly. One way to zoom in and out is to use the Zoom list on the Standard toolbar. You can either type a magnification value in the box, or expand the list and select a preset value, as shown in Exhibit 1-8. To expand the list, click the small black triangle on the right side of the Zoom box.

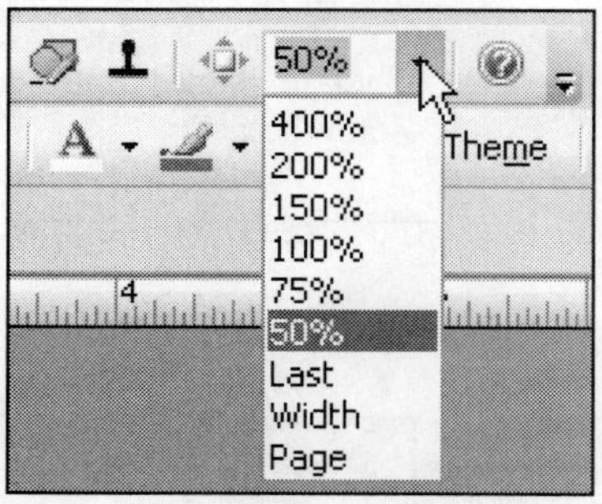

Exhibit 1-8: The Zoom list on the Standard toolbar.

You can also zoom in and out of drawings efficiently by using combined keyboard commands and mouse clicks. To zoom in, press Ctrl+Shift and click the drawing. To zoom out, press Ctrl+Shift and right-click the drawing.

Panning

You can also use *panning* to navigate a drawing. The Pan & Zoom window magnifies a portion of a drawing, and you can use the mouse to move the page freely in any direction, without using the scrollbars. To open this window, choose View, Pan & Zoom Window, or click the Pan & Zoom Window button on the View toolbar.

Do it!

- Short cut: Hold CTRL + mouse scroll to zoom
- Hold Shift key and roll mouse wheel to scroll left + right

B-2: Changing view settings

Here's how	Here's why
1 Right-click anywhere on the toolbars at the top of the work area	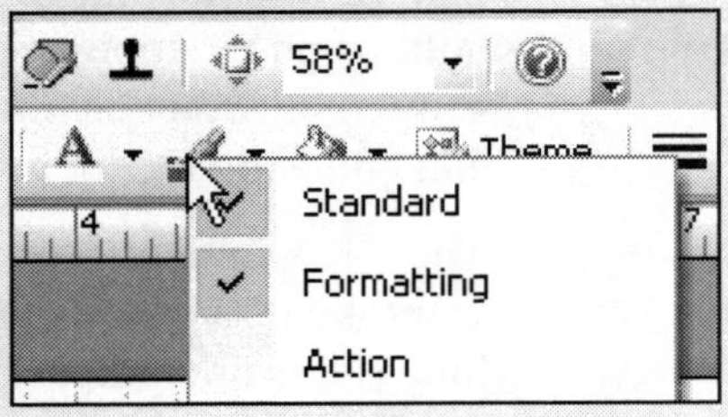 To display the toolbar list.
Choose **View**	To display the View toolbar.
2 On the toolbar, click [Grid button]	(The Grid button.) To deselect it and hide the drawing grid.
Click the button again	To show the drawing grid again.
3 On the Standard toolbar, expand the Zoom list, as shown	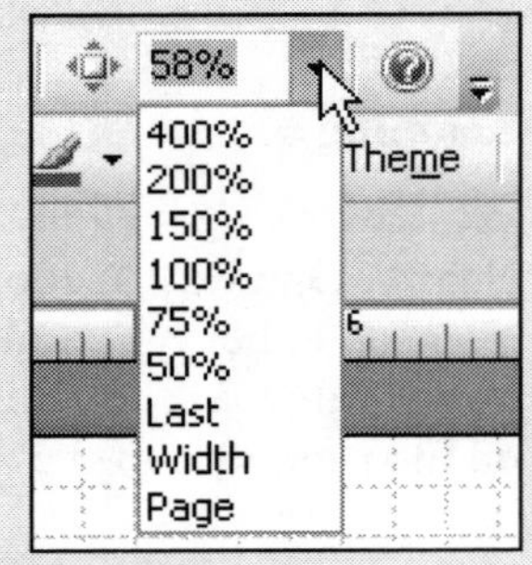 Click the small triangle on the right side of the Zoom box.
Select **150%**	To zoom in on the drawing.
4 Click the Zoom box	To select the value.
Enter **102**	 To specify a magnification value that is not available in the Zoom list.
Press ENTER	To zoom to 102% magnification.
5 From the Zoom list, select **Page**	To see the page in full view.

6	Press and hold CTRL + SHIFT	The mouse pointer changes to a magnifying glass.
	Near the center of the drawing, point to the diamond shape and click three times	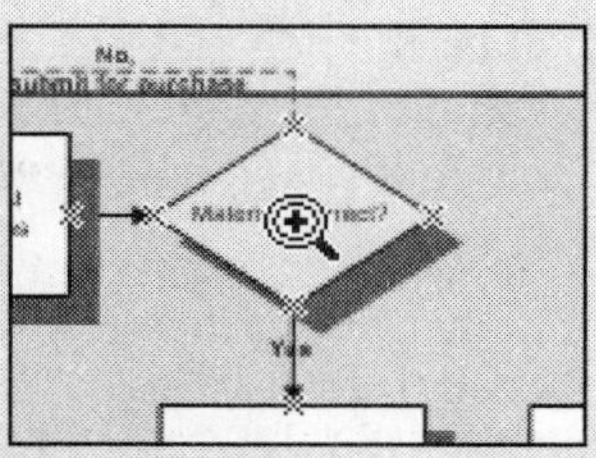 (While continuing to hold Ctrl+Shift.) To zoom in on the diamond shape.
7	While holding CTRL + SHIFT right-click the diamond shape twice	To zoom out. You'll now use a similar technique to reposition the drawing without using the scrollbars.
8	While holding CTRL + SHIFT, press and hold the right mouse button	
	Drag the mouse pointer across the page	(While continuing to hold Ctrl+Shift and the right mouse button.) The mouse pointer changes to a small hand and drags the page around the drawing area.
9	Release both keys and the mouse button	You can also reposition the drawing page and change magnification by using the Pan & Zoom window.
10	On the View toolbar, click 	(The Pan & Zoom Window button.) The Pan & Zoom window is docked by default in the upper-right corner. A red rectangle shows the area currently visible in the drawing window.
11	In the window, drag anywhere within the red rectangle	To reposition the drawing.
	On the right side of the window, drag the zoom slider up and down	To change the magnification.
12	Close the Pan & Zoom window	Click the small "x" in the lower-right corner.
13	View the entire page again	If necessary. (From the Zoom list, select Page.)

Page navigation

Explanation

Some drawings contain more than one page. To navigate through a multi-page drawing, click the page tabs at the bottom of the work area. If your file contains many pages, some of the page tabs might be hidden, and you'll have to scroll to view them. You can navigate page tabs by using the controls on the left side, as shown in Exhibit 1-9.

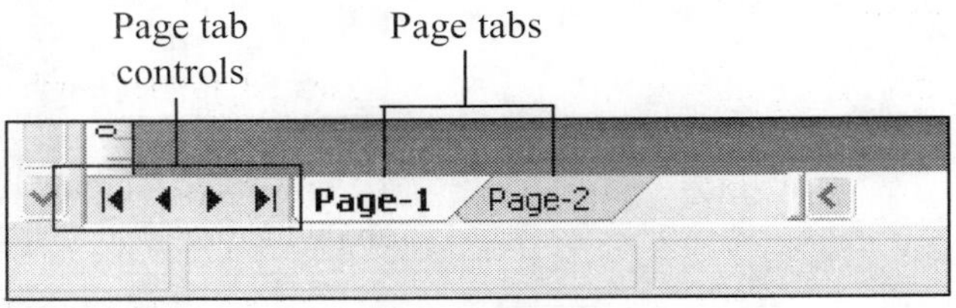

Exhibit 1-9: Page tabs and controls

You can also cycle through drawing pages by pressing Ctrl+Page Up, Ctrl+Page Down, or Ctrl+Alt+Tab.

Renaming drawing pages

By default, pages are numbered (Page-1, Page-2, etc), but you can rename them more descriptively. Renaming pages is useful if the drawing has many pages, because you can locate the exact chart or diagram you want based on the page title instead of cycling through to find the one you want.

To rename a page:

1 Right-click the page tab you want to rename.

2 From the shortcut menu, choose Rename.

3 Type a new name for the page tab.

4 Press Enter.

Do it!

* To INSERT A Page (Like a worksheet in Excel)

B-3: Navigating among drawing pages

Here's how	Here's why
1 At the bottom of the drawing area, click the **Page-2** tab	To switch to the second page.
2 Press CTRL+PAGE DOWN	To switch to the third page.
Press CTRL+PAGE DOWN again	To switch to the fourth page.
3 Observe the page tabs	As you moved through the pages, some of the page tabs became hidden (Page-1 and Page-2).
4 In the page controls, click the back arrow, as shown	 To see the Page-2 tab again.
Click the back arrow again	To see the Page-1 tab.
5 Click the **Page-1** tab	To return to the first page.
	You'll rename the first page.
6 Right-click the **Page-1** tab	To display the shortcut menu.
Choose **Rename Page**	
7 Type **Production** and press ENTER	To specify a new name for the page.

Topic C: Using windows and stencils

Explanation

As you work with Visio, you'll likely want to change the default layout of windows and stencils.

Anchored windows vs. docked windows

As you might have already noticed, there are variations in the way that windows snap to the edges of the work area. You can either dock windows or anchor them. A *docked* window is attached to an edge of the work area, and the window stretches across the entire height or width of the screen, regardless of the content. The default position of the Shapes window is an example of a docked window.

An *anchored* window is similarly attached to the edge of the work area, but you can change the width and height of the window. Also, you can temporarily hide or expand anchored windows by clicking the AutoHide button, shown in Exhibit 1-10. With AutoHide activated, the window's contents are shown only when you point to the window. When you point outside the window, it automatically collapses.

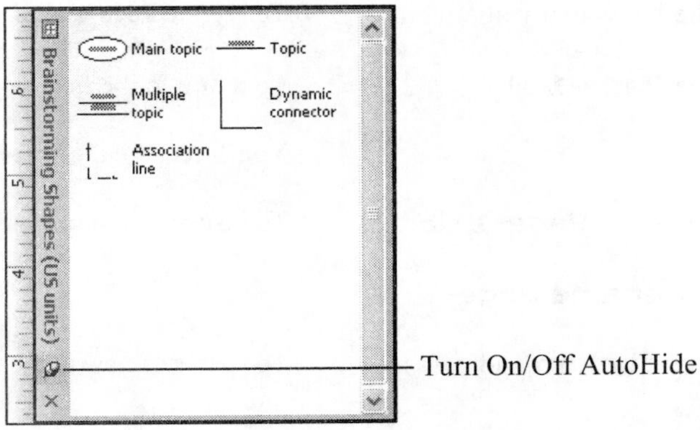

Exhibit 1-10: An anchored window

Manipulating windows

You can manipulate windows in the following ways:

- To float a docked or anchored window, drag its title bar toward the center of the work area. You can also right-click the window's title bar and choose Float window. After you've floated a window, you can position it anywhere in the work area. However, if you drag too close to an edge of the work area, the window will automatically snap to that edge and will be either anchored or docked. To prevent this from happening, press and hold Ctrl as you drag.
- To anchor a floated window, slowly drag it toward an edge of the work area until it snaps into place.
- To dock a floated window, drag it past the edge of the work area. You can also right-click the window's title bar and choose Dock Window.

Stencils

Each time you create a drawing based on a template, only the stencils associated with the template are shown. You can open new stencils by choosing them from the File, Shapes submenu. To close a stencil, right-click its title bar and choose Close. By default, open stencils are grouped together in the Shapes window, and only one set of stencil shapes is visible at a time. To switch stencils, click the title bar of the stencil you want to view.

You can also manipulate stencils by using the same techniques you use to manipulate windows. For example, to float a stencil, drag its title bar from the Shapes window to the center of the work area. After you've floated a stencil, you can anchor or dock it the same way you would anchor or dock other windows. You can also regroup stencils by dragging them back into the Shapes window.

Do it!

Adding Shapes: Navigate to desired shapes and then click and drag to display w/o changing stencils. Dock it (attach) to ruler by dragging right next to ruler. It will hide when not in use.

C-1: Manipulating stencils

Here's how	Here's why
1 Observe the Shapes window	Two stencils are open: Basic Flowchart Shapes and Network and Peripherals. The shapes in the Basic Flowchart Shapes stencil are visible.
2 Click the title bar of the **Network and Peripherals** stencil	The title bar for the Basic Flowchart Shapes stencil drops to the bottom of the window, and the shapes in the Network and Peripherals stencil are shown.
3 At the bottom of the window, click the title bar of the **Basic Flowchart Shapes** stencil	To view the stencil again. You can open and close stencils as you need them.
4 Choose **File**, **Shapes**, **Business**, **Brainstorming**	To display a submenu of the stencils in this group.
From the submenu, choose **Brainstorming Shapes (US units)**	To open the Brainstorming Shapes stencil. The three stencils are grouped in the Shapes window. You can float and/or anchor the entire window, or float and/or anchor the stencils individually. First, you'll float the Shapes window.
5 Double-click the title bar of the Shapes window, as shown	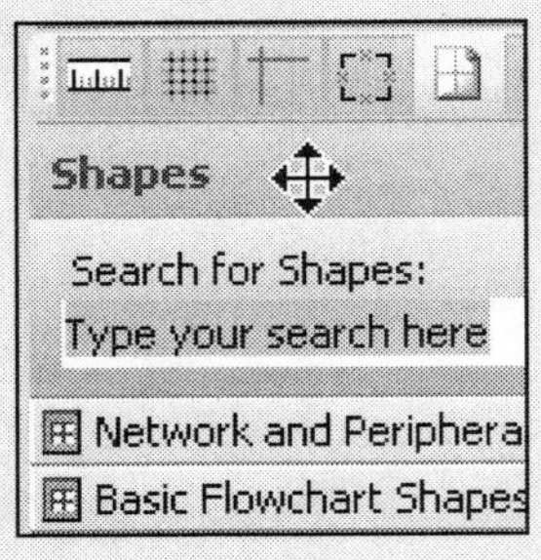 The Shapes window changes to a small window that you can move around the screen and resize as needed.
6 Press CTRL and drag the window to the center of the drawing area	Pressing Ctrl as you drag prevents the window from docking to other parts of the work area.
7 Double-click the title bar again	To dock the Shapes window. Next, you'll float one of the stencils.
8 Drag the title bar of the Brainstorming Shapes stencil to the right, toward the center of the drawing area	As you drag, the stencil breaks away from the Shapes window and becomes a small floating window. You'll anchor the stencil to the left edge of the drawing area.

TIP
View | Pan and Zoom
then drag red box to Zoom in on certain areas.

9 Slowly drag the floating stencil window to the left until it snaps to the left edge of the drawing area, as shown

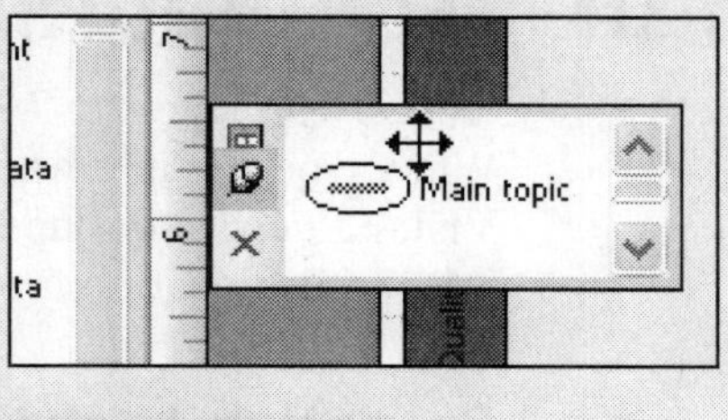

10 Drag the bottom-right corner of the window down and to the right

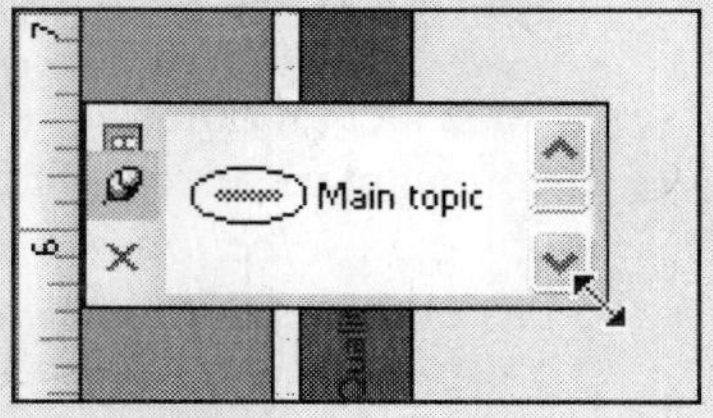

To enlarge the window and view the stencil shapes.

11 In the lower-left corner of the window, click [button]

The Turn On AutoHide button.

12 Point away from the anchored window

When you move the pointer away, the window automatically collapses so that just the title bar is visible.

Point to the **Brainstorming Shapes** title bar

To expand the window again.

13 Using the title bar, drag the Brainstorming Shapes stencil back to the Shapes window

So that the stencil is docked again with the other two stencils.

Topic D: Manipulating objects

Explanation

When working in drawings, you need to select objects before you can change them. In Visio, *objects* are shapes, connector lines, or any other items in the drawing. After you select an object or a group of objects, you can move or resize them.

TIP
Hold shift key down to select multiple shapes

Selection techniques

To select an object, first verify that the Pointer tool is selected and then click the object you want to select. (The Pointer tool is on the Standard toolbar.) When you select an object, a *selection box* appears around it, as shown in Exhibit 1-11. The selection box has eight *selection handles.* You can use the handles to resize or rotate the object.

*The one (shape) selected first matters.

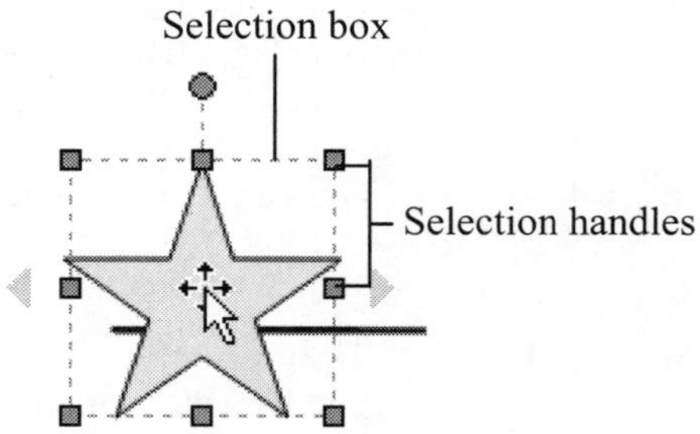

Exhibit 1-11: A selected object

Sometimes you might want to select more than one object. For example, you might want to move them simultaneously or change their color. Instead of selecting and changing each object individually, you can select them all and then make the changes.

You can select multiple objects by:

- Holding the Shift key as you click the objects
- Dragging a marquee around the objects
- Using the Multiple Select tool, which is located in the Pointer Tool list

Moving an object

After selecting one or more objects, you can drag them to a new location in the drawing. When you want to move an object, remember to point to the middle of the object. Otherwise, if the pointer gets too close to a selection handle, you might accidentally resize the object instead of moving it. If you inadvertently resize or move an object, press Ctrl+Z to undo the change, or click the Undo button on the Standard toolbar.

Do it!

D-1: Selecting and moving objects

Here's how	Here's why
1 Open Selection.vsd	From the current unit folder.
2 On the Standard toolbar, click [Pointer tool button]	(If necessary.) To ensure that the Pointer tool is selected.

Like Edit undo button (takes you back a step.

Step	Do it!	Here's why
3	Click the yellow star	To select it. Green selection handles appear around the shape.
4	Drag the selected star to the bottom of the drawing	
5	Press CTRL + Z	To undo the move.
6	Point between the blue triangle and the star	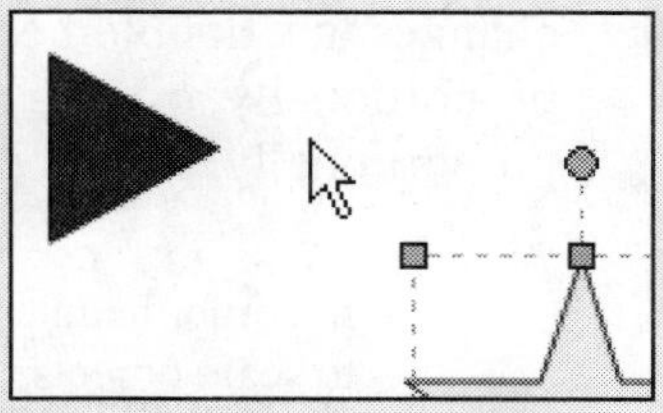 You'll drag to select the star, square, polygon, and line shapes.
7	Drag the pointer diagonally (down and to the right) to select the three shapes and the line	(Do not include the text.) A pink border appears around each object, and green selection handles appear around the entire group of objects.
8	Point to the square	It's always best to drag from the middle of the selected object or group.
	Drag the objects below the text	
9	Click a blank area of the drawing	To deselect the objects. Next, you'll practice using the Multiple Select tool to select multiple objects.
10	On the Standard toolbar, display the Pointer tool menu, as shown	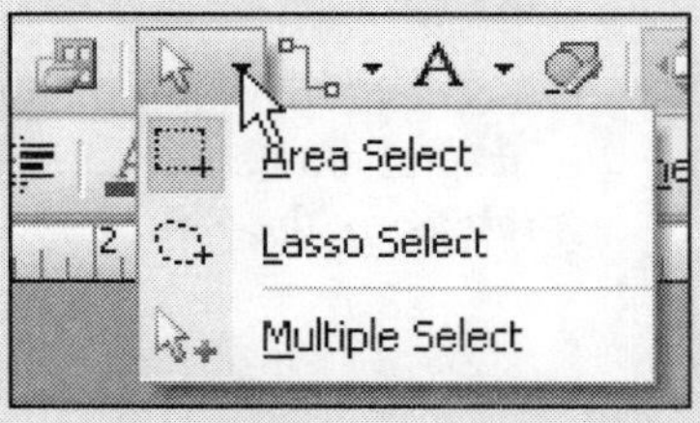
	Choose **Multiple Select**	To select the Multiple Select tool. The Pointer tool icon changes to the Multiple Select icon.
11	Click the star, square, line, and polygon shapes	To select all of these objects.
	Move the objects above the text	
12	Deselect the objects	Click a blank area of the drawing.

Scaling and resizing

Explanation

Scaling and resizing are actions you perform by dragging an object's selection handles, shown in Exhibit 1-12. Scaling maintains the height-to-width proportions, while resizing changes the size without maintaining the proportions.

Scaling an object

To scale an object, select it and point to any corner selection handle until the pointer changes to a double-headed arrow. Then, drag away from the object to increase the size proportionally, or drag toward the center of the object to decrease the size proportionally.

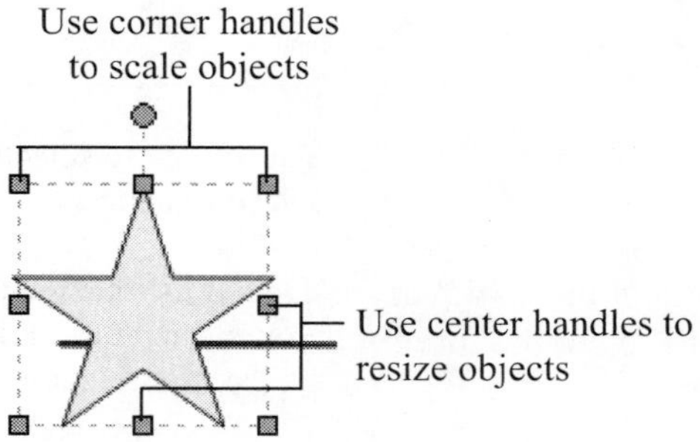

Exhibit 1-12: Scaling and resizing an object

Resizing an object

You use the center selection handles to resize an object without maintaining its proportions. This is useful if you want to stretch an object or otherwise change one of the proportions. To resize an object, point to any of the center selection handles and drag.

You can maintain the proportions of an object by holding down the Shift key and dragging a center selection handle. Remember to release the mouse button before releasing the Shift key.

Do it!

D-2: Scaling and resizing an object

Here's how	Here's why
1 Select the star	
2 Point to a corner selection handle	The pointer changes to a double-headed arrow.
Drag the handle away from the shape	(When you're done, release the mouse button.) To increase the size of the star. Notice that it's scaled proportionally.
3 Deselect the star	Click a blank area of the drawing.
4 Select the polygon	
5 Point to the center selection handle at the top of the shape	
Drag the handle up	To increase the height of the polygon.
Observe the polygon	You've increased the height without changing the width. Unlike rescaling the star, this isn't a proportional change.
Deselect the polygon	
6 Select the square	
Press and hold SHIFT	
Point to a center selection handle, and drag toward the center	(While continuing to hold Shift.) To decrease the size of the square proportionally.
Release SHIFT	
7 Release the mouse	

Saving files

Explanation

When you are working in Visio, you should save your work regularly. This is especially critical if you are working on a complex drawing. To save a file, you have two options: Save and Save As.

When you use the Save command, Visio saves the open file with its current name and in its current location. You can use the Save command on the File menu or click the Save button on the Standard toolbar.

Use the Save As command to save the active file with a different name and/or in a different location. (This creates a copy of the file, unless you're saving it for the first time.) If you're working on a new drawing that has never been saved, you'll automatically be prompted to provide a name and location for the file in the Save As dialog box.

Closing a file and Visio

When you have finished working with a file, you close it by choosing File, Close. To close Visio, choose File, Exit.

Do it!

D-3: Saving and closing a drawing

Here's how	Here's why
1 Choose **File**, **Save As...**	To open the Save As dialog box.
2 Navigate to the current unit folder	If necessary.
3 In the File name box, enter **My selection**	To specify the name.
4 Click **Save**	To save the file with the new name.
Observe the window's title bar	The name of the file appears in the title bar.
5 Choose **File**, **Close**	To close the file.
6 Close all open files	
7 Choose **File**, **Exit**	To close Visio.

Unit summary: The Visio environment

Topic A

In this topic, you learned that Visio is a **vector-based** illustration tool. You learned how to start Visio and create a file. You also learned about the Visio work area and the Visio Help system.

Topic B

In this topic, you learned how to open a Visio file and navigate in a drawing. You learned how to change the view settings by using the Zoom tool. You also learned how to use **page tabs** to navigate between pages.

Topic C

In this topic, you learned how to manipulate **windows** and **stencils**. You learned how to reposition stencils in the Shapes window and how to float and dock stencils in the work area.

Topic D

In this topic, you learned how to select objects by dragging a selection marquee and by using keyboard shortcuts. You also learned the difference between **scaling** and **resizing** objects. Then you learned how to save and close a file and close Visio.

Independent practice activity

In this activity, you'll open a file in Visio, change view settings, and change zoom settings. You'll rename a page, move shapes, move among pages, and resize a shape.

1. Start Visio.
2. Open Selection practice (from the current unit folder).
3. Save the file as **My selection practice** (in the current unit folder).
4. Change the view setting for the Shapes window to **Icons Only**.
5. Change the zoom setting to **65%.**
6. Rename Page-1 as **MyPage**.
7. Move the triangle and the square shapes together to the bottom of the page, without moving the circle.
8. Go to the More shapes page.
9. Resize the star shape.
10. Update the drawing.
11. Close the drawing. (Don't close Visio.)

Review questions

1 Which of the following is not true about Visio?

A Visio is a vector-based drawing program.

B Most new drawings are based on templates.

C Visio cannot work with bitmap images.

D Stencils are used to draw common shapes.

2 What basic elements do templates contain?

3 The three types of Visio files are ___________, stencils, and templates.

4 Which of the following view techniques magnifies a portion of a drawing and enables you to move the page freely in any direction, without using the scrollbars?

A Interactive zooming

B Panning

C Scaling

D Magnifying

5 Where are stencils located by default?

6 Name two ways to select multiple objects.

7 What is the difference between scaling and resizing?

Unit 2

Drawing tools

Unit time: 45 minutes

Complete this unit, and you'll know how to:

A Draw and manipulate shapes.

B Work with compound lines and use several methods to duplicate objects.

C Align, distribute, group, and rotate objects.

Topic A: Basic shapes and lines

Explanation

TIP
Hold shift key to make a proportional square or circle; unnecessary w/ rectangle or oval shapes

Visio provides tools for drawing any type of shape. If the stencils don't provide all the shapes you need, you can draw your own.

The Drawing toolbar

To draw shapes, you need to use the tools on the Drawing toolbar. To activate the toolbar, click the Drawing Tools button on the Standard toolbar. The drawing tools are listed in the following table:

Tool	Button	Used to...
Line		Create single-segmented lines.
Arc		Create simple arcs.
Rectangle		Draw rectangles and squares. If you hold the Shift key while using this tool, you constrain the tool to create a square.
Ellipse		Create ovals and circles. If you hold the Shift key while using this tool, you constrain the tool to create a circle.
Pencil		Draw lines and arcs without changing tools, and reshape other objects.
Freeform		Create multi-segmented curved lines.

To create basic shapes, select the Rectangle, Ellipse, Arc, or Line tool, and then drag in the drawing. An example is shown in Exhibit 2-1.

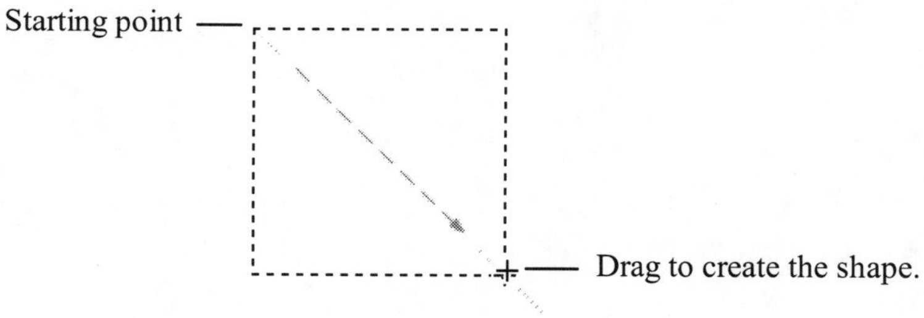

Exhibit 2-1: Using a drawing tool to create a basic shape

Do it!

A-1: Drawing basic shapes

Here's how	Here's why
1 Open Drawing.vsd	From the current unit folder.
Save the file as **My drawing**	In the current unit folder.
Observe the first page	The outlines of rectangles and squares are guides to help you practice drawing.
2 On the Standard toolbar, click	(The Drawing Tools button.) To activate the Drawing toolbar.
Dock the Drawing toolbar to the right of the Formatting toolbar	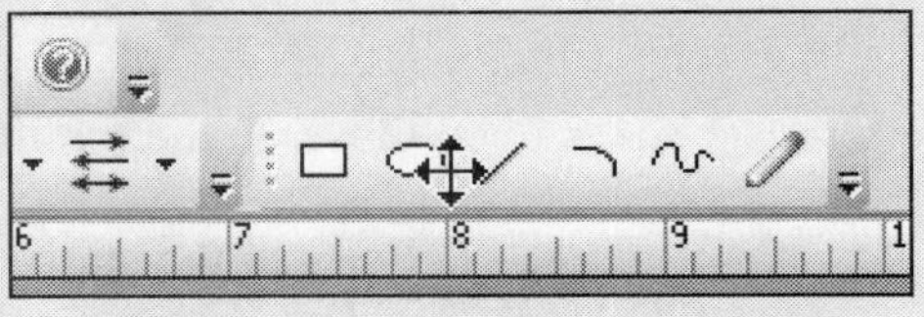 Drag the toolbar up and to the right to dock it.
3 On the Drawing toolbar, click	(The Rectangle tool.) The pointer changes to a crosshair with a small rectangle next to it.
4 Point to the upper-left corner of the rectangle	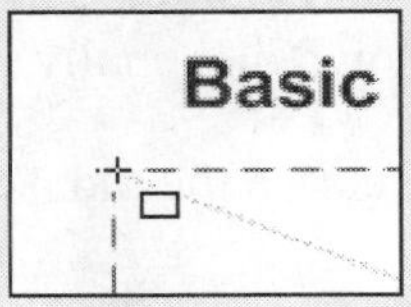 You'll begin drawing from this corner.
5 Drag the pointer diagonally to the lower-right corner of the rectangle	A black, dashed line appears, outlining the shape you're drawing. As you drag, the status bar displays information about the size of the object.
Release the mouse button	To view the rectangle with control handles.
6 Click a blank area of the drawing page	To deselect the rectangle.
7 Observe the shape of the pointer and the Drawing toolbar	The crosshair still has a rectangle beside it, and the Rectangle tool is still selected. You'll now draw a square.
8 Point to the upper-left corner of the square	

9	Press and hold SHIFT	Notice that the shape next to the crosshair changes to a square.
	While holding SHIFT, drag to the lower-right corner of the square	To draw the square.
	Release the mouse button	Be sure to release the mouse button before releasing the Shift key; otherwise you'll lose the constraint.
	Release SHIFT	You'll also draw an ellipse and a circle.
10	Click 	The Ellipse tool is on the Drawing toolbar.
	Observe the pointer	The crosshair now has an ellipse next to it.
11	Point to the starting point of the red guideline for the ellipse, as shown	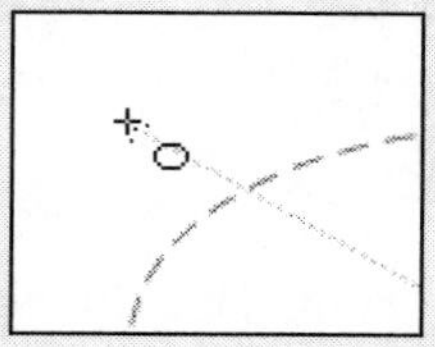
12	Following the guideline, drag down diagonally	
	Release the mouse	To complete the ellipse shape. (You can click the Undo button or press Ctrl+Z if you want to start over.)
	Deselect the ellipse	
13	Using the same technique, draw the circle	To draw the circle, you'll need to press and hold the Shift key.
14	Update the drawing	Click the Save button on the Standard toolbar.

Lines and arcs

Explanation

You can create and edit lines and arcs by using the Line or Arc tools. To draw straight lines, select the Line tool and drag in the drawing. By default, Visio is configured to snap lines to 45-degree increments. When the line is at a 45-degree angle, a gray guideline appears and extends across the page. To constrain lines to 45-degree increments *only*, press and hold the Shift key as you drag.

You can draw curved lines with the Arc tool. The direction of the arc depends on the direction you drag, as demonstrated in Exhibit 2-2. For example, if you drag up and to the right, the arc will bend up and to the right. If you drag slightly down, and then up and to the right, the arc will bend in the opposite direction.

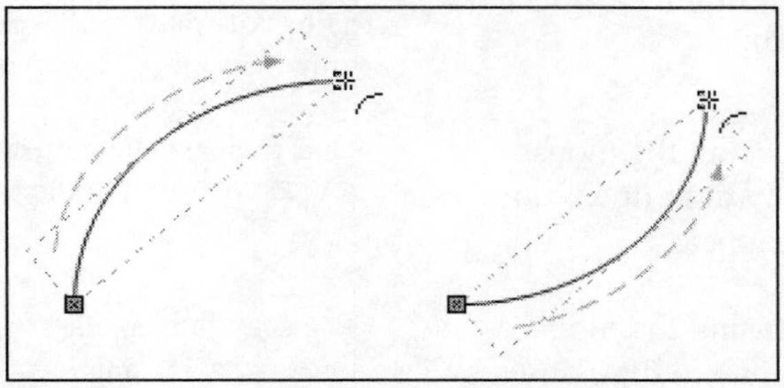

Exhibit 2-2: Drawing curved lines with the Arc tool

Do it!

A-2: Creating lines and arcs

Hold Shift to get a straight line at a perfect angle

TIP

use pointer tool to move shape around.

Here's how	Here's why
1 Switch to Page-2	At the bottom of the drawing, click the Page-2 tab.
2 On the Drawing toolbar, click [Line tool button]	The Line tool.
3 Point to a blank area near the upper-left side of the page; then drag to the right to begin creating a horizontal line	Don't release the mouse button. As you drag, the line automatically snaps to the grid, keeping the line horizontal. A gray guideline extends across the page, indicating that the line you're drawing will be horizontal.
4 Without releasing the mouse button, slowly drag down until the gray line disappears	Don't release the mouse button. The line is no longer snapping to the horizontal grid.
5 Without releasing the mouse button, continue to drag down and to the left until the line snaps to a 45° angle	The gray line appears again, indicating that the line is at a 45° angle.
6 Without releasing the mouse button, press and hold SHIFT, and then drag to the left or right	To constrain the line to 45° increments.
7 When the line is at a 45° angle, release the mouse button	Endpoints appear at both ends of the line.
Release SHIFT	
8 Select the Pointer tool	
Point to one of the endpoints	The pointer changes to four arrows pointing in opposite directions.
9 Drag the endpoint up or down	To change the angle of the line. Again, the line snaps to 45° angles, similar to the way it did when you were using the Line tool. You can change the length of the line. Next, you'll draw an arc.
10 On the Drawing toolbar, click [Arc tool button]	(The Arc tool.) An arc appears next to the crosshair.

11 In a blank area near the upper-right side of the page, drag slightly up, and then drag up and to the right in the shape of an arc

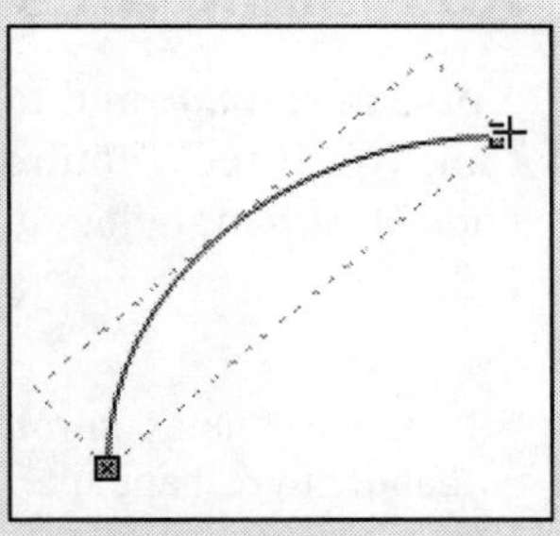

When you complete the arc, release the mouse button. Endpoints will appear at both ends of the arc.

The direction you drag determines the direction of the arc.

12 Press CTRL + Z

To undo the arc.

13 In the same area, drag slightly down, and then drag up and to the right

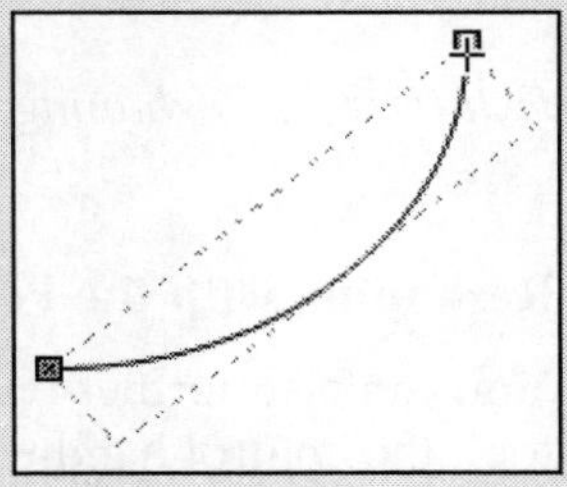

To create an arc that mirrors the first arc you drew. When you complete the arc, release the mouse button.

14 Update the drawing

Reshaping arcs

Explanation

You can reshape and rotate arcs to suit your needs. If you select an arc with the Pointer tool, you'll see a control handle in the middle of the arc, in addition to endpoints at both ends. To change the curve of the arc, drag the center control handle, as shown in Exhibit 2-3.

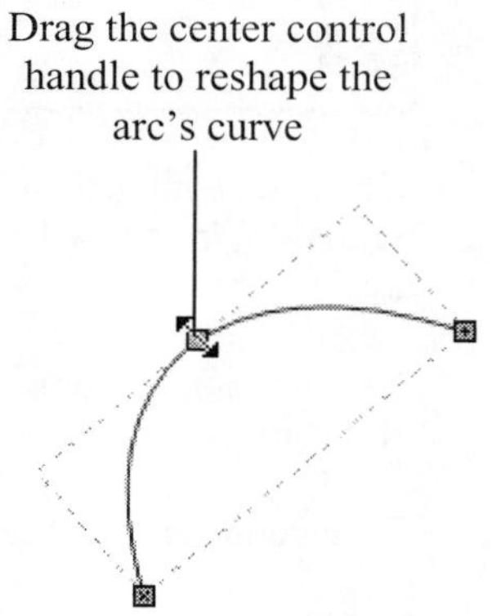

Exhibit 2-3: Reshaping an arc

Reshaping with the Pencil tool

You can also further reshape arcs by using the Pencil tool. When you select the Pencil tool, the control handle in the center of the arc changes from a square to a circle, and eccentricity handles extend from it, as shown in Exhibit 2-4. You can drag the eccentricity handles to reshape the arc's curve.

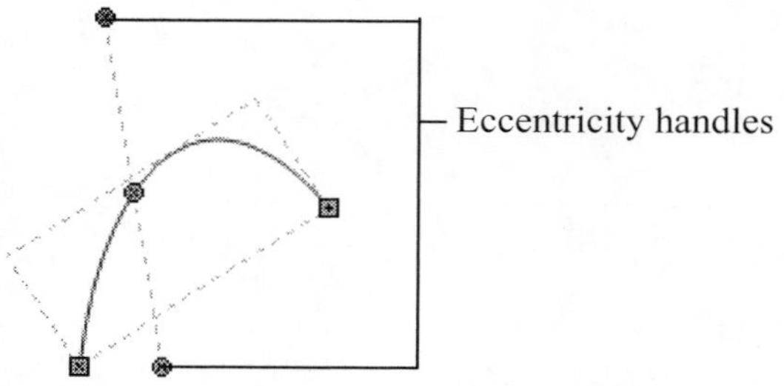

Exhibit 2-4: Adjusting an arc with the Pencil tool

Do it!

A-3: Reshaping an arc

Here's how	Here's why
1 Select the Pointer tool	
2 Click the arc	(If necessary.) To select it. Endpoints appear at both ends, and a control handle appears in the center.
3 Drag one of the endpoints up or down	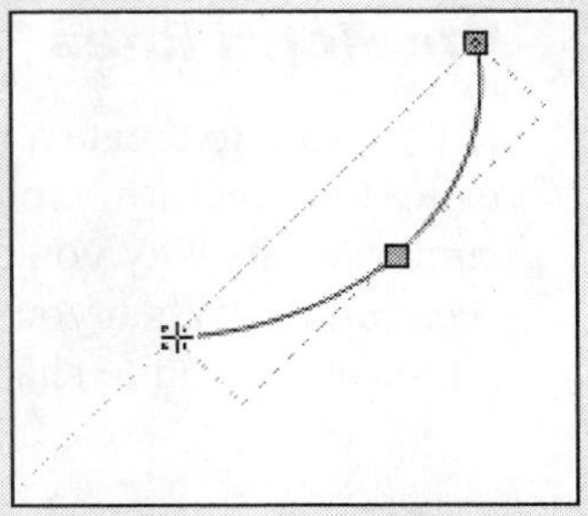 The arc pivots on its other endpoint and snaps to 45° angles, similar to the way lines do, and you can change the arc's width. If you drag around in a circle, you can rotate the arc.
4 Release the mouse button	
5 Point to the control handle in the center of the arc	The pointer changes to a two-headed arrow.
Drag the control handle	To reshape the arc's curve. You can adjust the arc more precisely by using the Pencil tool.
6 On the Drawing toolbar, click 	(The Pencil tool.) When you select the tool, the control handle in the arc changes from a square to a circle.
7 Click the center control handle	When you select the control handle, two eccentricity handles appear, extending out from it.
8 Drag one of the eccentricity handles up or down	To change the shape of the curve.
9 Update the drawing	

Topic B: Compound lines

Explanation

Simple lines consist of a single line segments. Compound lines consist of multiple line segments. You can create two types of compound lines in Visio. You can create a freeform line with the Freeform tool, or you can connect line segments by using the Line, Arc, and Pencil tools.

Freeform lines

If you want to create a more free-flowing compound line, you can do so quickly by using the Freeform tool. The tool creates exactly what you draw as you drag the pointer, similar to the way you draw with a pencil and paper. This feature is called *gesture recognition*. When you drag with the tool, Visio automatically creates multiple control points as needed to shape the curves, as shown in Exhibit 2-5.

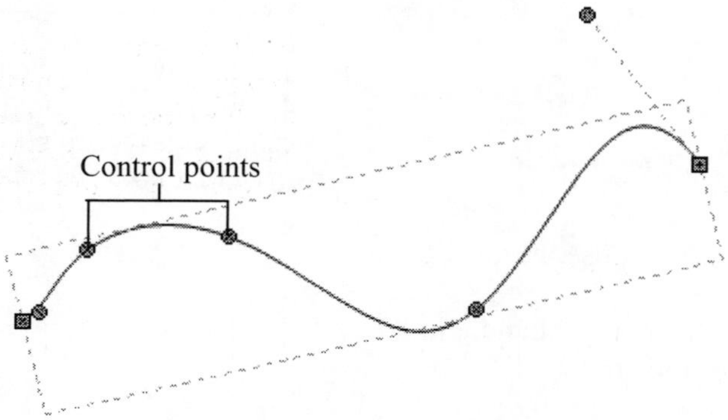

Exhibit 2-5: A freeform line

Do it!

B-1: Creating a freeform line

Here's how	Here's why
1 Switch to Page-3	
2 On the Drawing toolbar, click 	The Freeform tool.
3 Point to the left end of the curved line at the top of the page	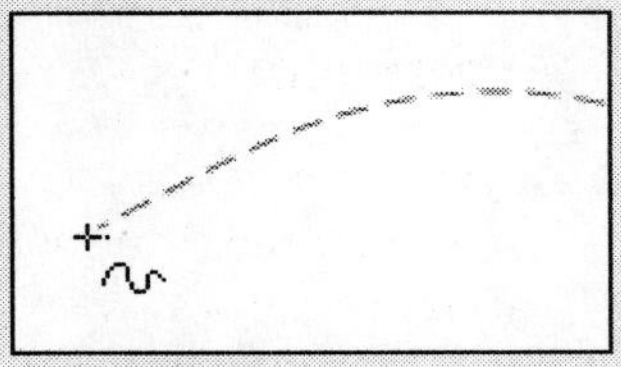
Using a smooth motion, drag to trace the curves of the line	As your hand changes direction, the line bends with it.
4 Observe the line	(Do not worry if the line you created does not exactly match the template line. You'll continue to adjust the line later in the unit.) Visio automatically created control points as necessary to control the curves of the line.
5 Update the drawing	

Using the Line and Arc tools to create compound lines

Explanation

Another way to create compound lines is to use the Line and Arc tools. To do this, select the tool you want and then create each segment in succession. To begin a new segment, point to the endpoint of the previous segment and then drag. When you use this technique, the segments are connected by *vertex points*, which look like small green diamonds, as shown in Exhibit 2-6.

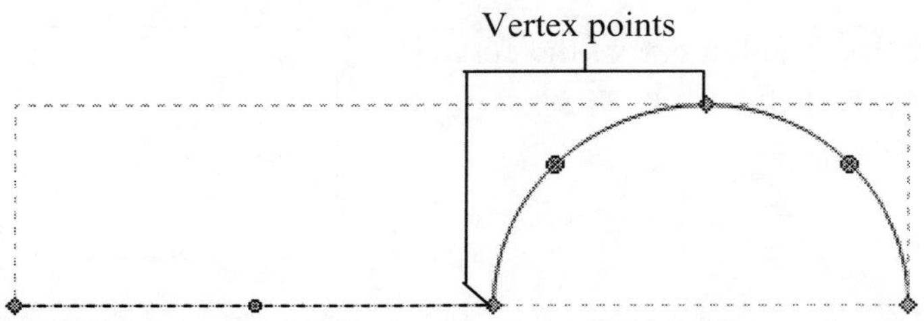

Exhibit 2-6: A compound line drawn with the Line and Arc tools

Do it!

B-2: Creating a compound line with the Line and Arc tools

Here's how	Here's why
1 On the Drawing toolbar, select the Line tool	
2 Drag to draw the straight, horizontal portion of the compound line at the bottom of the page, as shown	You can use the Shift key, if desired.

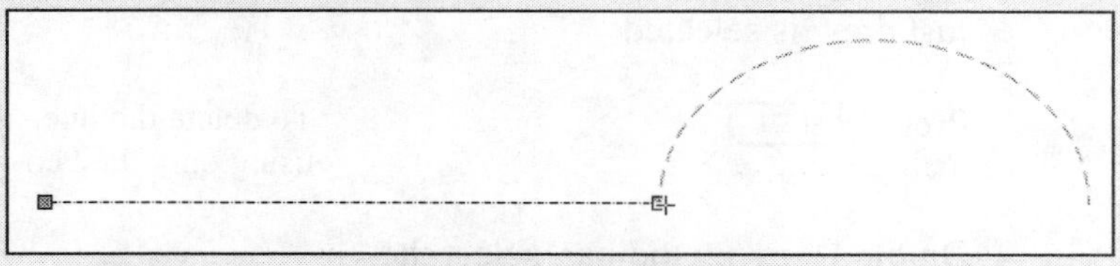

Here's how	Here's why
3 Select the Arc tool	
4 Point to the right endpoint of the new line	You'll continue the line by drawing the first half of the arc.
Drag to the center point of the tracing arc	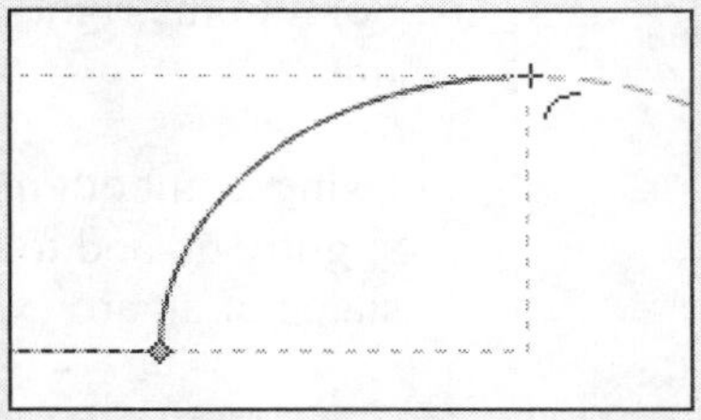 (Drag slightly to the left before you begin following the curve of the arc.) To draw the first half of the arc. The endpoints of both lines change to vertex points, indicating that the line is now a compound line.
5 Using the same technique, draw the second half of the arc	Start at the vertex point at the end of the first arc.
Observe the line	There are four vertex points.
6 Update the drawing	

Using the Pencil tool to create compound lines

Explanation

You can also create compound lines with the Pencil tool, which can function as both the Line and Arc tools combined. The type of line segment you create is controlled by the way you drag with the tool. For example, drag in a straight line to create straight line segments, and drag in the shape of an arc to create curved segments.

Do it!

B-3: Creating a compound line with the Pencil tool

Here's how	Here's why
1 Verify that the compound line you just drew is selected	If the line isn't selected, click it to select it.
Press DELETE	To delete the line. You'll create the same line by using only the Pencil tool.
2 On the Drawing toolbar, select the Pencil tool	
3 Draw the straight portion of the compound line	You can use the Shift key, if desired.
4 Point to the right endpoint of the line	You'll create the first part of the curve.
Using a smooth motion, drag slightly up and to the right in the shape of an arc	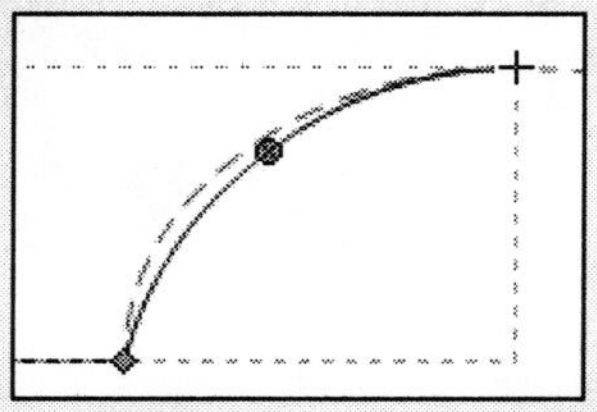 Similar to the way you would with the Arc tool.
5 Using the same technique, draw the second half of the arc	Again, don't worry if the curves don't exactly match the template line.
6 Update the drawing	

Adjusting compound lines

Explanation

You can adjust compound lines by manipulating the control and vertex points. If you created a freeform line, you can make adjustments by moving the control points with either the Pointer tool or the Pencil tool. If you created a compound line with the Line, Arc, or Pencil tools, you can move control points as well as vertex points.

In both types of compound lines, you can convert control points to vertex points, and you can add vertex points where there previously weren't any. To do both, you need to use the Pencil tool. To convert a control point to a vertex point, Ctrl+click the control point you want to convert. To add a vertex point, point to a location on a segment where you want to add the point, and then Ctrl+click the segment.

Do it!

B-4: Manipulating compound lines

Here's how	Here's why
1 On the freeform line, point to one of the control handles	
2 Drag one of the control points	To change the curve for a portion of the line.
Reposition the control points	If necessary, to more precisely align the curves of the line with the curves in the template line.
3 Press and hold CTRL, and click a blank portion of the line	To create a new vertex point. Eccentricity handles extend from the vertex point.
Drag the eccentricity handles to change the shape of the line, as shown	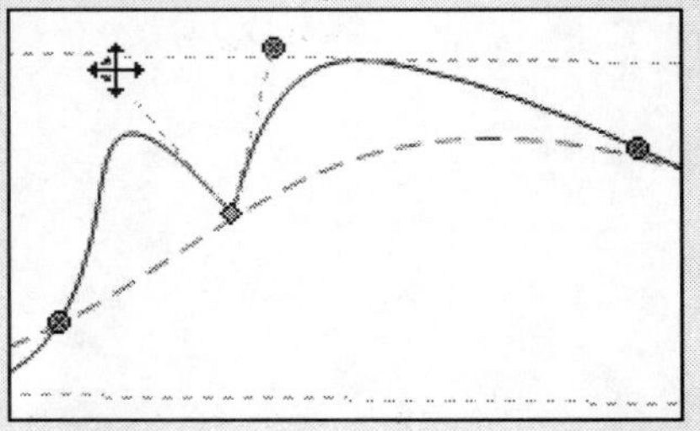
4 Click the compound line at the bottom of the page	To select it.
5 Drag the control point on the left side of the curve, as shown	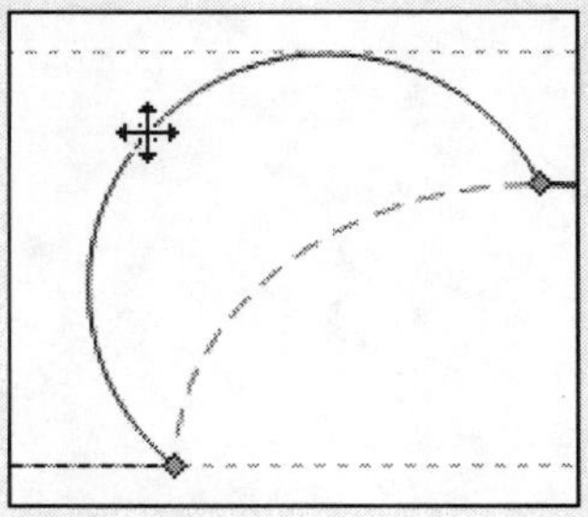 To change the curve.
6 Press and hold CTRL, and click the control point	To convert it to a vertex point. The segment is divided into two segments, and control points appear on both sides of the vertex point.

7 Drag the right control point down, as shown

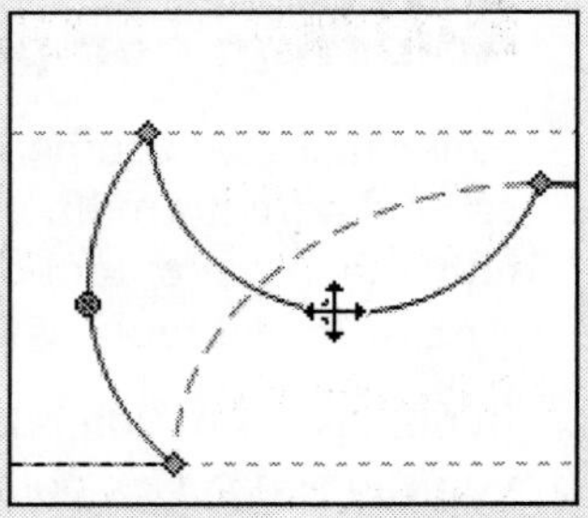

To completely change the direction of the second segment.

8 Click a blank area of the page

To deselect the line and view the results.

9 Update the drawing

Topic C: Editing objects

Explanation

There are many ways to edit shapes and lines. Some of the basic techniques include aligning, distributing, grouping, and rotating.

Object duplication

You can duplicate objects by using several methods. You can use the Copy and Paste commands in the Edit menu (or use the keyboard shortcuts Ctrl+C and Ctrl+V). You can also press and hold Ctrl as you drag an object. When you do this, Visio creates a duplicate of the object. In addition, you can select an object and press Ctrl+D.

Maintain alignment when duplicating

If you duplicate an object by pressing Ctrl as you drag it, you can also use the Shift key to maintain alignment. Make sure you do not press Shift until you start dragging; otherwise, the tool will change to the Magnification tool.

The F4 key

The F4 key functions as a Repeat key. In many cases, it repeats your last action. This can be useful when you're duplicating an object by dragging because you not only get a duplicate of the object, but you also duplicate the distance you dragged that object.

Do it!

Click shape | CTRL. to copy/duplicate a shape; Just hold CTRL key and drag.

F4 - repeats last step to include space, format, etc.

C-1: Duplicating objects

Here's how	Here's why
1 Switch to Page-4	
Select the Pointer tool	If necessary.
2 Click the circle	To select it. You'll duplicate it.
3 Point to the center of the circle; then press and hold CTRL	A plus sign appears next to the pointer.
Drag the circle to the other end of the dotted line	To create a copy of the circle on the other end of the dotted line.
Release the mouse button; then release CTRL	
4 Press CTRL + D	To create a duplicate circle that is offset from the original.
Press CTRL + D two more times	To create two more duplicate circles.
5 Select the leftmost circle	The original circle.
6 Point to the center of the circle; then press and hold CTRL	A plus sign appears next to the pointer.
Slowly begin dragging down	To begin creating a duplicate.
As you drag, press and hold SHIFT	To maintain vertical alignment for the duplicate circle.
7 Position the duplicate circle as shown; then release the mouse button	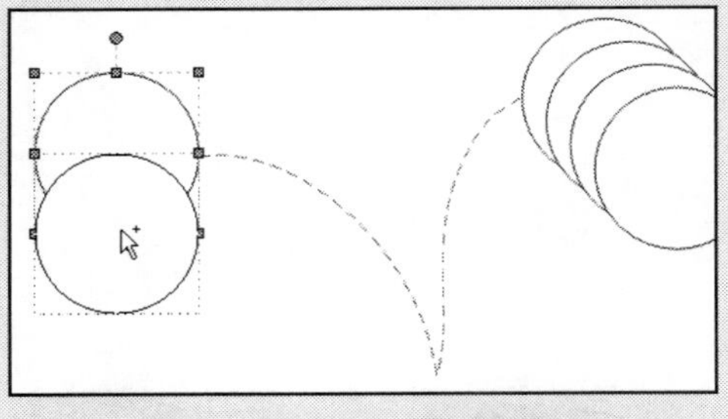 After you release the mouse button, you can also release the Ctrl and Shift keys. You'll use the F4 key to create additional duplicates with the same spacing.

8 Press F4	To create a duplicate circle that is spaced the same distance that you spaced the original.
Press F4 two more times	To create two more evenly spaced duplicates.
9 Update the drawing	

Object alignment

Explanation

You'll probably spend a lot of time moving and aligning objects in your drawings. Although Visio offers many ways to accomplish these actions, one of the easiest ways to align objects is to use the Align Shapes command in the Shape menu. The command opens a dialog box you can use to align objects horizontally (left to right) or vertically (top to bottom).

To align shapes:

1. Select the objects you want to align.
2. Choose Shape, Align Shapes to open the Align Shapes dialog box, shown in Exhibit 2-7.
3. Click the button (or buttons) for the desired alignment. For example, you can align objects vertically and horizontally at the same time.
4. Click OK.

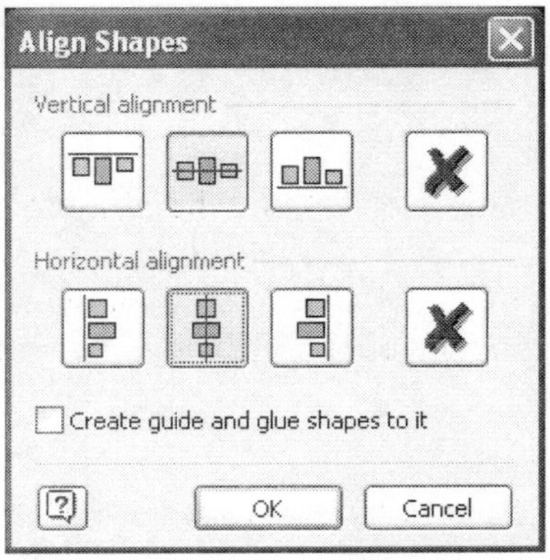

Exhibit 2-7: The Align Shapes dialog box

The following table lists the buttons in the dialog box and explains their functions.

Button	Function
	Aligns selected objects with the top of the reference object (the first object you select in the group of objects you're aligning).
	Horizontally aligns selected objects with the center of the reference object.
	Aligns selected objects with the bottom of the reference object.
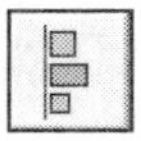	Aligns selected objects with the left side of the reference object.
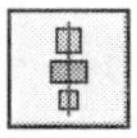	Vertically aligns selected objects with the center of the reference object.
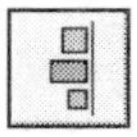	Aligns selected objects with the right side of the reference object.
	Clears your selections from the dialog box.

Reference objects

When you align objects, the order in which you select them is critical. The first object you select is the *reference object:* all other objects you select will be aligned with it. The reference object has a thick pink border, while the other selected objects have thin pink borders, as shown in Exhibit 2-8.

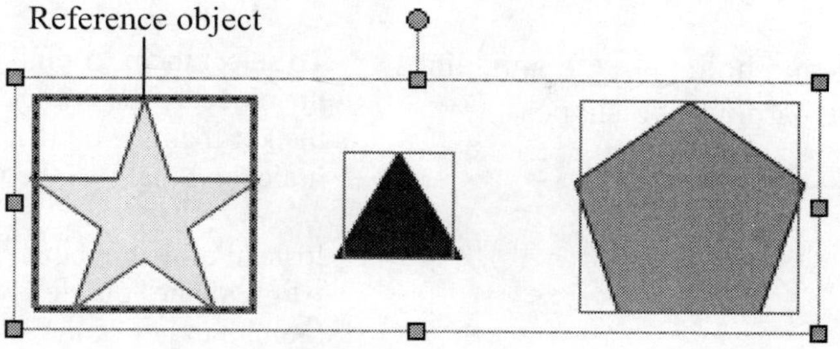

Exhibit 2-8: A reference object in a group of selected objects

Use the Shift key to select multiple objects

Earlier you learned how to select multiple objects by dragging to create a marquee. However, suppose you want to select specific objects, but leave others unselected. To do this, you can press the Shift key and click the objects you want to select. You can also remove an object from a group of selected objects by Shift+clicking it.

The Action toolbar

Aligning and distributing objects is a common task, so to make the process easier, you can open the dialog boxes by using buttons on the Action toolbar, shown in Exhibit 2-9. The Action toolbar also provides quick access to other basic editing commands, such as Rotate, Group, Flip, and Align.

Exhibit 2-9: The Action toolbar

Do it!

C-2: Aligning objects

Here's how	Here's why
1 Switch to Page-5	You'll left-align the three shapes.
2 Select the yellow shape	You'll use this shape as the reference object.
3 Press and hold SHIFT, and click the remaining two shapes	To select them. A pink border appears around all the objects. The border for the yellow shape is thicker than the border for the other shapes, indicating that it is the reference object.
	Instead of using the menu command to open the Align Shapes dialog box, you'll open the Action toolbar and click the Align Shapes button.
4 Right-click the Standard toolbar	To display a list of toolbars.
Choose **Action**	To activate the Action toolbar.
5 Verify that the objects are still selected	
On the Action toolbar, click 	(The Align Shapes button.) To open the Align Shapes dialog box.
6 Under Horizontal alignment, click 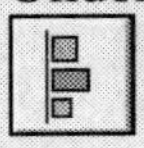	This setting will align the selected objects with the left side of the reference object.
Click **OK**	To apply the alignment and close the dialog box. The selected objects are aligned with the left side of the yellow shape.
7 Press CTRL + Z	To undo the alignment. This time you'll vertically center the shapes.
8 On the Action toolbar, click the Align Shapes button	To open the Align Shapes dialog box.
Under Vertical alignment, click 	This setting will align the selected objects horizontally with the center of the reference object.
Click **OK**	
9 Update the drawing	

Object distribution

Explanation

Distributing objects evenly spaces them from either their centers or their edges. The distance between the first and last objects determines the overall distance. All other objects are distributed evenly to fill the space between the first and last objects. You can distribute objects vertically or horizontally by using the Distribute Shapes dialog box. To open this dialog box, use the Shape menu or the Distribute Shapes button on the Action toolbar.

The following table shows the buttons you'll find in the Distribute Shapes dialog box and explains their functions:

Button	Function
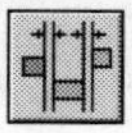	Left and right inside edges are spaced evenly apart.
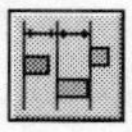	Left edges are spaced evenly apart.
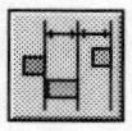	Right edges are spaced evenly apart.
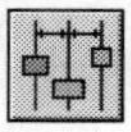	Horizontal centers of objects are spaced evenly apart.
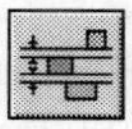	Top and bottom inside edges are spaced evenly apart.
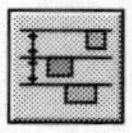	Top edges of objects are spaced evenly apart.
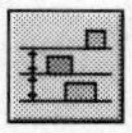	Bottom edges are spaced evenly apart.
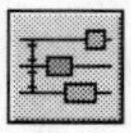	Vertical centers of objects are spaced evenly.

Do it!

C-3: Distributing objects

Here's how	Here's why
1 Switch to Page-6	
2 Select all of the light blue shapes	You'll distribute these shapes vertically.
3 On the Action toolbar, click 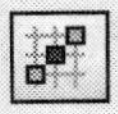	(The Distribute Shapes button.) To open the Distribute Shapes dialog box.
4 Under Vertical distribution, click 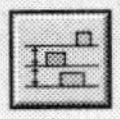	This setting will distribute the selected shapes evenly based on their bottom edges.
5 Click **OK**	
6 Select the dark blue shapes	
Add the light blue diamond shape to the selection	You'll distribute the shapes horizontally.
7 On the Action toolbar, click the Distribute Shapes button	To open the Distribute Shapes dialog box.
Under Horizontal distribution, click 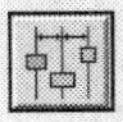	This setting will distribute the selected shapes evenly according to their horizontal centers.
Click **OK**	The diamond shape is no longer vertically aligned with the lighter blue shapes. The vertical alignment is off because of the horizontal distribution. To fix this, you'll realign the light blue shapes, using the diamond shape as a reference object.
8 Deselect the shapes	
Select just the light blue diamond shape	
Add the remaining light blue shapes to the selection	
9 On the Action toolbar, click the Align Shapes button	To open the Align Shapes dialog box.
Under Horizontal alignment, click 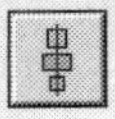	This setting aligns the selected objects vertically with the center of the reference object.
Click **OK**	The shapes are now aligned vertically under the diamond, so the shape arrangement is no longer staggered.
10 Update the drawing	

Grouping

Explanation

You can avoid the problem of staggered arrangements by *grouping* objects before aligning or distributing them. Grouping holds the objects together and allows them to act as one. Then, when you distribute or align the group, all of the objects in the group move together. Grouping is also useful when you want to create a new item based on a variety of shapes and you need them to act as one object, such as when you create a logo.

To group objects, select the objects you want to group and choose Shape, Grouping, Group. To ungroup the objects, choose Shape, Grouping, Ungroup. You can also group and ungroup objects by clicking the Group or Ungroup buttons on the Action toolbar or by using the keyboard shortcuts Ctrl+G (to group) and Shift+Ctrl+U (to ungroup).

Do it!

TIP

Shapes | operations | union. To combine shapes into one.

C-4: Grouping objects

Here's how	Here's why
1 Switch to Page-7	
2 Select the orange diamond and the shapes below it	
3 Align the selected shapes from top to bottom based on their centers	Use the Align Shapes dialog box.
4 Press CTRL + G	To place the selected shapes in a group. Notice that there is only one set of selection handles around the group.
5 With the group selected, press and hold SHIFT	You'll select the other yellow objects.
Select each of the remaining yellow objects	Click them.
Release SHIFT	
6 Distribute the shapes horizontally based on their centers	(Use the Distribute Shapes dialog box.) The yellow shapes are distributed uniformly, but the shape arrangement is not disrupted because of grouping.
7 Close the Action toolbar	To close the toolbar, right-click any toolbar and choose Action from the shortcut menu.
8 Update the document	

Object rotation

Explanation

You rotate objects around a point called the *center of rotation* by using special rotate handles. When you select an object with the Rotate tool, the center of rotation appears in the middle of the object. In addition, a round Rotate Shape tool appears at the top of the selected object. You can use this tool to rotate the object clockwise or counterclockwise around the center of rotation.

Moving the center of rotation

You can move an object's center of rotation. You might want to do this if you need to rotate one object around another. To move a center of rotation, you drag it to a new location. It's still associated with the original shape.

Do it!

C-5: Rotating an object

Here's how	Here's why
1 Switch to Page-8	
2 Select the airplane	A green circle appears above it. 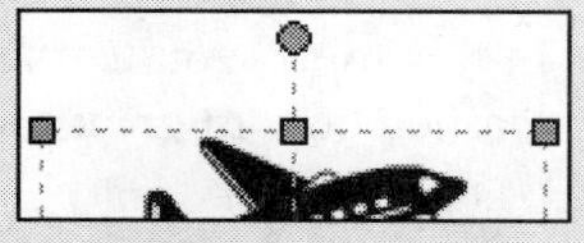
3 Point to the green circle	To activate the Rotate Shape tool. You'll use it to rotate the airplane around its center of rotation.
Drag clockwise until the plane is rotated approximately 45 degrees	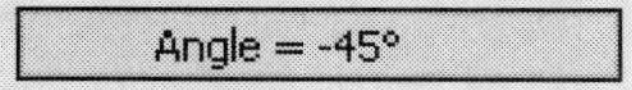 Use the status bar to determine the angle.
4 Press CTRL + Z	To undo the rotation.
Point to the green circle	(If necessary.) To activate the Rotate Shape tool again.
5 Point to the plane's center of rotation	Located in the middle of the plane shape. 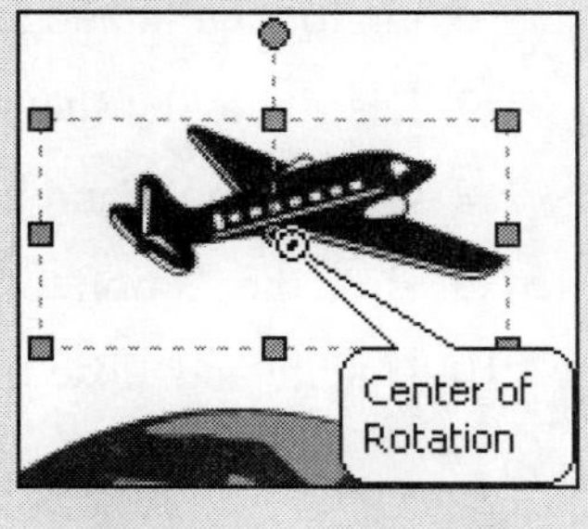
Observe the pointer	It changes to a Center of Rotation icon.
6 Drag the center of rotation to the center of the earth shape	To move the center of rotation.
Rotate the plane	Around the earth shape.
7 Update and close the document	

Unit summary: Drawing tools

Topic A

In this topic, you learned how to use **drawing tools** to create different shapes. You drew closed and open shapes and objects, and you learned how to reshape objects.

Topic B

In this topic, you learned how to use the Freeform tool. You also created **compound lines** by using the Line, Arc, and Pencil tools.

Topic C

In this topic, you learned how to **duplicate**, **align,** and **distribute** objects. You also learned how to **group** and **rotate** objects.

Independent practice activity

In this activity, you'll draw and duplicate shapes. You'll also align, distribute, and rotate shapes.

1. Open Drawing practice (from the current unit folder).
2. Save the file as **My drawing practice**.
3. Use the drawing tools to draw the shapes on Page-1. (*Hint*: Use the Freeform tool for Shape D.)
4. Go to Page-2 and draw the compound line shape. (*Hint*: You can use the Arc and Line tools or the Pencil tool.)
5. Go to Page-3 and create two duplicates of the circle. Place the duplicates under the original, and group the duplicates.
6. Go to Page-4 and align the shapes under the yellow diamond.
7. Distribute the shapes based on their vertical centers.
8. Go to Page-5 and rotate the sun around the earth.
9. Hide the Action toolbar.
10. Update and close the drawing. (Don't close Visio.)

Review questions

1 Which of the following tools can you use to draw a square in one stroke?

A Rectangle

B Line

C Arc

D Ellipse

2 What is the difference between simple and compound lines?

3 Which key can you use to constrain the Line tool to draw lines in 45-degree increments?

A Ctrl

B Alt

C Shift

D Ctrl+Shift

4 What is the difference between a control handle and an eccentricity handle?

5 What is gesture recognition?

6 Which of the following can you add to a freeform line to hold the line in place and provide control of each eccentricity handle?

A Eccentricity handles

B Vertex points

C Control handles

D Arc handles

7 Which of the following techniques holds objects together and allows them to act as one?

A Rotating

B Aligning

C Distributing

D Grouping

Unit 3
Basic diagrams

Unit time: 75 minutes

Complete this unit, and you'll know how to:

A Plan a diagram.

B Create a basic diagram.

C Use basic text features.

D Create an organization chart.

Topic A: Planning your diagram

Explanation

You can use Visio diagrams, or drawings, to present information graphically. One type of diagram is a flowchart. Typically, a flowchart represents a process, such as building a fan motor on an assembly line. Another type of diagram is an organization chart, which shows a company's structure. Visio provides other types of charts and diagrams to represent a variety of information. The type of information you want to illustrate, such as a process or an organizational structure, determines the kind of diagram to use.

Design tips

Effective design begins with analyzing your audience. Ask yourself these questions to identify and understand the audience:

- Who is going to use this diagram?
- Why are they going to use it?
- What information is most important to them?

The answers will help you target the right diagram for the right people. If you have a wide audience, the questions are harder to answer. No matter who your audience is, though, it's best to keep the diagram as simple as possible.

Next, consider the design and purpose of your diagram. Will it be distributed online across a company network? Will you be printing the diagram? If so, will you print in color or black and white? If you are printing in color, consider using highly contrasting colors. Make it easy for your audience to read the diagram.

Shapes

Each step, action, or idea in a diagram is represented by a shape. Some shapes, such as those used in process mapping, are standard across most processes. Others are not. If you're creating a flowchart, your company might have a standardized set of flowchart symbols that you can use as a guide. Visio stores commonly used shapes on stencils and then organizes these stencils with the type of diagram you're creating. When you choose a template in Visio, the stencils that contain the shapes most commonly used for that type of drawing are also opened.

Here are some tips on how to select a shape if you aren't sure what to use:

- First, check to see if the shape you want to use is a standard shape for a particular action or function. Often the shapes found on the Basic stencil are enough to get started. If they're not, many other stencils are available.
- Never reinvent the wheel. Research what your company has done in the past. Find out if there are any company standards you should be following.
- Choose a graphic whenever you can't find the right shape. Usually a graphic can convey a simple idea or action. Consider using a universal type of graphic, such as an industry icon. Remember, a picture is worth a thousand words.
- Don't worry about using something that isn't perfect. You might find a shape that is better suited to the idea you want to convey after you've created the drawing. You can always go back and replace a shape without rebuilding the entire diagram.

Do it!

A-1: Discussing diagram planning

Questions and answers

1 What kind of information is best represented by a flowchart? Processes

2 What is the first step you should take when planning a diagram?
Consider your audience: who will use it? why?
what is important to your audience?

3 If your diagram is going to be printed in color, what color scheme might work well? Any scheme with high contrast
Ex: Light colors on dark background or vice-versa

4 If you can't find the right shape to use, what is a good alternative?
- Get one from online
- Insert Clip Art
- Search online (google search shapes)

Topic B: Creating a basic diagram

Explanation

Master shapes are the basic building blocks of any Visio diagram or drawing. When you begin a drawing, stencils containing specific master shapes are automatically added to the work window.

Shape properties

Each master shape has "smart" behavior built in. That is, each shape is programmed to behave in a certain way in a particular context. For example, flowchart shapes have size ratios and connection points that are specific to flowchart diagrams.

All shapes contain three basic components: a *symbol*, a *text block*, and *connection points*, as shown in Exhibit 3-1. The following table explains each component's function in the context of a flowchart diagram:

Component	Description
Symbol	The graphic portion, which represents a function or process in the flowchart. Think of this component as the shape you see in the stencil.
Text block	The shape text used to label or define a function or process in a flowchart. When a shape is added to a drawing page, the name appears in the middle of the shape. You can edit the text to define each step in the process.
Connection point	A small blue x that appears on each side of a shape. Connection points provide a fast way to connect the shapes in a diagram.

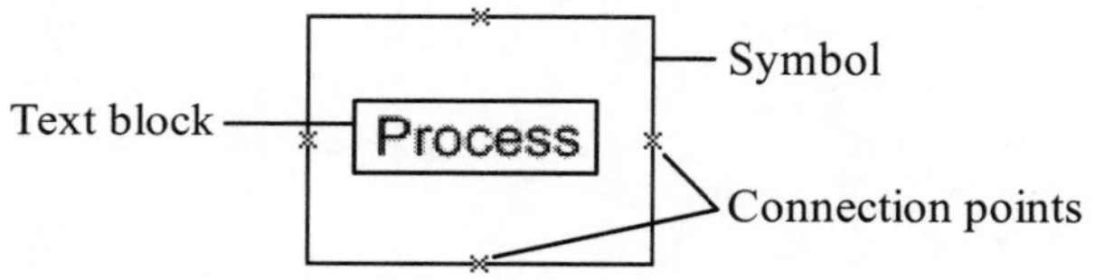

Exhibit 3-1: An example of a master shape

Shape placement

Add shapes to a diagram by dragging them from the stencils and positioning them on the page. Each shape serves a specific purpose and demonstrates a particular function in the chart. For example, decision shapes in flowchart diagrams represent decisions within a flow of events, while process shapes represent specific steps or tasks.

AutoConnect

You can save time by using AutoConnect to automatically connect shapes as you add them. To activate AutoConnect, click the AutoConnect button on the Standard toolbar, as shown in Exhibit 3-2.

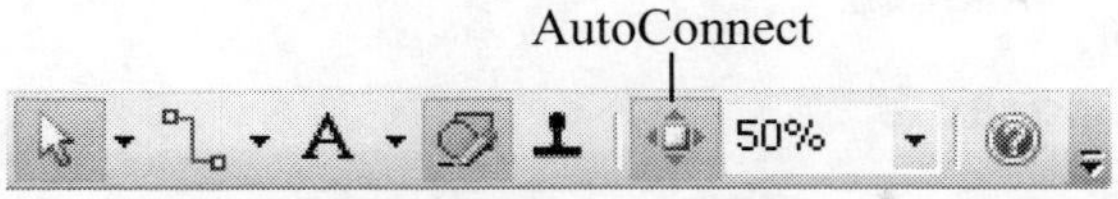

Exhibit 3-2: The AutoConnect button on the Standard toolbar

When AutoConnect is active, blue AutoConnect handles appear around shapes in the drawing when you point to them, as shown in Exhibit 3-3.

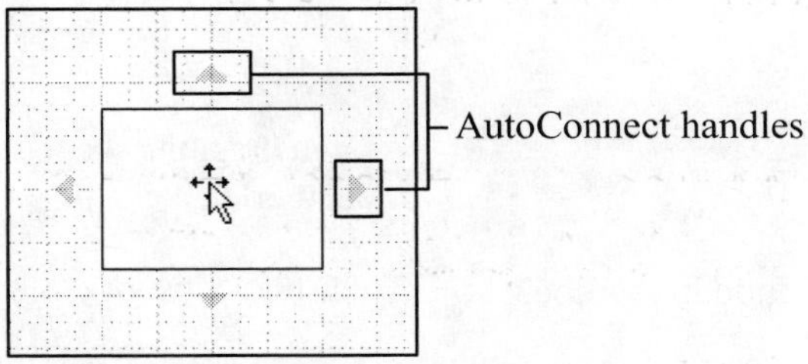

Exhibit 3-3: AutoConnect handles

You can add and connect new shapes by using a couple of techniques:

- While pointing to a shape on the drawing page, click one of the AutoConnect handles. When you do, the last shape you selected in the stencil will automatically be added to the drawing and connected to the shape you clicked.
- Drag a shape from the stencil and place it on top of an existing shape without releasing the mouse button. When you do this, the AutoConnect handles will appear. Drop the shape on one of the handles to add it to the drawing and to connect it to the shape you pointed to.

The View toolbar

As you work on a diagram, you might want to use certain visual aids, such as guides, rulers, or the grid. The *grid* is a series of horizontal and vertical lines, similar to graph paper, that help you accurately position shapes. The grid does not print when you print a drawing. You can show or hide visual aids by choosing them from the View menu or by clicking buttons on the View toolbar, as shown in Exhibit 3-4.

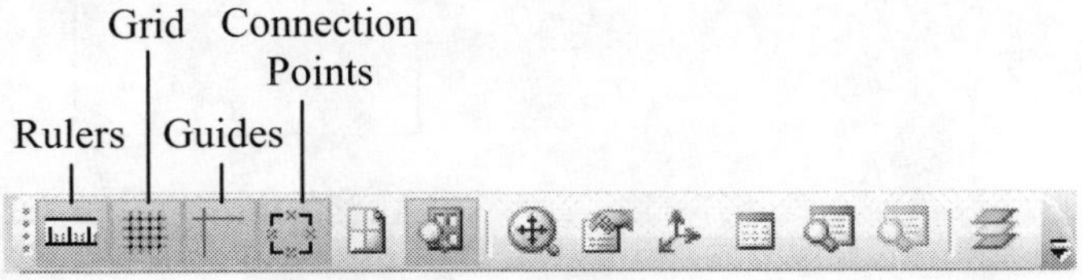

Exhibit 3-4: The View toolbar

Do it!

B-1: Adding shapes

Here's how	Here's why
1 Open Basic diagrams.vsd	From the current unit folder.
Save the file as **My basic diagrams**	
2 From the Basic Flowchart Shapes stencil, drag the **Process** shape on top of the outline for shape 1	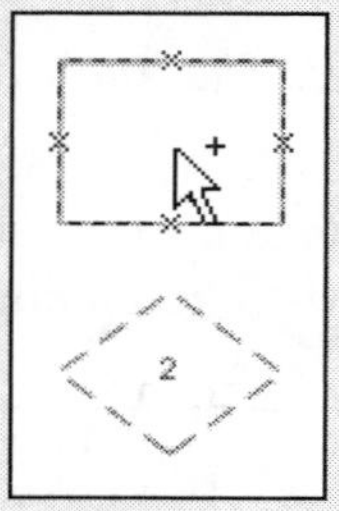 As you drag, the shape seems to snap to a hidden grid.
3 Right-click the Standard toolbar	To display a list of toolbars.
From the list, choose **View**	To activate the View toolbar, if necessary.
4 On the toolbar, click 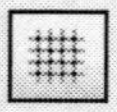	(The Grid button.) To turn on the grid, if necessary. By default, shapes will snap to the grid whether it's visible or not.
5 Point to the shape you added	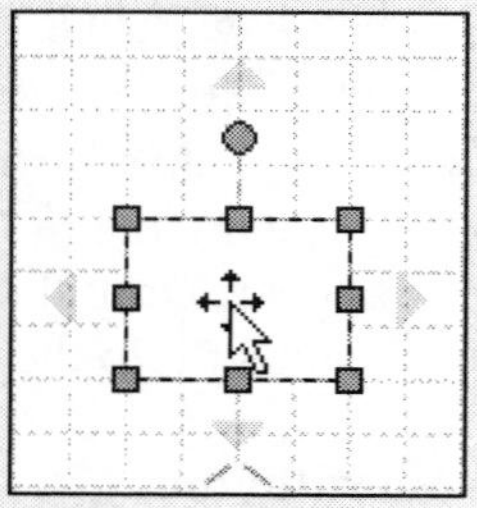 When you point to the shape, four blue AutoConnect handles appear: one on each side.
Click the bottom AutoConnect handle	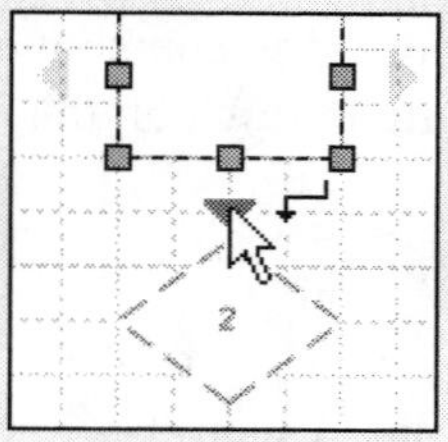 Another Process shape is added beneath the existing one. However, you want to add a Decision shape.
6 Press CTRL + Z	To undo the change.

7 Drag the Decision shape from the stencil and place it over the Process shape on the page	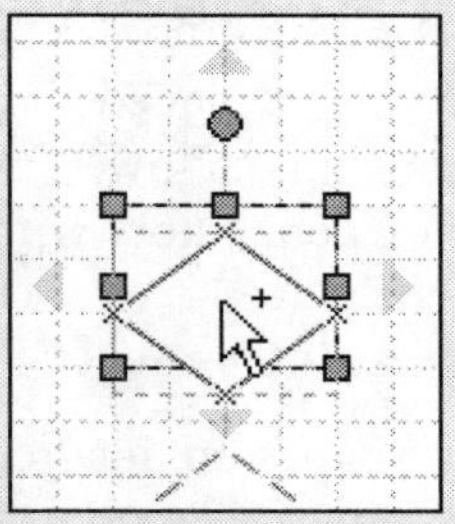 (Do not release the mouse button.) When you position the new shape over the existing one, the AutoConnect handles are visible again.
Point to the bottom AutoConnect handle; then release the mouse button	To add the shape.
8 Press ESC	To deselect the new shape. Because you used AutoConnect, the new shape is automatically connected to the previous one.
9 Drag a new Process shape from the stencil and place it on top of the outline for shape 3	
10 Add a new Process shape on top of the outline for shape 4	
11 Using AutoConnect, add Process shapes for the outlines for shapes 5, 6, and 8	Point to the Process shape at the top of the column; then click the bottom AutoConnect handle. Repeat the process for the bottom shape in the column. Click the right AutoConnect handle to add shape 8.
12 Using AutoConnect, add a Document shape for the shape 7 outline	Drag a Document shape from the stencil and place it over the Process shape at the top of the center column. Point to the right AutoConnect handle and release the mouse button.
13 Using AutoConnect, add a Decision shape for the shape 9 outline	
14 Press ESC	To deselect the shape and view the changes.
15 Update the drawing	

Connecting shapes with one another

Explanation

After you've placed shapes in a drawing, you can connect them to illustrate their relationship or flow. You can connect shapes by using AutoConnect or by manually drawing connectors with the Connector tool.

Using AutoConnect

If two shapes are near each other in a drawing, you can connect them by using AutoConnect. To do so, point to one of the shapes to display the AutoConnect handles; then click the handle that's between the two shapes.

Using the Connector tool

Sometimes you might need to connect shapes that are not next to each other. To do this, you can manually draw a connector with the Connector tool, shown in Exhibit 3-5.

Exhibit 3-5: The Connector tool on the Standard toolbar

To use the tool, drag the pointer from a connection point on one shape to a connection point on the shape to which you want to connect, as shown in Exhibit 3-6. It's important to remember to always connect the shapes in the direction of the process flow. By default, when an arrowhead is added to a connecting line, it points in the direction the connection was made in.

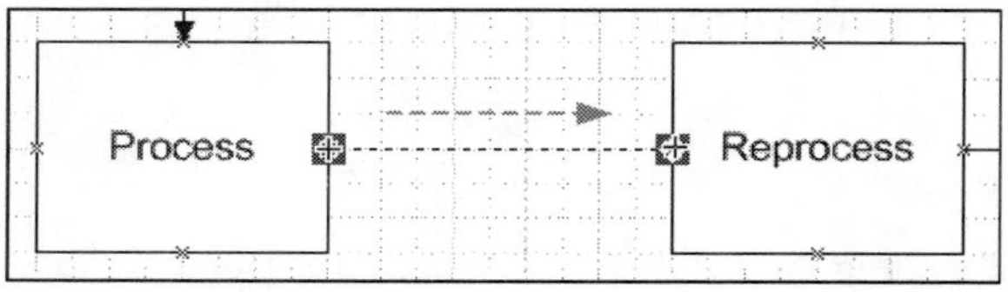

Exhibit 3-6: Connecting shapes by using the Connector tool

To ensure that the shapes are properly connected, you attach them at their connection points. When connected properly, the shapes are glued. *Gluing* secures the shapes together so that when a shape is moved, the connection is not broken.

Do it!

B-2: Connecting shapes

Here's how	Here's why
1 On the View toolbar, click 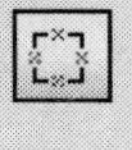	(The Connection Points button.) Small blue "x" marks appear on each side of the shapes.
2 Point to the Decision shape in the first column	AutoConnect handles appear on each side and on the bottom.
3 Point to the bottom AutoConnect handle	The Process shape below the Decision shape is outlined in red, indicating that it will be connected, rather than added as a new shape.
Click the bottom handle	To automatically connect the Decision shape to the Process shape.
4 Connect the Decision shape to the Process shape on the right side	Point to the Decision shape and click the AutoConnect handle on the right side. Now all the shapes are connected.
	You want to connect the bottom Process shape in the first column with an arrow pointing back to the top Process shape. You can't do this with AutoConnect, but you can draw the connector with the Connector tool.
5 On the Standard toolbar, click 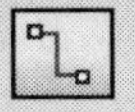	The Connector tool.
6 In the bottom Process shape, point to the connection point on the left side, as shown	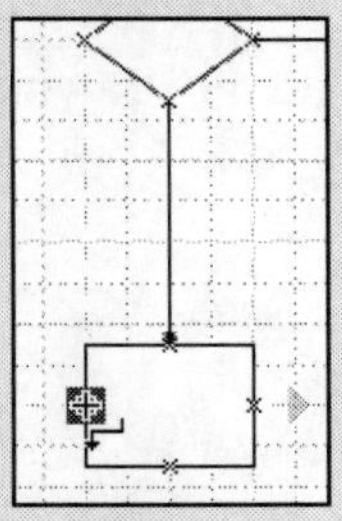 The connection point has a bold red box around it, and the pointer changes to a crosshair.
7 Slowly start dragging slightly to the left and up	To begin drawing a connection.

8 Point to the leftmost connection point in the top Process shape	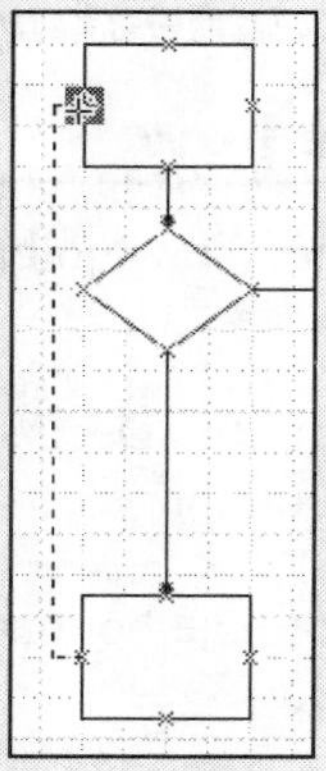 The connection point has a bold red box around it.
Release the mouse button	To make the connection. Two red boxes appear at the connections to indicate that the shapes are properly connected, or glued.
9 Select the Pointer tool and click a blank area of the page	To deselect the connection.
10 On the View toolbar, click 	(The Connection Points button.) To hide the connection points, so you can more clearly see the direction of the connections.
Click the Connection Points button again	To switch connection points back on.
11 Update the drawing	

Connector shapes

Explanation

You can use special connector shapes to connect other shapes, as shown in Exhibit 3-7. Connector shapes are located on various stencils, but you can quickly view them all on the Connectors stencil, which is available in the Visio Extras category. Some stencils have connector shapes that work especially well with the master shapes on them.

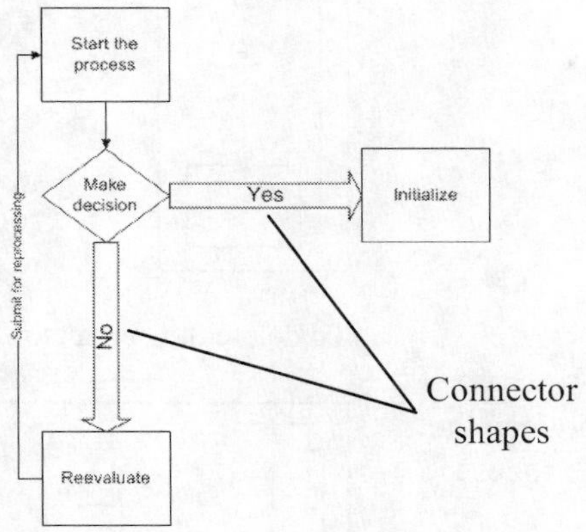

Exhibit 3-7: Two examples of connector shapes

Do it!

B-3: Using connector shapes

Here's how	Here's why
1 Click the connector between the Decision shape and the bottom Process shape in the first column	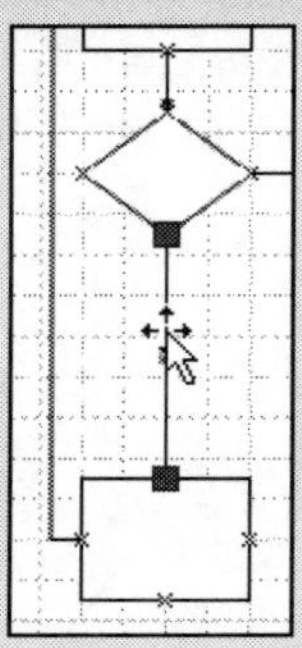
Press DELETE	To delete the connector.
2 Delete the connector between the Decision shape and the Process shape to the right	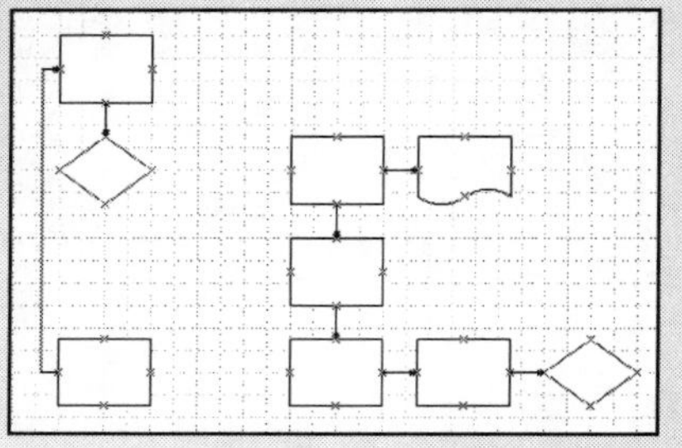 You'll use connector shapes to indicate the "Yes" or "No" decisions. To see common connector shapes, you'll need to open the Connectors stencil.
3 On the Standard toolbar, click 	(The Shapes button.) To expand the stencils list.
Select **Visio Extras, Connectors (US Units)**	To open the Connectors stencil.
4 In the Stencil, scroll down	(If necessary.) To view the connector shapes near the bottom of the stencil. You'll add a 1-D single connector shape.

Another way to add SHAPES to AN. Active Stencil —

5 From the stencil, drag a 1-D single connector to the connection point on the right side of the Decision shape	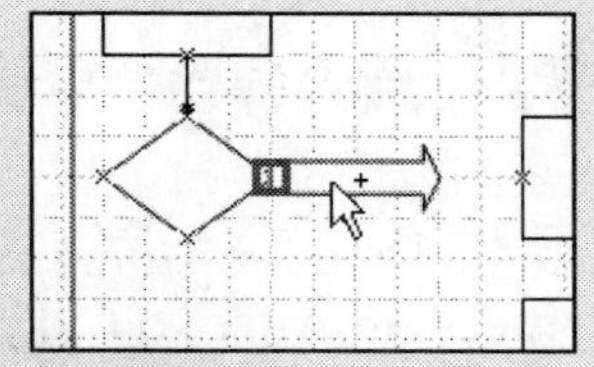 When the left side of the connector shape is over the connection point, it changes to red, indicating that the connector will be glued to the shape.
Release the mouse button	To glue the left side of the connector shape. A red glue point attaches the connector to the Decision shape, and a green control handle appears on the right side.
6 Drag the control handle to the right	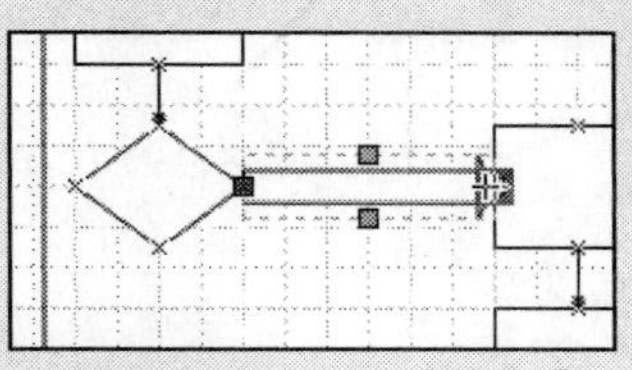 To glue the connector shape to the Process shape in the second column. You can also add connector shapes by using AutoConnect.
7 In the stencil, verify that the 1-D single connector shape is selected	
8 On the page, point to the Decision shape in the first column	To display the AutoConnect handles.
9 Click the bottom AutoConnect handle	To add the 1-D single connector shape as a link between the two shapes in the column.
10 Press ESC	To deselect any shapes.
11 Hide the connection points	On the View toolbar, click the Connection Points button.
12 Update the drawing	+

Topic C: Working with text

Explanation

Adding and formatting text in Visio is similar to doing those tasks in any word processor. After you add text to the drawing page or to a shape, you can format it.

Unlike in a word processor, text in Visio is contained in a *text block*. You can think of a text block as a container for the text. This means that when you place text in a drawing, there are two things at work: the text block and the text itself. Each has its own properties and can be formatted separately.

Text blocks

Text blocks are included with shapes, connector shapes, or any object containing text. Like objects, text blocks can be resized, formatted, and rotated. Exhibit 3-8 provides an example of different text placements in shapes and connectors.

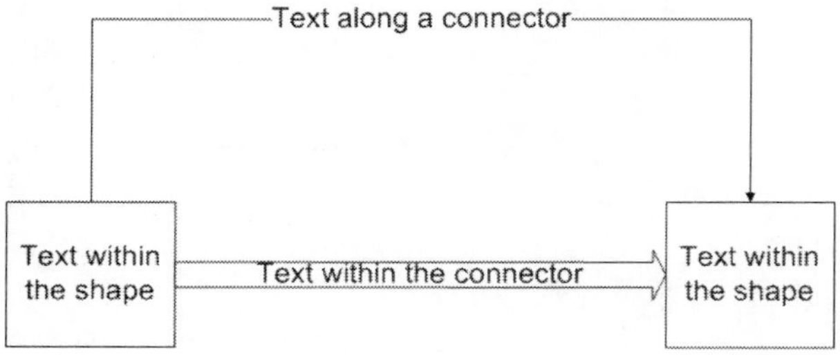

Exhibit 3-8: Examples of text in objects

Text blocks give you added flexibility in how text is displayed. This is especially beneficial when you have a shape with a horizontal orientation, but you need the text in a different orientation, as shown in Exhibit 3-9.

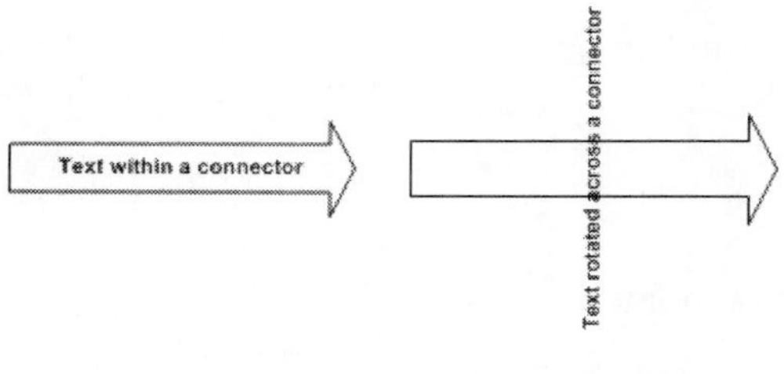

Exhibit 3-9: Text rotated across an object

Finally, a text block can be formatted independently of the shape with which it is associated. For example, a text block can be larger or smaller than its associated shape.

Text editing

If you decide to change text after you've added it to a drawing, you can return to text mode. Select the Text tool on the Standard toolbar and then click the text you want to edit. When you're finished editing, press Esc or click outside the text block.

You can resize the text box by selecting it and dragging a handle with the Pointer tool.

Do it!

C-1: Creating and editing a text block

Here's how	Here's why
1 On the Standard toolbar, click [A]	The Text tool.
2 Click the blank area at the top of the page, near the center	The page magnification automatically increases, and a text box with an insertion point appears.
Type **Outlander Work Processes**	
3 Press ESC	To exit text mode. Notice that the text has handles around it.
4 Double-click the text	To enter text mode again.
Click at the beginning of the text	To place the insertion point.
5 Type **New** and press SPACEBAR	The text wraps to a new line.
6 Press ESC	To exit text mode.
7 Select the Pointer tool	
Drag the right handle until the text fits on one line	
8 Press ESC	To deselect the text box.
Update the drawing	

Paragraph text

Explanation

To add larger amounts of text, such as a paragraph, it is often best to create a large text block. By doing this, you can control how large the text area will be before you add text. This avoids the problem of having a text block run into shapes on your diagram.

You create a text block by selecting the Text tool and dragging diagonally. The text will wrap when it reaches the end of the text block area. You can resize and move the block.

Do it!

C-2: Adding paragraph text

Here's how	Here's why
1 Select the Text tool	If necessary.
2 Point to the top-right area of the drawing page, under the 8" mark on the horizontal ruler	
Drag down and to the right to create a text box 2.25" wide and 2" high	Use the status bar to determine the size of the box.
3 Type **In an effort to increase productivity and quality, our company has decided to adopt these new work processes. They will take effect for a 90-day trial. During this time, any feedback would be appreciated.**	In the text block.
Press ENTER	To create a new line.
4 Type **To submit feedback:**	As the next line.
Press ENTER	
5 Type **Download the feedback form**	
Press ENTER	
6 Type **List your feedback**	
Press ENTER	
7 Type **Email the form to your manager**	
Press ESC	

8 Observe the text block area

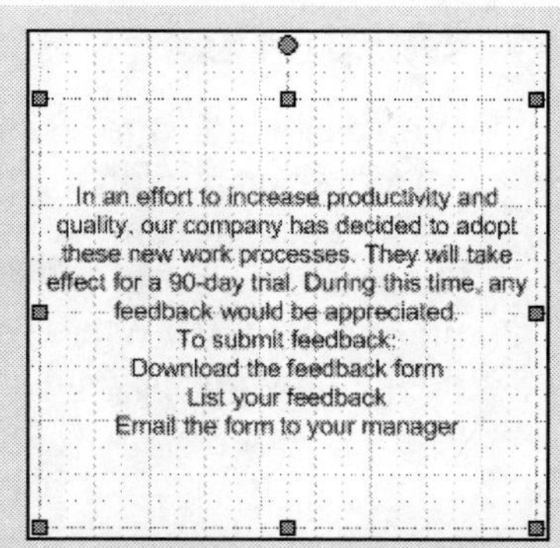

The text is centered.

9 Update the drawing

Shape text

Explanation

You can add text to shapes to describe the steps in your flowchart. To add text to a shape, select it with the Pointer tool or the Text tool; then start typing. As you type, Visio enters text mode and zooms in on the shape. You can also double-click a shape to enter text mode. Either way, as you type, the text block for the text is visible, as shown in Exhibit 3-10. When you are done adding text, press Esc to exit text mode and return to the previous page magnification.

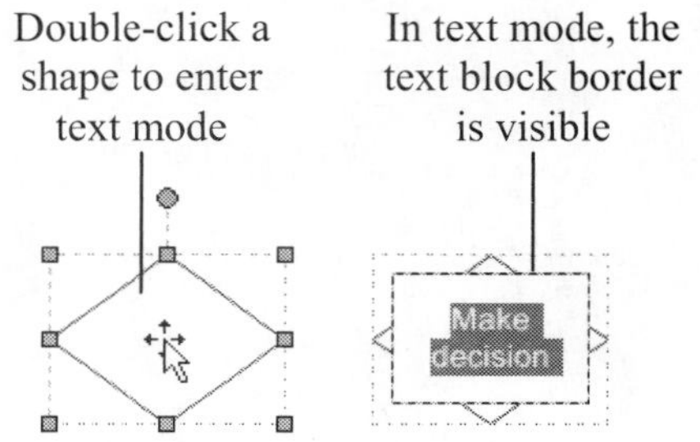

Exhibit 3-10: Adding text to a shape

Do it!

C-3: Adding text to shapes

Here's how	Here's why
1 Verify that the Text tool is selected	
2 From the Zoom list, select **Page**	To fit the entire page in the work area.
3 Click the top Process shape in the first column	The view zooms in again, and you are in text mode.
4 Type **Start the process**	
Press ESC	To exit text mode. The shape is still selected.
	You can also enter text in shapes without using the Text tool.
5 Select the Pointer tool	
6 Click the Decision shape below the Process shape	To select it.
Type **Make decision**	As soon as you begin typing, Visio automatically enters text mode.
7 Press ESC	To exit text mode and view the entire page again.

8 Select the bottom Process shape in the first column

Type **Reevaluate** and press ESC

9 Enter text in the rest of the shapes, as shown

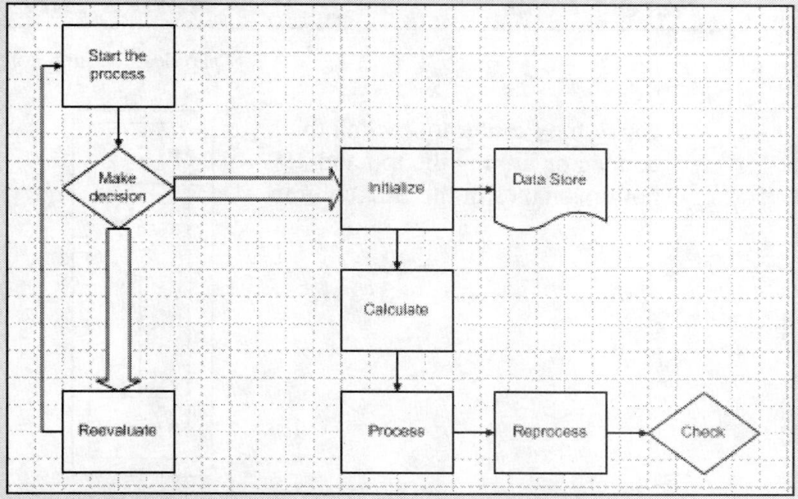

10 Update the drawing

Connectors and text

Explanation

In Visio, connectors are also considered shapes. This means you can add text to connectors by using the same methods you use for adding text to shapes. There are advantages to adding text to connectors: the text moves with the connector, and if the connector length is changed, the text is adjusted.

Do it!

C-4: Adding text to connectors

Here's how	Here's why
1 Press ESC	To deselect any selected objects.
2 Using the Pointer tool, click the connector linking the top and bottom shapes in the first column	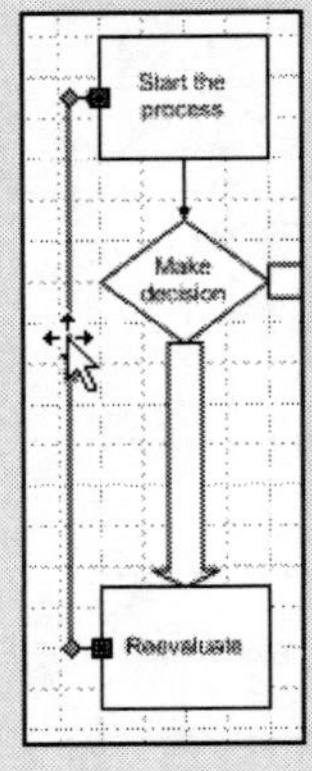
Type **Submit for reprocessing**	The text runs perpendicular to the connector.
3 Press ESC	To exit text mode.
4 Select the connector shape on the right side of the Decision shape	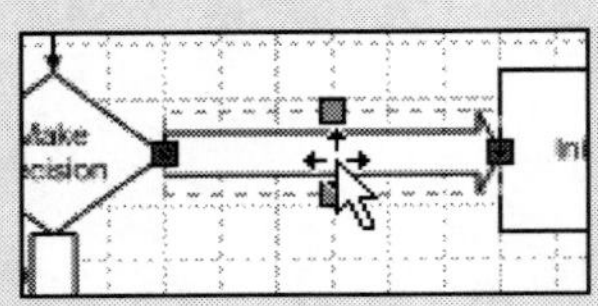
Type **Yes** and press ESC	To define the flow of the decision.
5 Select the connector shape on the bottom of the Decision shape	
Type **No** and press ESC	The text for the connector shape matches the direction the shape is pointing.

6 Select the connector shape going to the Document shape	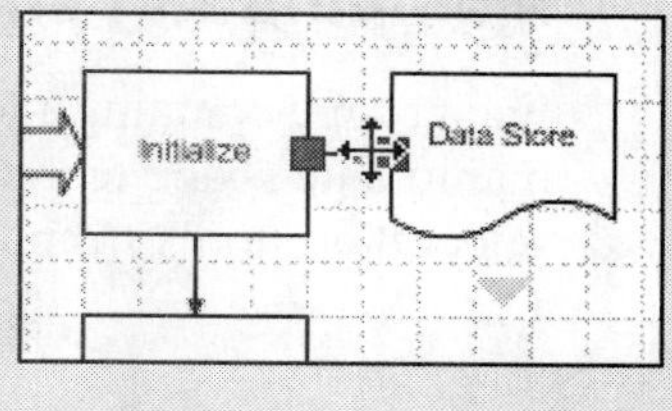
Type **Create report** and press ESC	
7 Press and hold CTRL + SHIFT and click the Document shape	To zoom in on it. The connector text overlaps both shapes.
8 Drag the Document shape approximately 1" to the right	(Use the Pointer tool.) The connector expands, and the text maintains its position relative to the center.
Press CTRL + Z	To undo the change.
9 View the entire page in the work area	In the Zoom list, select Page.
10 Update the drawing	

Manipulating shape text

Explanation

Each shape contains a text block area you can move and manipulate. You can manipulate shape text blocks with either the Text tool or the Text Block tool. You can select these tools from the Text Tool list on the Standard toolbar, as shown in Exhibit 3-11.

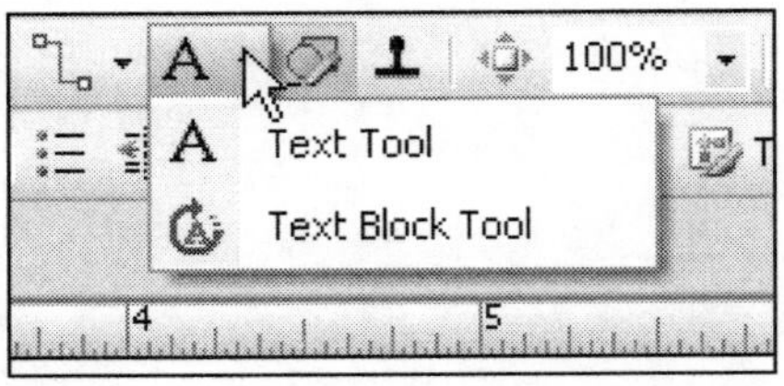

Exhibit 3-11: The Text Tool list on the Standard toolbar

The Text tool vs. the Text Block tool

The primary difference between the Text and Text Block tools is what happens when you select a text block. When you use the Text tool to select a text block, you immediately enter text mode. You can press Esc to end text mode and select the text block itself. When you use the Text Block tool to select a text block, you select the block itself, not the text contained in the block.

Do it!

C-5: Adjusting shape text

Here's how	Here's why
1 Double-click the **Create report** connector	To enter text mode.
Press END	To move to the end of the text.
2 Press ↵ ENTER	To move to the next line.
Type **confirmation**	
3 Double-click the Document shape	To enter text mode for the shape.
Edit the text to read **Document 1** and press ESC	To replace the previous text with "Document 1."
4 Point to the middle handle at the bottom of the text block	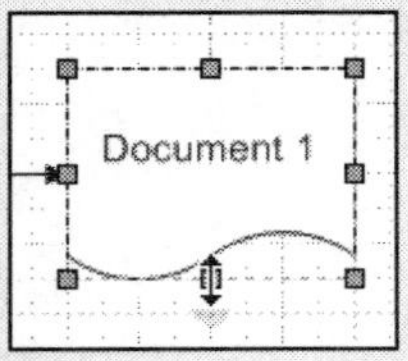 The pointer becomes a double-headed arrow.
Drag down slightly	To resize the text block.

To select Text only and then rotate

5 On the Standard toolbar, expand the Text Tool list, as shown

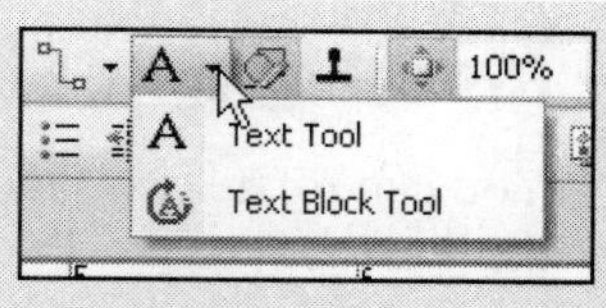

Select **Text Block Tool**

6 Point to the text in the Document shape

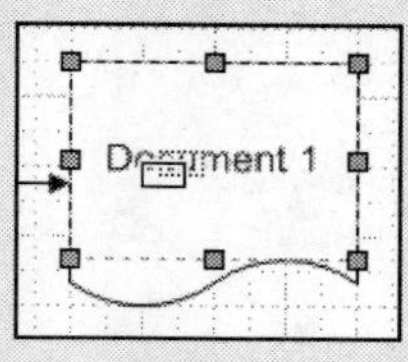

The pointer changes to two rectangles.

Drag the text down

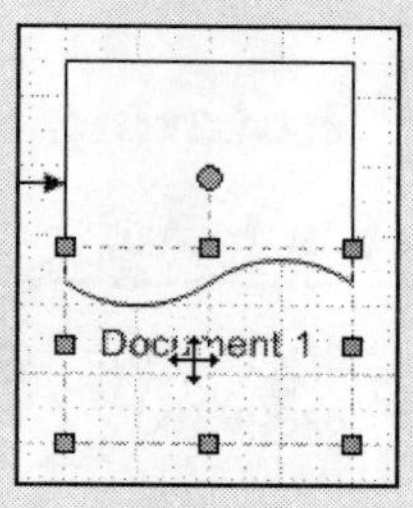

The text block moves below the Document shape.

7 Press ESC — To deselect the text block.

8 Update the drawing

Rotating text blocks

Explanation

You can rotate text blocks as you would any other shape. To do so, select the block with the Text tool or the Text Block tool. A round rotation handle appears outside the text block, as shown in Exhibit 3-12. Drag this handle to rotate the text.

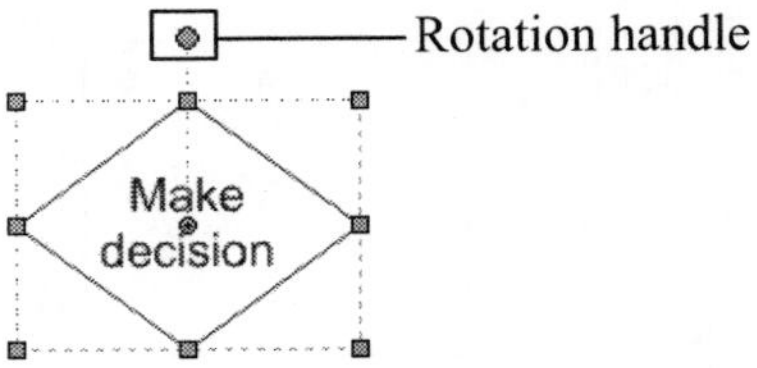

Exhibit 3-12: A shape rotation handle

Do it!

C-6: Rotating text

Here's how	Here's why
1 Verify that the Text Block tool is still selected	
2 Click the Document shape	A round rotation handle appears at the top of the text block.
3 Point to the rotation handle	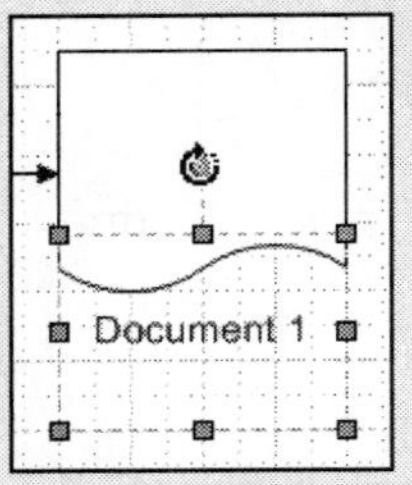 The pointer changes to the Rotate shape.
Drag clockwise until the text is perpendicular to the shape	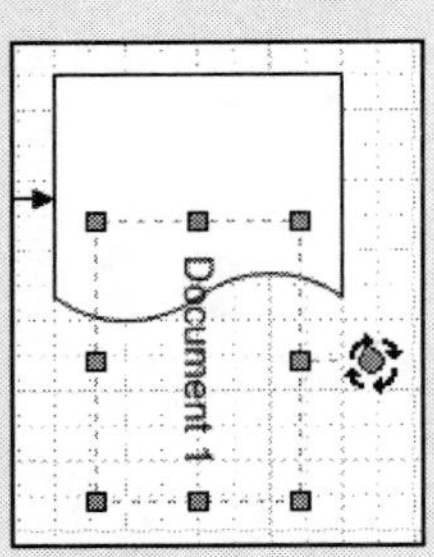
4 Move the text block up and to the left until it is inside the shape again	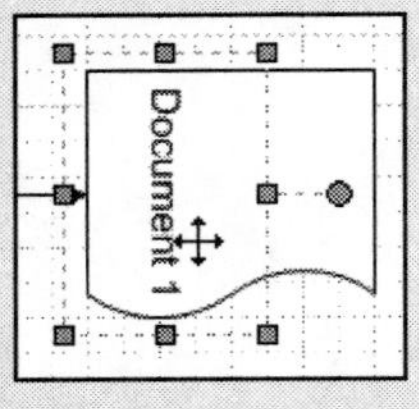
5 Scroll to the left	To view the first column of shapes in the diagram.

6 Select the **Submit for reprocessing** connector text

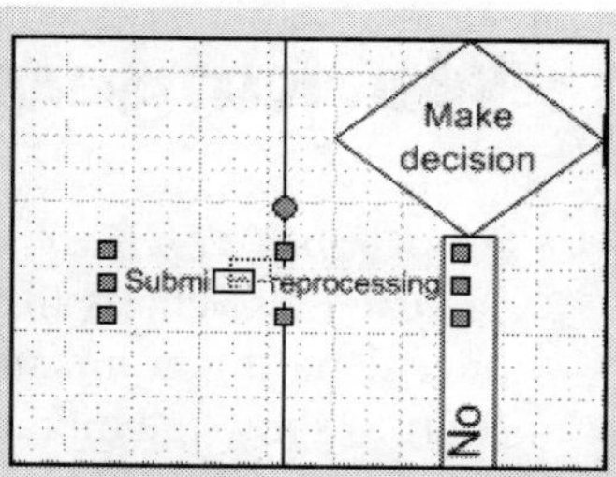

7 Rotate the text block counterclockwise so that it is parallel with the line

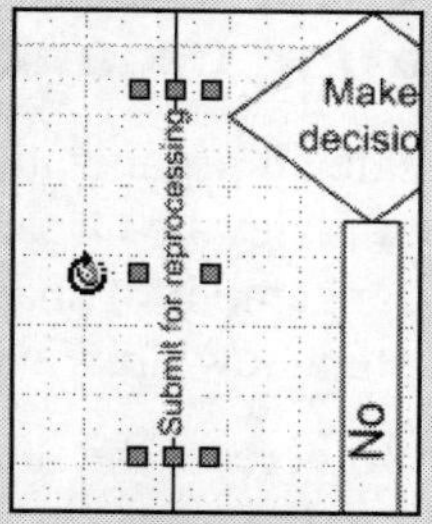

8 View the entire page in the work area

In the Zoom list, select Page.

9 Update and close the drawing

Topic D: Working with organization charts

Explanation

An *organization chart* depicts the systematic flow of authority and responsibility. You can use these charts to show superior-subordinate relationships, report hierarchies, and inter-department links in an organization. For example, you can use an organization chart to show the hierarchy of the department structure of your company.

Creating organization charts

To create an organization chart, you use the Organization Chart template. When you use this template, the Organization Chart stencil and toolbar open. Use the toolbar to change the arrangement of shapes on the drawing page. To use the Organization Chart template to create a new drawing, choose File, New, Organization Chart, Organization Chart.

After you create the drawing, create the organization chart by dragging shapes from the stencil to the page. An organization chart shape contains the name and title of the person represented by the shape. When you drag an organization chart shape to the page, the Connecting Shapes message box appears, advising you to drop the shape over the superior shape to connect the shapes. Check "Don't show this message again" to prevent the message from appearing every time you drag shapes from the stencil.

Adding multiple shapes

You can add more than one shape of the same type to your organization chart. For example, you might need five Manager shapes under an Executive shape. You can insert all of the Manager shapes by dragging the Multiple Shapes shape over the Executive shape. When you do this, the Add Multiple Shapes dialog box appears, as shown in Exhibit 3-13. In the dialog box, enter the number of shapes you want to create, select the shape type, and click OK. Visio automatically creates and links the shapes.

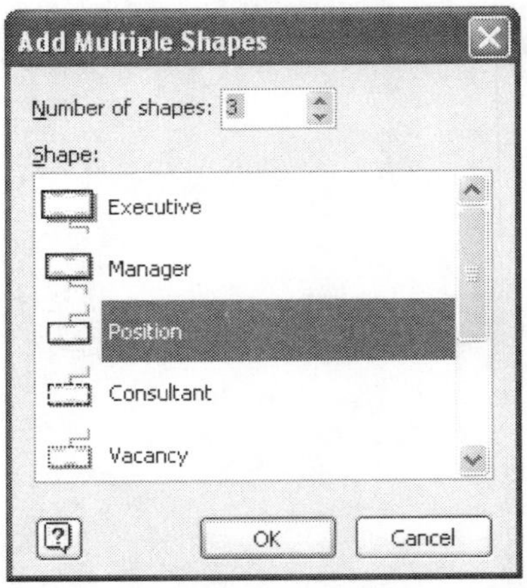

Exhibit 3-13: The Add Multiple Shapes dialog box

Do it!

D-1: Creating an organization chart

Here's how	Here's why
1 Choose **File**, **New**, **Business**, **Organization Chart (US Units)**	To create a file based on the Organization Chart template. The Organization Chart Shapes stencil appears in the Shapes pane, and the Organization Chart toolbar is floating in the work area.
Save the file as **My organization chart**	In the current unit folder.
2 Dock the Organization Chart toolbar	With the other toolbars at the top of the application window.
3 From the Organization Chart Shapes stencil, drag an Executive shape near the top center of the page	The Connecting Shapes message box appears.
Check **Don't show this message again**	(If necessary.) To prevent this message box from appearing each time you drag a shape from the Organization Chart Shapes stencil.
Click **OK**	
4 Type **Kathy Sinclair**	This is the name of the executive.
Press ENTER	To go to the next line within the shape.
Type **President**	To enter the title of the executive.
Press ESC	
5 On the Standard toolbar, click the AutoConnect button	(If necessary.) To make it active. You'll use a special master shape to add multiple shapes to the chart.
6 From the stencil, drag the Multiple Shapes shape and place it over the Executive shape on the page	To display the AutoConnect handles. (Don't release the mouse button.)
Point to the bottom AutoConnect handle and then release the mouse button	The Add Multiple Shapes dialog box appears.
7 From the Shape list, select **Manager**	You'll add multiple Manager shapes.

8 Increase the Number of shapes value to **4**	Click the up-arrow to the right of the box.
Click **OK**	To link four Manager shapes to the Executive shape.
9 Deselect the shapes	Press Esc.
10 Link two Position shapes to the leftmost Manager shape	Drag the Multiple Shapes shape from the stencil and place it over the leftmost Manager shape. Point to the bottom AutoConnect handle and then release the mouse button. In the dialog box, select Position, change the value to 2, and click OK.
11 Using the same technique, add two Position shapes to the third Manager shape	
12 Press and hold CTRL + SHIFT and click near the center of the shapes	To zoom in on them.
13 Add text to the shapes, as shown	

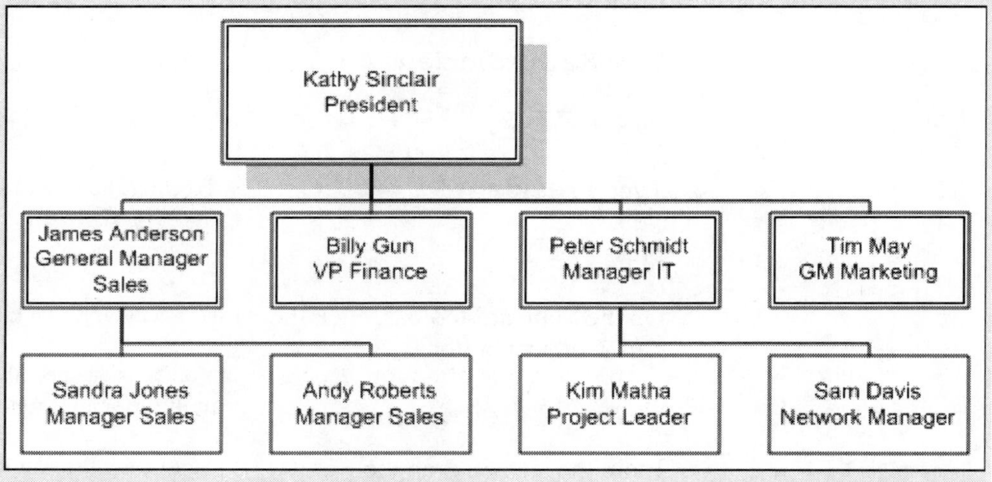

14 Update the drawing

Modifying layouts

Explanation

A *layout* in Visio defines the way in which shapes are arranged. You might need to change the layout of the shapes to change the hierarchy in an organization chart. The Organization Chart toolbar provides different layout styles, such as horizontal and vertical layouts, as shown in Exhibit 3-14. Changing the layout of a superior shape changes the layout of all subordinate shapes. To change the layout of the shapes, select a layout from the Organization Chart toolbar.

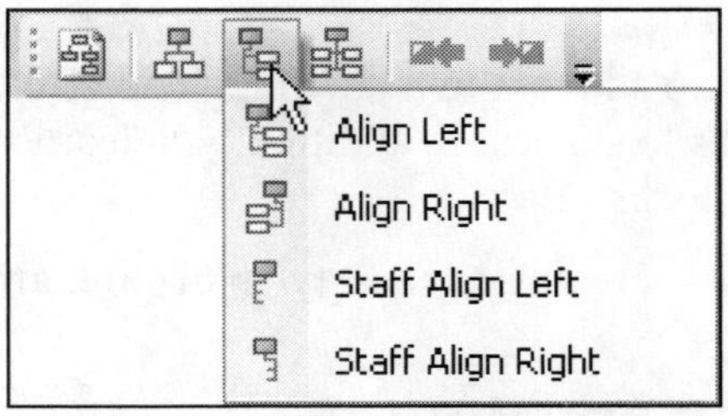

Exhibit 3-14: Some layout styles available from the Organization Chart toolbar

Do it!

D-2: Changing the layout of an organization chart

Here's how	Here's why
1 Select the **James Anderson** Manager shape	You'll change the layout of this shape and its subordinates.
2 On the Organization Chart toolbar, click 	(The Vertical Layout button.) To display a palette of vertical layout options.
Select **Align Right**	To right-align all the shapes under the James Anderson Manager shape.
3 Select the **Peter Schmidt** Manager shape	
From the Vertical Layout menu, choose **Align Left**	To left-align all subordinate shapes under the Peter Schmidt Manager shape.
4 View the entire page in the work area	From the Zoom list, select Page.
5 Update and close the drawing	

 VISGUY.COM = search google for shapes

Unit summary: Basic diagrams

Topic A In this topic, you learned how to plan a basic flowchart. You also learned some tips for using **flowchart shapes**.

Topic B In this topic, you created a **basic diagram**. You placed shapes on a page by dragging from stencils and by using **AutoConnect**. You linked shapes by using both AutoConnect and the **Connector tool**. Finally, you connected shapes by using **connector shapes**.

Topic C In this topic, you learned how to add text to a drawing. You also learned how to create **text labels** and add **text blocks** to shapes. In addition, you learned how to edit text and how to move and rotate text blocks.

Topic D In this topic, you learned how to create and modify an **organization chart**.

Independent practice activity

In this activity, you'll create a diagram by adding shapes and connector lines. You'll also add and manipulate text to complete the diagram.

* Remember to start in the pointer tool

1. Open Shapes practice (from the current unit folder in the Student Data folder). Save the file as **My shapes practice**.
2. Add the shapes to the drawing page. Link the shapes so they're similar to the example in Exhibit 3-15. (*Hint*: By using AutoConnect, you can link the shapes as you add them; you can then reposition them on the page. Or you can position the shapes first and then use AutoConnect to link them.)
3. Using the Connector tool, add a connector line to connect the bottom Process shape in the second column to the Process shape in the first column, as shown in Exhibit 3-16.
4. Open the Connectors stencil and add 1-D single connector shapes, as shown in Exhibit 3-17.
5. Add text to the shapes and connectors, as shown in Exhibit 3-17.
6. Add the text **New Process** at the top of the drawing.
7. Move the text to the lower-left side of the page, and rotate it at a 60-degree angle.
8. Hide the View toolbar.
9. Update and close the drawing.

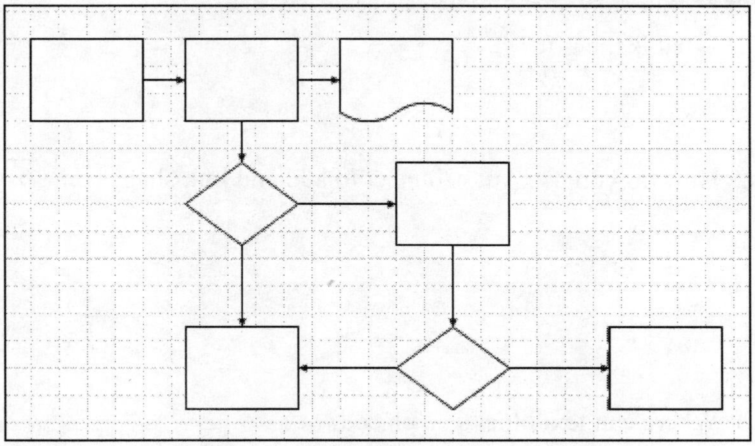

Exhibit 3-15: The diagram after Step 2

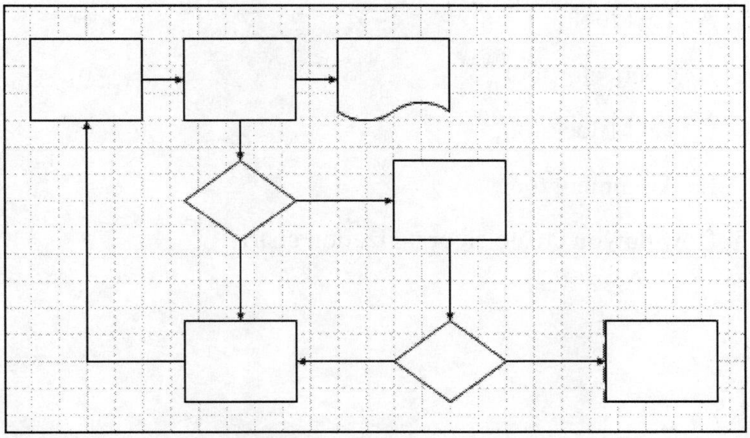

Exhibit 3-16: The diagram after Step 3

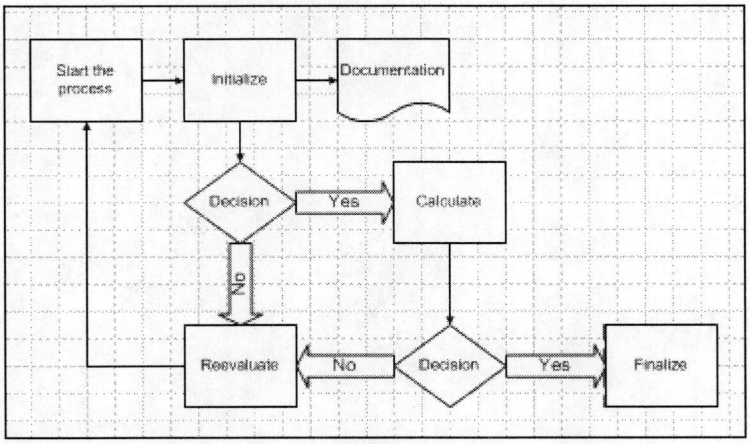

Exhibit 3-17: The diagram after Step 4

Review questions

1 What is the grid?

2 How do you use AutoConnect to add and link shapes on a page?

3 Where can text blocks be placed?

4 Which tools can you use to reposition a shape text block? [Choose all that apply.]

A Text tool

B Connector tool

C Text Block tool

D Alignment tool

5 How do you create an organization chart?

Unit 4

Formatting drawings

Unit time: 55 minutes

Complete this unit, and you'll know how to:

A Use text formatting options.

B Format text blocks.

C Format shapes and lines.

Topic A: Formatting text

Explanation

A Visio drawing has three basic elements: shapes, lines, and text. To make your diagrams attractive, you can improve the appearance of these elements. This is known as *formatting*. It includes changing colors, adding shadows, changing line properties, and changing the size and font used.

To format objects, you use dialog boxes or toolbars. Dialog boxes offer extensive options for formatting, while toolbars provide shortcuts to many of the common formatting commands. If you want to apply multiple formats to an object, using a dialog box is a better option because you can change multiple attributes in a single dialog box.

The Formatting toolbar

By default, the Formatting toolbar appears below the Standard toolbar when you start Visio. The Formatting toolbar provides shortcuts to the most commonly used formatting commands. Some of the buttons on the Formatting toolbar have an arrow next to them. Clicking the arrow displays a list or palette of additional options. The most recent option you've chosen from the list or palette appears as the active option on the toolbar. The following table describes some of the toolbar options.

Formatting toolbar option	Used to...
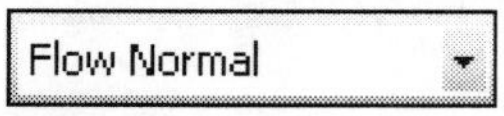 Style list	Apply a named style to the selected text. *Styles* are pre-designed groups of formatting attributes.
 Font list	Change the font of the selected text.
 Font size list	Change the size of the selected text. You can select the desired size from the list or enter it directly in the box.
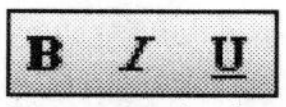 Text style buttons	Make the selected text bold, italic, or underlined.
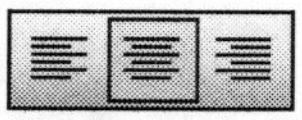 Horizontal alignment buttons	Align the selected text to the left, right, or center.
 Text Color button	Change the color of the selected text. Click the arrow to display the color palette, and then choose a color.

The Format Text toolbar

In addition to the Formatting toolbar, Visio provides the Format Text toolbar, which contains options for formatting text. To display this toolbar, right-click any toolbar in the Visio window and choose Format Text. The following table describes some of the options on the toolbar.

Format Text toolbar option	Used to...
 Increase/decrease font size buttons	Increase or decrease the size of the selected text incrementally based on settings in the Font size box.
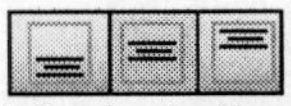 Vertical alignment buttons	Change the top-to-bottom alignment of text.
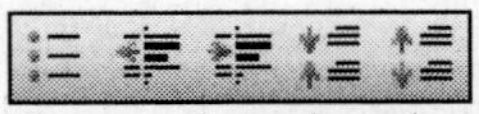 Paragraph options buttons	Add bullets, change indents, and set line spacing.

You can format the text in a section or format each word separately to draw attention to it. To format text by using the toolbar, select the text you want to format and then click the appropriate toolbar button.

Do it!

A-1: Formatting text by using toolbars

Here's how	Here's why
1 Open Formatting.vxd	
Save the file as **My formatting**	In the current unit folder.
2 Right-click any toolbar and choose **Format Text**	To display the Format Text toolbar.
3 Using the Pointer tool, select the text label near the top of the drawing area	The label reads "New Outlander work processes."
4 On the Format Text toolbar, click  twice	(The Increase Font Size button.) The text is larger, which forces it to wrap to two lines. You'll expand the text box so that the text fits on one line.
5 Drag the right-side handle until the text fits on one line	
Move the text so that it fits comfortably in the space at the top of the page	If necessary.
6 Select the upper-left Process shape	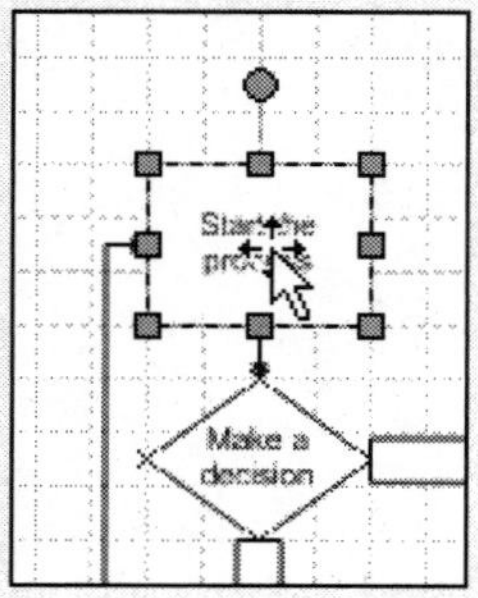 You'll change the text to a blue color.
7 On the Formatting toolbar, expand the Text Color list, as shown	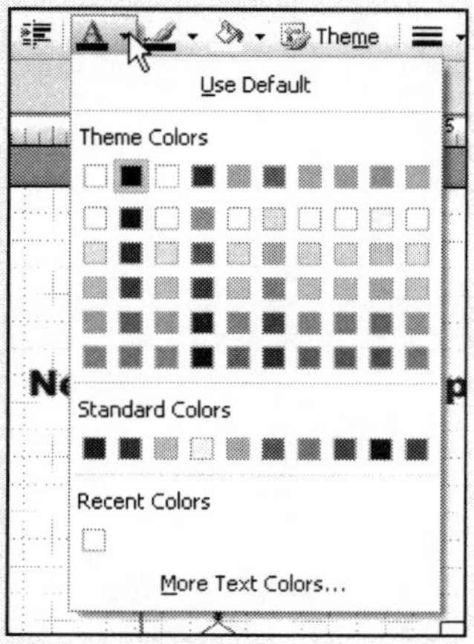 Click the down-arrow on the Text Color button.

8 Select a blue color	The text in the shape changes to blue.
9 On the Formatting toolbar, click **B**	(The Bold button.) To make the text bold.
10 Select the Decision shape below the first Process shape	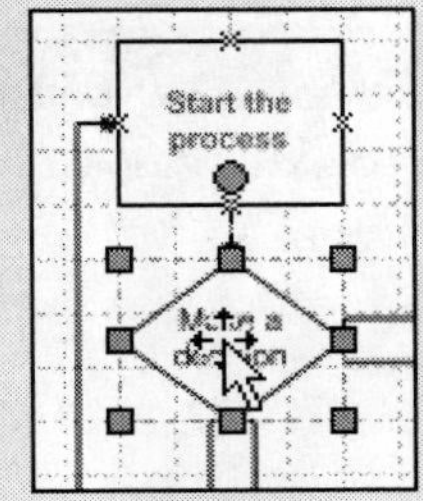
11 Select the Text tool	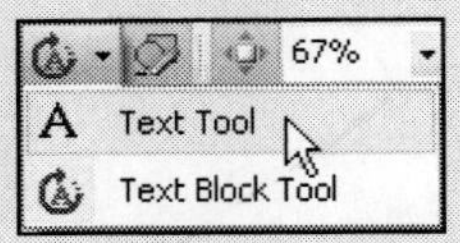 (Click the arrow beside the Text Block tool, if necessary, and select the Text tool.) To enter text mode.
12 Double-click the word **decision**	To select it. You'll apply formatting to this word only and not to the rest of the text.
On the Formatting toolbar, click **B**	To make the selected word bold.
Press ESC twice	To exit text mode and deselect the shape.
13 Press and hold CTRL + SHIFT and click the Decision shape	To zoom in on it and view the changes.
Press and hold CTRL + SHIFT and right-click anywhere on the diagram	To zoom out again.
14 Update the drawing	

The Text dialog box

Explanation

Although toolbars provide shortcuts to many formatting options, it can be time-consuming to apply multiple formats. If you need to make extensive formatting changes, it is sometimes easier to use the Text dialog box, shown in Exhibit 4-1.

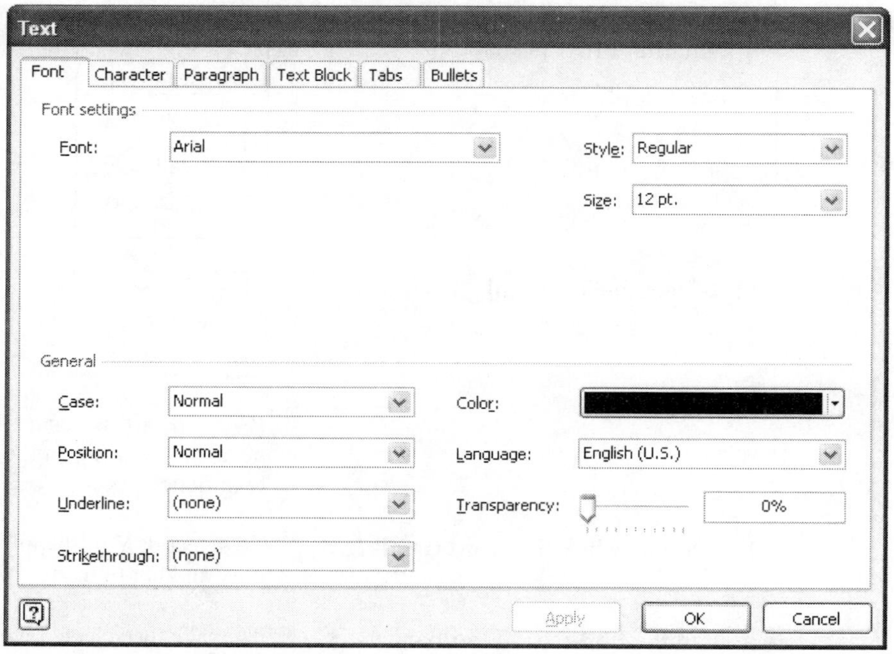

Exhibit 4-1: The Text dialog box

The Text dialog box contains six tabs. You choose options from each tab and then apply them by clicking Apply. When you're finished selecting options, click OK to apply all text changes and close the dialog box. The tabs and their functions are described in the following table:

Tab	Used to...
Font	Specify font and style characteristics.
Character	Set character spacing and scaling.
Paragraph	Specify paragraph alignment, spacing, and indentation.
Text Block	Set margins and vertical spacing for text blocks.
Tabs	Define the position and alignment of tab stops in text blocks.
Bullets	Select a bullet style.

To use the Text dialog box:

1. Select the shape or text you want to format.
2. Choose Format, Text to open the Text dialog box.
3. On the various tabs, select the formatting options you want to apply.
4. Click Apply to view your changes without closing the dialog box.
5. Click OK.

Do it!

A-2: Formatting text by using the Text dialog box

Here's how	Here's why
1 Using the Pointer tool, select the bottom Process shape in the middle column	
2 Choose **Format**, **Text...**	To open the Text dialog box. The Font tab is active by default.
3 From the Font list, select **Verdana**	To choose a different font type.
4 From the Style list, select **Bold**	To make the text bold.
5 From the Size list, select **12 pt.**	To increase the font size.
6 From the Color list, select a blue color	
7 Click **Apply**	To view the formats without closing the dialog box. (You might have to move the dialog box in order to see the selected shape.)
8 Click **OK**	To close the dialog box.
9 Update the drawing	

Topic B: Formatting text blocks

Explanation

Text blocks are shapes without borders. You can format them by using buttons on the Standard toolbar or by using options on the Text Block tab in the Text dialog box, as shown in Exhibit 4-2. When you format text blocks by using the Text dialog box, you can set alignment, margin, and background options.

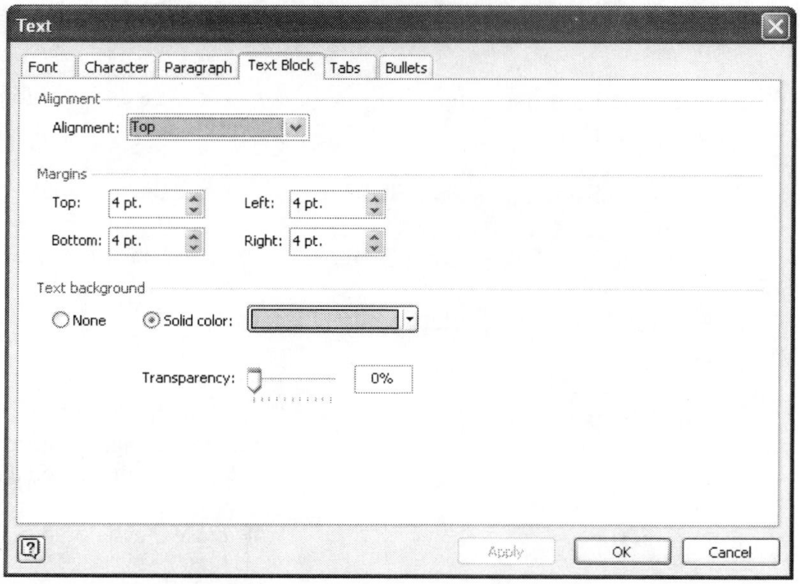

Exhibit 4-2: Text block formatting options in the Text dialog box

The following table describes the options on the Text Block tab:

Area	Used to...
Alignment	Position text vertically within the text box. Options include top, middle, and bottom.
Margins	Specify the distance between the text and the border of the text box. This option is helpful when you are using borders around text blocks. You can set top, bottom, left, and right margins for a text block.
Text background	Specify a color for the background of a text box. You can also specify a transparency level for the background.

Do it!

B-1: Formatting a text block

Here's how	Here's why
1 On the Standard toolbar, from the Zoom list, select **Page**	To view the entire page in the work area.

2	Select the text block in the upper-right corner of the drawing	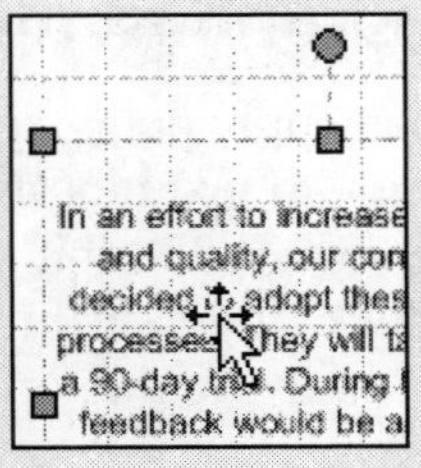 You'll apply text block formatting.
3	Choose **Format**, **Text...**	To open the Text dialog box.
	Activate the Text Block tab	
4	Under Alignment, select **Top**	
5	Set all the margins to **4 pt.**	Click the up-arrow next to each value three times.
6	Under Text background, select **Solid color**	
	From the Solid color list, select a light orange color	
7	Click **Apply**	To apply the formatting without closing the dialog box.
8	Activate the Font tab	To display the font formatting options.
	From the Font list, select **Times New Roman**	To change the font.
	Change the font size to **12 pt.**	
9	Click **Apply**	The text expands beyond the boundaries of the text block, but is still visible.
10	Click **OK**	To apply the changes and close the dialog box. You can use the same technique to format connector shapes.
11	Select the Yes connector shape linking the left Decision shape to the Process shape in the middle column	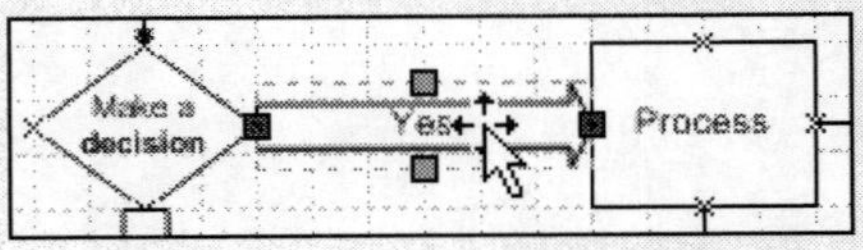
12	Open the Text dialog box and activate the Text Block tab	Choose Format, Text and click the Text Block tab.
	Set the text background color to a light green	
	Click **OK**	
13	Update the drawing	

Paragraph formatting in text blocks

Explanation

You can apply paragraph formats—such as horizontal alignment, indents, and spacing—to text blocks by using the options on the Paragraph tab of the Text dialog box, shown in Exhibit 4-3. The formatting you apply affects all text that is part of the text block. If you want to format only a section of text, select only the desired section before applying the formatting.

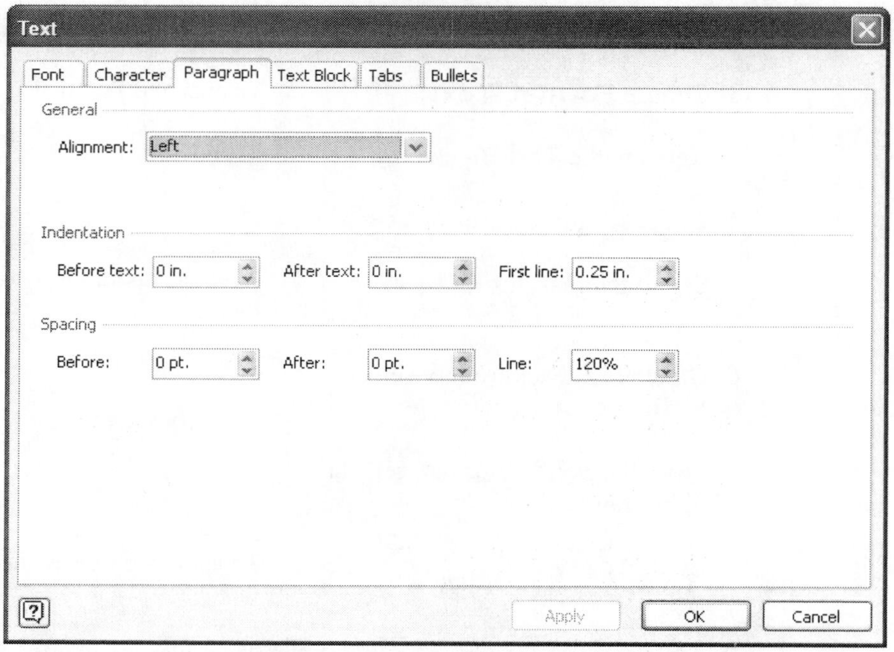

Exhibit 4-3: Paragraph options in the Text dialog box

The following table describes the options on the Paragraph tab:

Option	Used to...
General	Align the selected paragraphs horizontally. The options are left, right, centered, justified, or distributed.
Indentation	Specify the paragraph indentation. You can indent from the left or the right margin, or only the first line of a paragraph.
Spacing	Specify the gap between paragraphs.

Do it!

B-2: Applying paragraph formatting to a text block

Here's how	Here's why
1 Select the orange text block in the upper-right corner of the drawing	
2 Open the Text dialog box	Choose Format, Text.
Activate the Paragraph tab	
3 From the Alignment list, select **Left**	
4 Under Indentation, in the First Line box, triple-click the value	To select it.
Enter **.25**	
5 Click **Apply**	To view the change.
6 Click **OK**	To close the dialog box.
7 Select the Text tool	To enter text mode.
8 Triple-click the text **To submit feedback:**	To select it.
9 Open the Text dialog box and activate the Paragraph tab	
10 Under Spacing, edit the Before box to read **12**	To add space before the selected paragraph.
Click **Apply**	
Click **OK**	To close the dialog box.
11 Update the drawing	

Bullets

Explanation

You can apply predefined bullets to your text blocks by using the Bullets tab of the Text dialog box, shown in Exhibit 4-4. Bullets are used to present independent pieces of information that might be related or categorized.

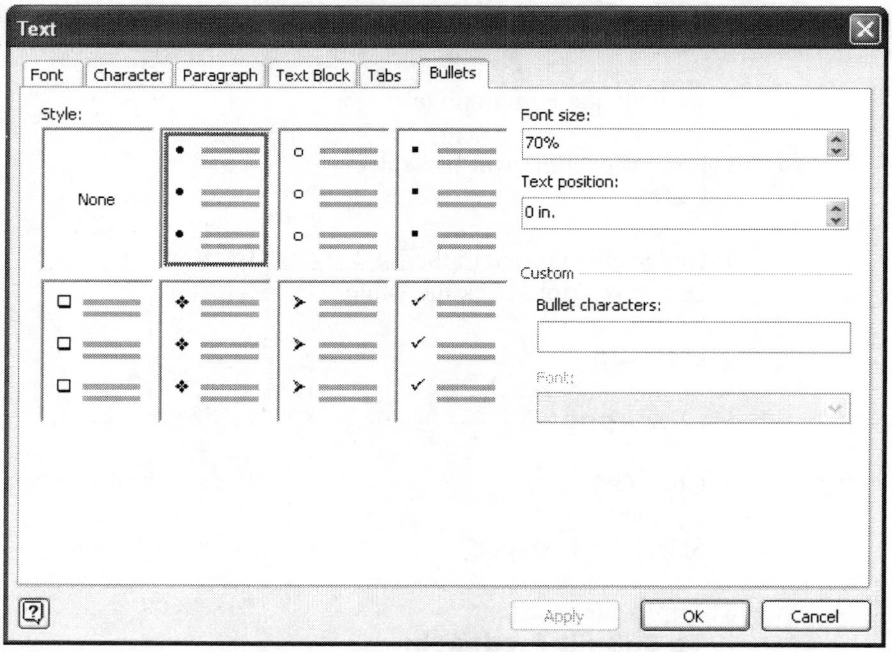

Exhibit 4-4: Bullet options in the Text dialog box

Do it!

B-3: Adding bullets to a text block

Here's how	Here's why
1 Using the Text tool, select the last three paragraphs of the large text block	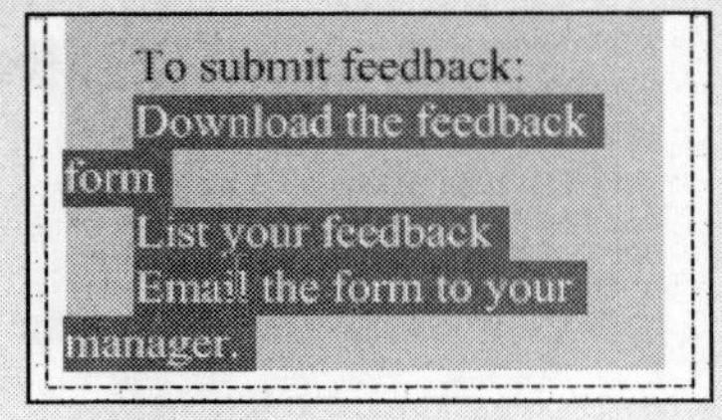
2 Open the Text dialog box	
Activate the Bullets tab	To view predefined bullets.
3 Select the first bullet style	
Click **Apply**	The last three lines are bulleted.
4 In the Font Size list, click the down-arrow to set the size of the bullets to **70%**	
Click **Apply**	The bullets are smaller.
5 Click **OK**	To close the dialog box.
6 On the Standard toolbar, click 	(The Increase Indent button.) The bullets line up under the word "To" in the paragraph above the bulleted text.
7 Using the Pointer tool, expand the width of the text block	(Select the Pointer tool; then drag the right control handle to the right.) Expand the width so that each bulleted paragraph fits on one line.
8 Reposition the text block in the upper-right corner	If necessary.
9 Update the drawing	

Topic C: Formatting shapes and lines

Explanation

You can format shapes and lines in Visio by changing colors, stroke weights, and line ends. You can apply these formats by using the buttons on the Standard toolbar, shown in Exhibit 4-5.

Exhibit 4-5: Basic shape and line formatting options on the Standard toolbar

Do it!

C-1: Formatting a shape

Here's how	Here's why
1 Using the Pointer tool, select the leftmost top Process shape	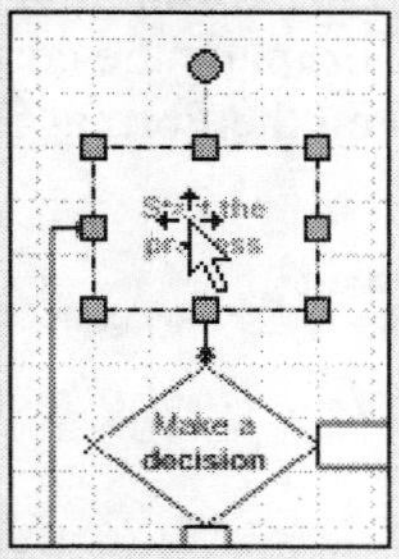
2 On the Formatting toolbar, expand the Fill Color list	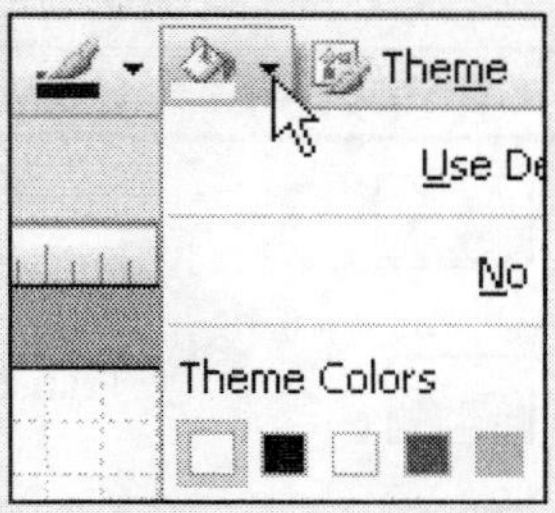
Select a light blue color	(Under Theme Colors, we chose Tint 10%.) To change the color of the shape.
3 On the toolbar, click 	(The Line Color button.) To apply a thin, black stroke around the shape. Because the shape is selected, the stroke color might not be visible.
4 On the toolbar, from the Line Weight list, select **Line Weight 9**, as shown	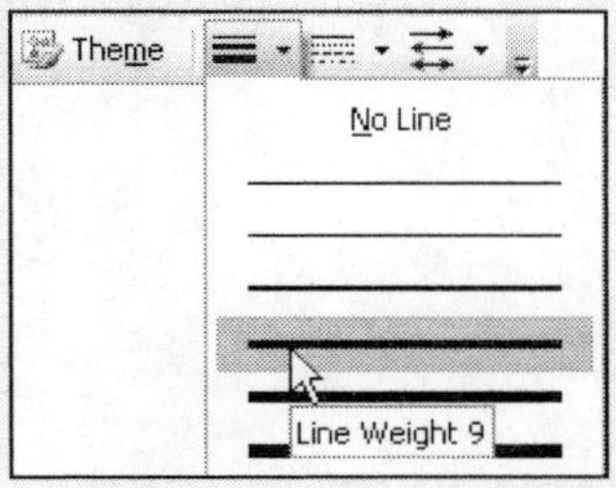 The line weight names are visible when you point to the lines. You'll change the line color to a dark blue.
5 On the toolbar, from the Line Color list, select a dark blue color	
6 Deselect the shape	To preview the results.
7 Update the drawing	

The Format Shape toolbar

Explanation

Sometimes you might want to use formatting options that aren't available on the Standard or Formatting toolbars. For example, you might want to add a shadow behind a shape or make the corners of a shape look more rounded. You can do this by using the buttons on the Format Shape toolbar, shown in Exhibit 4-6.

Exhibit 4-6: The Format Shape toolbar

The following table describes some of the options on the toolbar.

Component	Name	Used to...
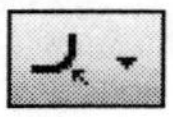	Corner Rounding button	Round the corners of shapes and lines.
	Transparency button	Change the opacity of the fill color for a shape.
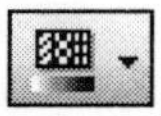	Fill Pattern button	Set the fill pattern of selected shapes.
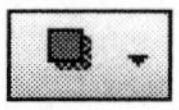	Shadow Color	Select and apply a drop shadow and set its color.

Do it!

C-2: Customizing a shape

Here's how	Here's why
1 Using the Pointer tool, select the leftmost top Process shape again	The shape you just formatted.
2 Display the Format Shape toolbar	(Right-click any toolbar and choose Format Shape.) You'll begin customizing the shape by rounding the corners.
3 On the toolbar, expand the Corner Rounding list	The expanded list shows a series of curve choices.
4 From the list, select the indicated option	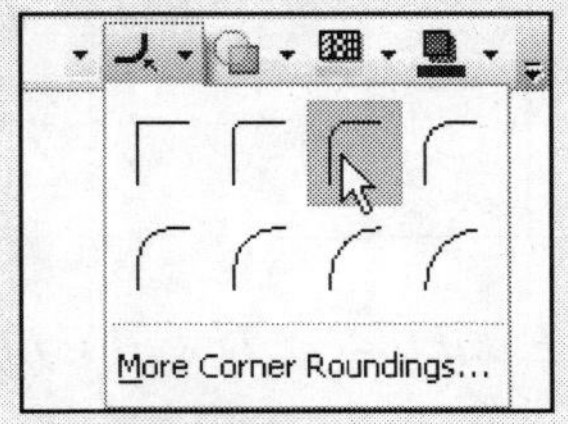 To make the corners of the shape more rounded. You'll also add a drop shadow to the shape.
5 On the Format Shape toolbar, click	(The Shadow Color button.) To add a gray drop shadow to the shape.
6 Expand the Shadow Color list, as shown	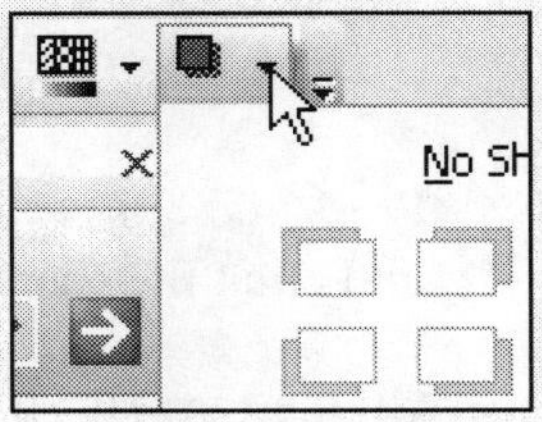
Select a dark blue color	
7 Deselect the shape	To preview the results.
8 Update the drawing	

The Fill, Line, and Shadow dialog boxes

Explanation

As with formatting text, sometimes you might want apply multiple formatting options to shapes, and it can be tedious to select each option individually by using toolbars. To make complex formatting easier, you can use the Fill, Line, and Shadow dialog boxes, shown in Exhibit 4-7. You can open the dialog boxes in several ways. You can choose Line, Fill, or Shadow from the Format menu, or you can select More from the corresponding button lists on the Formatting or Format Shape toolbars.

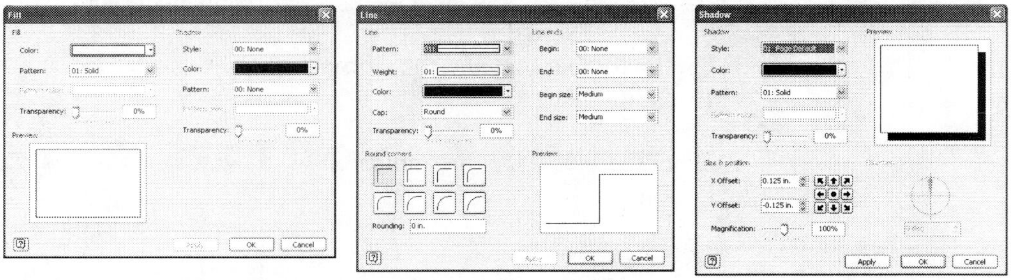

Exhibit 4-7: The Fill, Line, and Shadow dialog boxes

Do it!

C-3: Using the Fill and Shadow dialog boxes

Here's how	Here's why
1 Using the Pointer tool, select the leftmost top Process shape again	The shape you just formatted. You'll make some more precise adjustments for the shadow.
2 Press and hold CTRL + SHIFT and click the shape	To zoom in on it.
3 On the Format Shape toolbar, expand the Shadow Color list	The list shows basic shadow choices as well as color choices.
Choose **More Shadow Settings...**	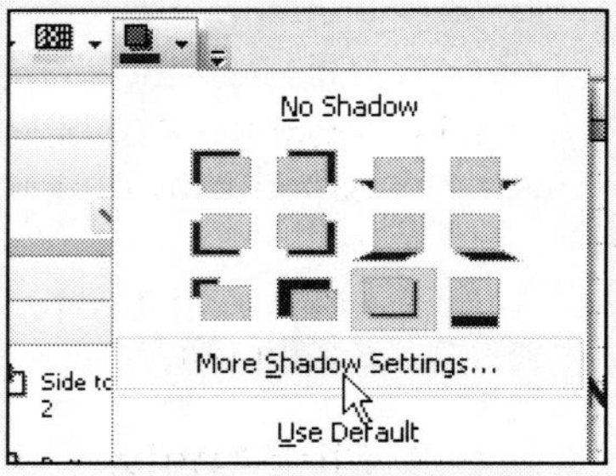 To open the Shadow dialog box.
4 From the Style list, verify that 01: Page default is selected	The preview on the right shows the fill and shadow colors currently applied to the shape. You'll make the shadow more transparent.
5 Drag the Transparency slider to approximately 50%	

6 Click **Apply**	To preview the shadow on the shape in the drawing. (You might have to move the dialog box to see the shape.) You also want to decrease the amount by which the shadow is offset.
7 Under Size & Position, triple-click the value in the X Offset box	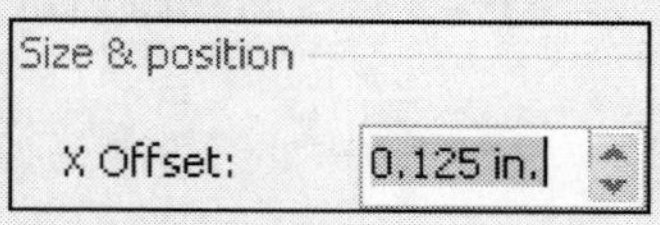 To select it.
Enter **.05**	To decrease the offset amount for the X axis.
8 Change the value in the Y Offset box to **-.05** (negative)	Be sure to enter a negative value: –.05 instead of just .05.
9 Click **Apply**	To preview the change.
Click **OK**	To close the dialog box. Next, you'll apply a fill pattern to the shape.
10 On the Format Shape toolbar, expand the Fill Pattern list	
Choose **More Fill Patterns…**	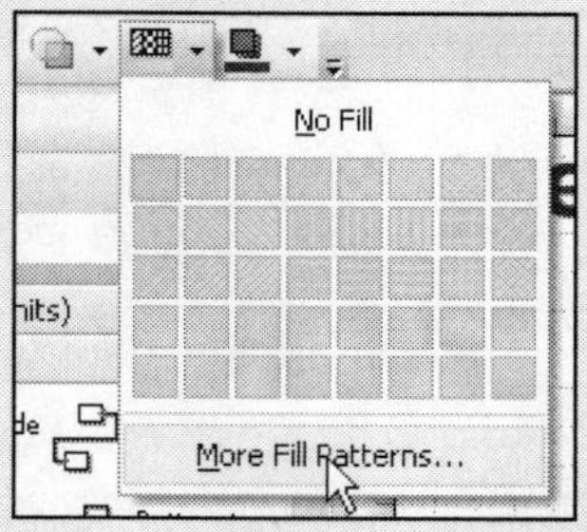 To open the Fill Pattern dialog box.
11 From the Pattern list, select pattern #13	The pattern has subtle horizontal stripes.
From the Pattern Color list, select a light purple	To alternate the stripe colors.
12 Click **Apply**	To preview the change.
Click **OK**	To close the dialog box.
13 Deselect the shape	To preview the results.
14 Update the drawing	

The Format Painter

Explanation

After you format a shape, you'll likely want to apply the same formatting to other shapes in the drawing. You can do this by using the Format Painter tool, located on the Standard toolbar, shown in Exhibit 4-8.

Format Painter

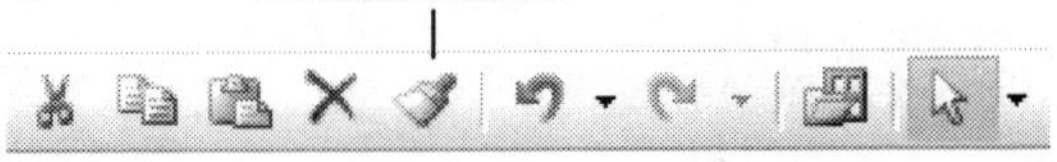

Exhibit 4-8: The Format Painter button on the Standard toolbar

The Format Painter tool enables you to copy formatting attributes from one shape to another. To use the tool, select the shape that contains the formatting attributes you want to copy, click the Format Painter button, and then click another shape in the drawing to apply the same formatting.

If you want to format multiple shapes, double-click the Format Painter button. This prevents Visio from switching back to the previous tool after you format a shape. To deselect the Format Painter, press Esc.

Do it!

C-4: Formatting multiple shapes

Here's how	Here's why
1 View the entire page in the work area	On the Standard toolbar, from the Zoom list, select Page.
2 Using the Pointer tool, select the leftmost top Process shape again	The formatted shape.
3 On the Standard toolbar, click 	(The Format Painter button.) To copy the formatting of the selected shape.
4 Click the Decision shape directly below the formatted Process shape	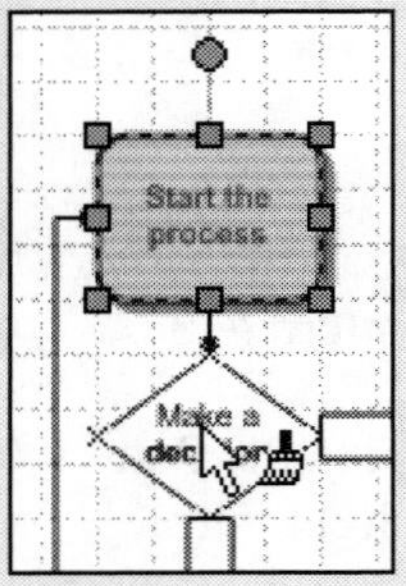 To apply the same formatting. You'll apply this formatting to the rest of the shapes.
5 Verify that the Decision shape is selected	The shape you just formatted.
6 On the Standard toolbar, double-click the Format Painter button	To select the Format Painter so you can format multiple shapes without reselecting the tool.

7	Click the remaining shapes	To format them.
	Press ESC	To deselect the shapes. You'll remove the rounded corners from the Decision and Document shapes.
8	Ctrl+click the two Decision shapes and the Document shape	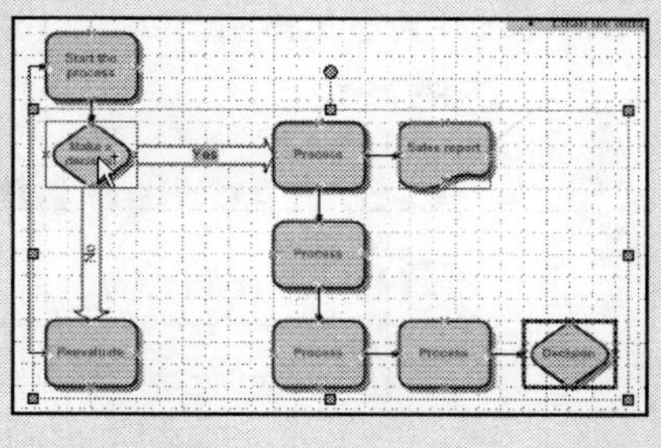 To select them.
9	On the Format Shape toolbar, expand the Corner Rounding list	
	Select the first option, as shown	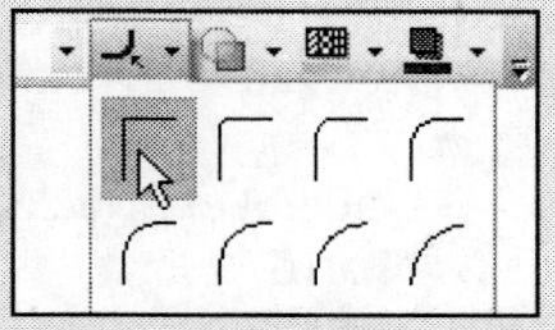 To remove the curve from the corners of the shapes.
10	Deselect the shapes	(Press Esc.) To preview the changes.
11	Update the drawing	

Fill and line formatting for text blocks

Explanation

Earlier, you learned how to format the background of a text block by using the Text Block tab in the Text dialog box. However, text blocks are similar to shapes, and you can often format them more effectively by using the same formatting techniques. For example, you can add backgrounds and strokes to them by using the buttons on the Formatting or Format Shapes toolbars or by using the Line, Fill, and Shadow dialog boxes.

Do it!

C-5: Adding fill and line attributes to a text block

Here's how	Here's why
1 Select the large text block in the upper-right corner of the page	You'll format the block so that it has a background color and a stroke around it. Previously, you used the Text dialog box to apply a background color. You'll remove that formatting.
2 Choose **Format**, **Text...**	To open the Text dialog box.
3 Activate the Text Block tab	
4 Under Text Background, select **None**	 To remove the orange background color. You'll also increase the margins.
5 Set all margins to **10 pt.**	Click the up-arrow next to each value once.
Click **OK**	To apply the changes and close the dialog box.
6 Choose **Format**, **Fill...**	To open the Fill dialog box.
7 Under Fill, from the Color list, select a light orange color	
Click **OK**	To apply the color and close the dialog box.
8 Choose **Format**, **Line...**	To open the Line dialog box.
9 From the Color list, select a dark orange color	
10 From the Weight list, select a thicker line weight	We chose 17.
11 Under Round Corners, select a slightly rounded corner option	

12 Click **Apply**	To preview the results. (You might have to move the dialog box to see the changes.)
Click **OK**	To close the dialog box. Some of the text at the bottom of the text block is cut off, but you can fix this by expanding the text block.
13 Using the bottom control handle, drag the bottom of the text box down	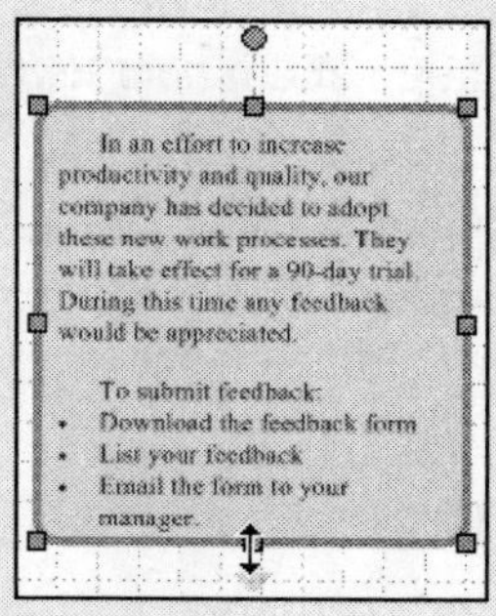 Until the text is centered in the box.
14 Deselect the text block	To view the changes.
15 Update and close the drawing	

Unit summary: Formatting drawings

Topic A In this topic, you learned how to format text by using **colors** and **styles**. You also learned how to increase the size of text and use the Text dialog box to apply **multiple text formats** at the same time.

Topic B In this topic, you learned how to format **text blocks**, change their margins, and apply a background color. You also learned how to use **paragraph formatting** in a text block to align and indent text, set line spacing, and add bullets.

Topic C In this topic, you learned how to format shapes and lines. You added **drop shadows** and fill patterns and learned how to use the Format Painter to **copy formatting**. You also learned how to change the appearance of a text block by using the same techniques for formatting shapes.

Independent practice activity

In this activity, you'll format text and resize shapes containing text. You'll also apply color to connector lines and shape backgrounds.

1 Open Formatting practice (from the current unit folder). Save the file as **My formatting practice**.

2 Increase the size of the text in all of the shapes to **14 pt**.

3 Resize the shapes to accommodate the text, if necessary, and adjust the connectors.

4 Format the text over the connectors as **Verdana**, **14 pt.**, **Bold**, and change the color to dark green.

5 Change the color of all connector lines to blue.

6 Apply a yellow background to all of the shapes.

7 Apply a solid red background to the shape text in both Decision shapes.

8 Format the label text on the lower-left side as **Comic Sans MS**, **30 pt**., **Red**, and **Bold**.

9 Hide the Format Shape toolbar and the Format Text toolbar.

10 Update and close the drawing.

Review questions

1 What is the difference between dialog boxes and toolbar buttons when it comes to formatting Visio objects?

2 What types of formatting can be applied with buttons on the Format Text toolbar?

3 When you work with text blocks, what are the two major components that can be formatted?

4 What are two ways you can open the Line, Fill, or Shadow dialog boxes?

5 How can you format multiple shapes by using the Format Painter?

A Click the Format Painter button and then click the shapes you want to format.

B Select all the shapes you want to format and then click the Format Painter button.

C Click the Format Painter button and then Ctrl+click the shapes you want to format.

D Double-click the Format Painter button and then click the shapes you want to format.

Review questions

Unit 5

Working with pages

Unit time: 50 minutes

Complete this unit, and you'll know how to:

A Set file properties for a new drawing.

B Create background pages.

C Work with detail pages and links.

D Use Print Preview mode and print a diagram.

Topic A: Creating and setting up a drawing

Explanation

When you're creating a diagram, you should begin by planning your page layout. This is often dictated by your printer's capabilities and the content of your drawing. You must also consider the file properties, the page and printer setups, and the page properties.

File properties

When you create or open a file, you can edit its *properties*. File properties include the file's location and creation date, the name of the file's author, and the file's subject and content. You can edit these properties by using the Properties dialog box, shown in Exhibit 5-1. To open this dialog box, choose File, Properties.

Exhibit 5-1: The Properties dialog box

The Properties dialog box contains three tabs, described in the following table:

Tab	Description
General	Stores information such as location, creation date, size, and the template used to create the drawing.
Summary	Contains fields for user-defined data, such as the subject, author name, name of the author's company, keywords, and a description of the file.
Contents	Lists the pages and master shapes contained in the drawing.

Do it!

A-1: Creating a drawing and setting file properties

Here's how	Here's why
1 Choose **File**, **New**, **General**, **Basic Flowchart (US units)**	
Save the drawing as **My page settings**	In the current unit folder.
2 Choose **File**, **Properties**	To open the Properties dialog box. By default, the Summary tab is active.
3 In the Subject box, enter **Company flowchart**	This is the subject of the flowchart diagram.
In the Author box, enter your name	
4 In the Company box, enter **Outlander Spices**	
5 Click **OK**	To add the user-defined information to the file's properties.

Page and printer setup

Explanation

Before creating a drawing, you should consider the page size and layout. The page layout defines how to print a drawing according to its dimensions. For example, for a drawing that is wider than it is long, you should change the page layout to landscape to make sure that the entire drawing is printed on one page. Page layout is also limited by the capabilities of your printer and the size of the drawing page. You define the page and printer settings in the Page Setup dialog box, shown in Exhibit 5-2.

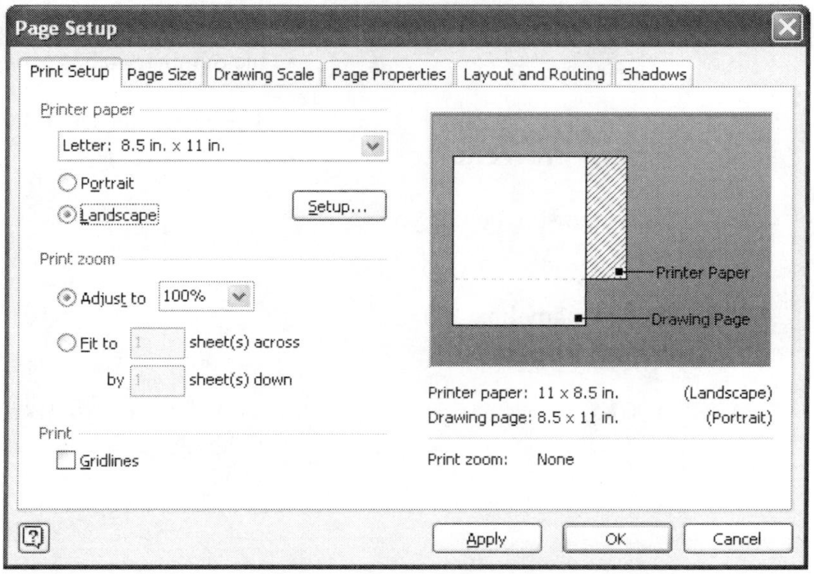

Exhibit 5-2: The Page Setup dialog box, showing Print Setup options

The Page Setup dialog box contains six tabs, described in the following table:

Tab	Description
Print Setup	Contains settings for the current printer. The Preview window shows the orientation of the paper and the drawing page.
Page Size	Contains size and orientation settings for the drawing page. You can define page size for each page in a drawing. The Preview window shows the orientation of the paper and the drawing page.
Drawing Scale	Used to define a scale for the drawing. This is helpful for floor plans and other architectural drawings.
Page Properties	Used to set the name of the page, apply the drop shadow effect, and assign background pages.
Layout and Routing	Used to define how shapes and lines will appear in print.
Shadows	Used to define shadow settings for a page.

When you set a page layout, you also set the page orientation. *Page orientation* defines whether a page will print in portrait orientation (8.5"×11") or landscape orientation (11"×8.5"). The default settings automatically synchronize the page size and orientation to work with a standard desktop printer. The Preview window shows the orientation of the paper and the drawing page.

Do it!

A-2: Defining printer settings and page size

Here's how	Here's why
1 Choose **File**, **Page Setup…**	To open the Page Setup dialog box.
2 Activate the Page Size tab	
Observe the settings	The default selection is "Same as printer paper size." Any changes you make in the size or orientation of the printer paper will automatically be updated on the Page Size tab.
Observe the Page orientation options	They are unavailable.
3 Select **Pre-defined size**	You can now define custom size and orientation settings for the page.
4 Activate the Print Setup tab	
Under Printer paper, select **Landscape**	If necessary.
Observe the Preview window	The paper orientation is now landscape, as shown in Exhibit 5-2.
Set the paper orientation back to **Portrait**	Under Printer paper, select Portrait.
5 Activate the Page Size tab	
Under Pre-defined size, from the second list, select **Legal: 8.5 in. x 14 in.**	To change the size of the page.
Observe the Preview window	The drawing page is longer than the printer paper.
6 Activate the Print Setup tab	
Change the size of the Printer paper to **Legal 8.5 in x 14 in.**	(From the Paper size list, select Legal 8.5 in. × 14 in.) The size of the printer paper increases to match the size of drawing page.
Click **OK**	To close the Page Setup dialog box.
7 Update the drawing	

Page properties

Explanation

You can define foreground and background page types in Visio. You create drawings on *foreground pages*. *Background pages* hold and display elements such as page numbers and borders that are common to one or more foreground pages. You designate the page type on the Page Properties tab in the Page Setup dialog box, shown in Exhibit 5-3.

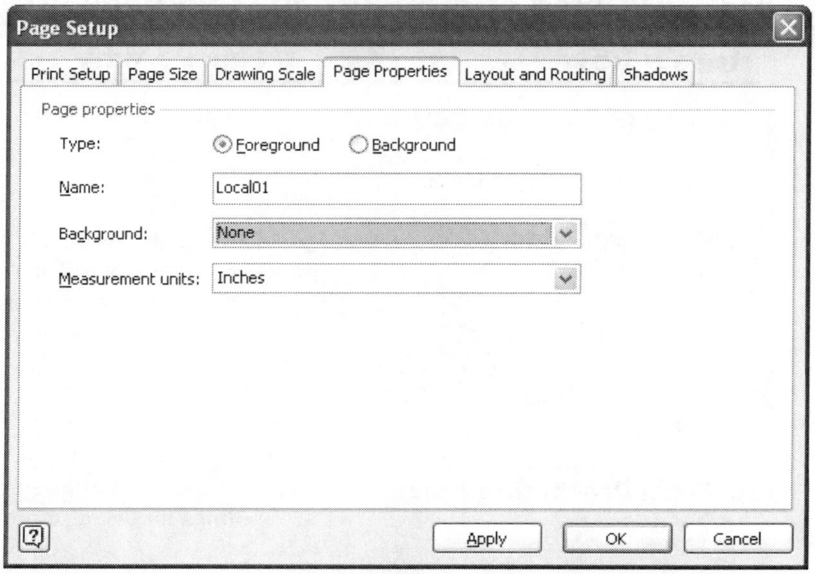

Exhibit 5-3: The Page Properties tab in the Page Setup dialog box

You can also use the Page Properties tab to change the name of a page, assign a background page and a foreground page, and change measurement units.

Do it!

A-3: Setting page properties

Here's how	Here's why
1 Open the Page Setup dialog box	Choose File, Page Setup.
Activate the Page Properties tab	By default, pages are added as foreground pages.
2 In the Name box, enter **Local01**	To change the name on the page tab for this page.
3 Click **Apply**	
Observe the page tab	The name has changed.
4 Click **OK**	To close the Page Setup dialog box.
5 Update the drawing	

Topic B: Working with background pages

Explanation

In addition to using drawing pages, you can add *background pages* to display information you want to repeat on multiple pages in a drawing.

Overview of background pages

Background pages provide additional information for foreground pages. When you designate a page as background, the fields added to the page also appear on foreground pages, as shown in Exhibit 5-4. Background pages typically contain information such as a company name, page numbers, or information specified in the Properties dialog box. You can have more than one background page in a file, but you can apply only one background page to a foreground page. The same background page is automatically applied to each new page added to a drawing. Use the Page Properties tab in the Page Setup dialog box to remove a background page from a foreground page.

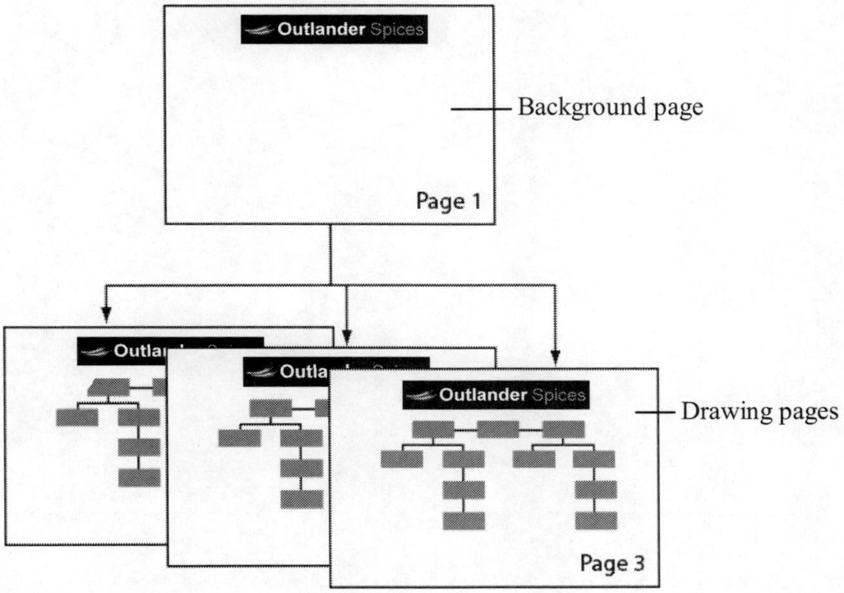

Exhibit 5-4: A background page and foreground pages

Headers and footers

You use background pages to create headers and footers in your drawings. *Headers* appear at the top of each page, and *footers* appear at the bottom of each page.

Do it!

B-1: Creating a background page

Here's how	Here's why
1 Choose **Insert**, **New Page...**	To open the Page Setup dialog box. You'll insert a new page in the drawing.
2 Select **Background**	To create a background page.
3 In the Name box, enter **Header/Footer**	You'll use this background page to display headers and footers.
4 Click **OK**	To add the Header/Footer page to the drawing file.
Update the drawing	

Fields

Explanation

Fields are placeholders that can store details about your drawing file, such as the company name, the file name, or the file location. You also use fields to display information such as the current date, page numbers, and time, as shown in Exhibit 5-5. When field data changes, it is automatically updated in the drawing. After adding fields, you format them as you would format other text.

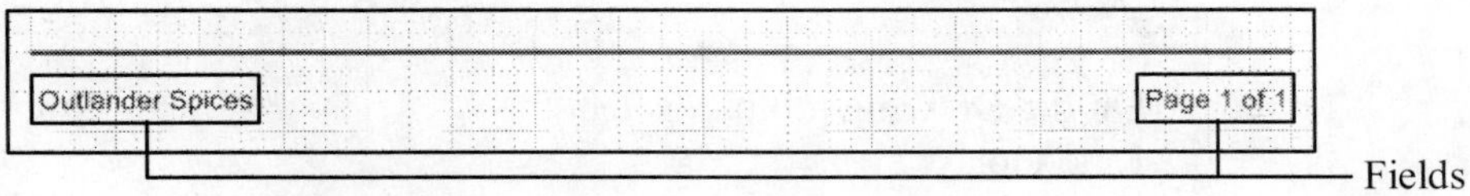

Exhibit 5-5: Fields used in a footer

To add a field:

1 Using the Text tool, create a text box or select a text box in the drawing.
2 Choose Insert, Field to open the Field dialog box, shown in Exhibit 5-6.
3 In the Category section, select a category for the information you want to add.
4 In the Field name section, select a field.
5 Click OK.

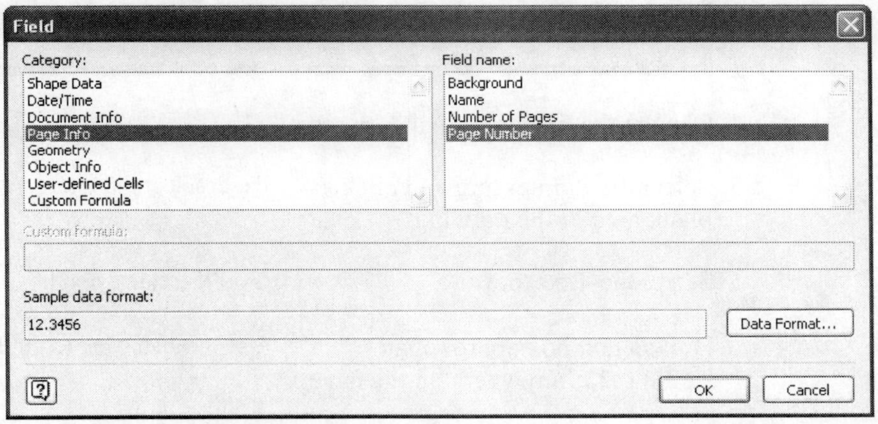

Exhibit 5-6: The Field dialog box

Page breaks

Displaying page breaks can help you lay out your drawing. With page breaks showing, you can avoid placing objects or fields too close to margins. You can also determine where to place shapes if you're nearing the end of a page. Page breaks are determined by the current printer setup for the computer.

Do it!

B-2: Adding fields to a background page

Here's how	Here's why
1 Choose **View**, **Page Breaks**	Thick gray lines appear around the edges of the page.
2 Change the magnification to **75%**	On the Standard toolbar, from the Zoom box, select 75%.
On the Drawing toolbar, select the Line tool	
3 Point to the 1" mark on the vertical ruler	You might need to scroll to the bottom of the page.
Drag to draw a line near the bottom of the drawing page, leaving a half-inch space on either side of the drawing	Use the horizontal ruler to determine the spacing on either side of the page. The line will extend from 0.75" to 7.75" on the horizontal ruler.

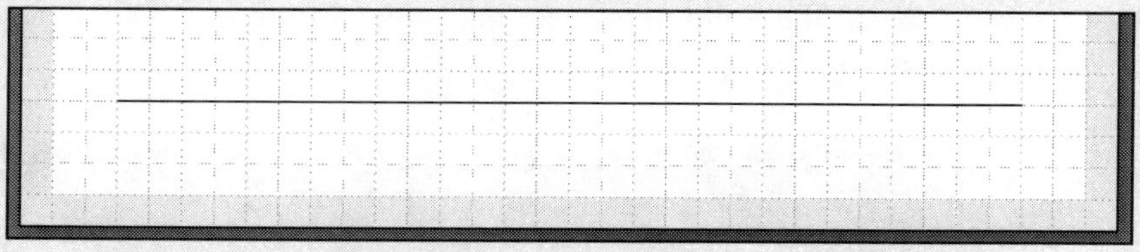

Here's how	Here's why
4 Change the line color to a dark red	
5 Select the Pointer tool and click a blank area of the drawing	To deselect the line.
6 Select the Text tool	You'll create a text box.
Draw a text box approximately 2.5" × 0.25" anywhere on the page	Use the status bar to guide you.
7 Choose **Insert**, **Field...**	To open the Field dialog box.
8 Under Category, select **Document Info**	To display a list of fields in this category.
Under Field name, select **Filename**	You'll insert the name of the file as a field.
Click **OK**	To insert the Filename field in the footer.
9 Click at the beginning of the file name	To move the insertion point.
Open the Field dialog box	Choose Insert, Field.

10	Display the fields in the Document Info category	Select the Document Info category from the Category list.
	From the Field list, select **Directory**	To insert the Directory field.
	Click **OK**	To add the file location to the footer.
11	Press ESC	To end text mode.
12	Select the Pointer tool	
	Move the text box to the lower-left corner of the page, under the red line, as shown	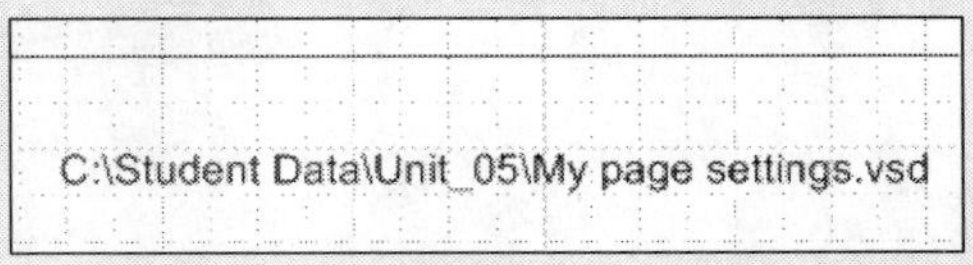
13	Verify that the text box is still selected	
	Press CTRL + D	To duplicate the text box.
14	Drag the duplicate to the right side of the drawing page	Under the right edge of the red line.
15	Select the Text tool	The next characters you type will replace the contents of the text box.
	Type **Page**	You'll add page numbers to the footer.
	Press SPACEBAR	
16	Open the Field dialog box	
	Display the fields for the Page Info category	
	From the Field list, select **Page Number**	To insert the Page Number field in the footer.
	Click **OK**	The page number is zero because you are on a background page.
17	Press SPACEBAR	
	Type **of**	
	Press SPACEBAR	
18	Insert the **Number of Pages** field	From the Page Info category.

19 Right-align the text	On the Formatting toolbar, click the Align Right button.
Press ESC	
20 Update the drawing	

Applying background pages to drawing pages

Explanation

After you create a background page, you can apply it to any drawing page. You must manually apply each background page to the desired drawing page by using the Page Properties tab in the Page Setup dialog box. After you apply a background page, each new foreground page you add to the drawing will use this background.

Do it!

B-3: Applying a background page

Here's how	Here's why
1 Switch to the Local01 page	Click the Local01 page tab.
2 Choose **File**, **Page Setup...**	
Activate the Page Properties tab	
3 From the Background list, select **Header/Footer**	To apply this page as the background page for your drawing.
4 Click **OK**	To close the Page Setup dialog box.
Observe the page	(Zoom in, if necessary.) The items from the background page appear.
5 Select the red line	You cannot select the line because it's on the background page.
Update the drawing	

Background page editing

Explanation

A background page functions the same way as a drawing page or foreground page. You can edit the shapes on a background page the same way you would edit them on a drawing page. You can also add graphics, such as a logo, to a background page, as shown in Exhibit 5-7. You can add simple line drawings or complex graphic images, such as photographs. Visio can use any graphic format.

To insert a graphic on a page:

1. Go to the page where you want to add the graphic.
2. Choose Insert, Picture, From File.
3. Navigate to the location of the file you want to use.
4. Select the file and click Open.
5. Resize and position the graphic if necessary.

Exhibit 5-7: Adding a title and a graphic to a background page

Do it!

B-4: Editing a background page

Here's how	Here's why
1 Switch to the Header/Footer background page	Click the Header/Footer page tab.
2 Select the Text tool	
Click a blank area of the drawing page	
3 Enter **New Processes**	
4 Open the Text dialog box	Choose Format, Text.
5 Select the bold style	
Change the font size to **18 pt.**	
Change the font color to a dark red	
Click **OK**	To apply the formatting to the selected text.
6 Select the Pointer tool	
Resize the text block so that the text fits on one line	
Center the text block near the top of the page	As shown in Exhibit 5-7. You'll also add a graphic above the text.
7 Choose **Insert**, **Picture**, **From File…**	
Navigate to the current unit folder	
8 Select **Outlanderlogo**	This is a .jpg file.
Click **Open**	To insert the file.
9 Place the logo above the text as shown	
10 Switch to the Local01 page	Click the Local01 page tab.
11 Update and close the drawing	

Topic C: Working with links

Explanation

When you create a complex drawing in Visio, the drawing might extend over several pages. If this happens, you can link the pages. You can also link diagrams to other Visio files, to Internet addresses, or to files of other types, such as Excel worksheets.

Detail pages

When a detailed drawing does not fit on one page, you can create additional pages, each of which contains varying degrees of detail. Typically, you begin with an overview and then expand the detail based on logical portions. For example, the main drawing page might depict an organization's structure, and additional pages would show the structure of the various departments.

Page links

You link multiple pages by using shapes as the activation point. You do this by modifying the shape's behavior. To link pages:

1. Select the shape you want to use as the activation point.
2. Right-click the shape and choose Format, Behavior to open the Behavior dialog box, shown in Exhibit 5-8.
3. Activate the Double-Click tab.
4. Select Go to page and select a page from the list.
5. Click OK.

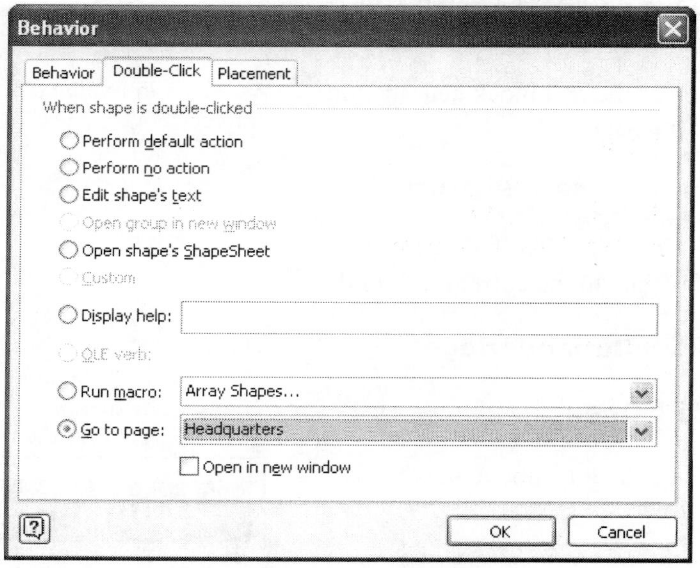

Exhibit 5-8: The Behavior dialog box

Do it!

C-1: Adding a page link

Here's how	Here's why
1 Open OutlanderOrg.vsd	From the current unit folder.
Save the file as **MyOutlanderOrg**	
2 Select the Pointer tool	If necessary.
Right-click the **East Coast Regional Headquarters** shape	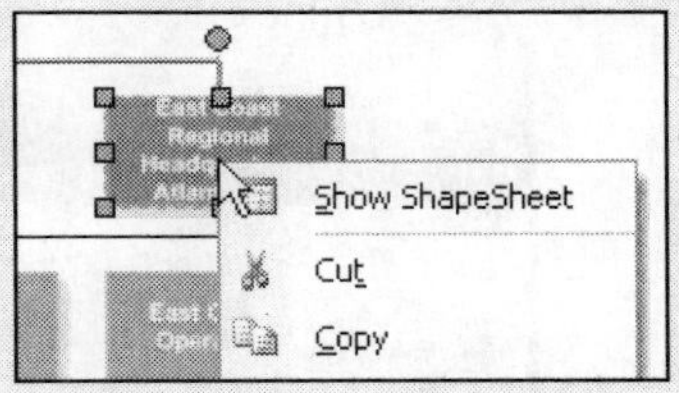
Choose **Format**, **Behavior...**	To open the Behavior dialog box.
3 Activate the Double-Click tab	By default, when you double-click an object, you switch to text mode.
Select **Go to page**	At the bottom of the dialog box.
From the list, select **EC Operations**	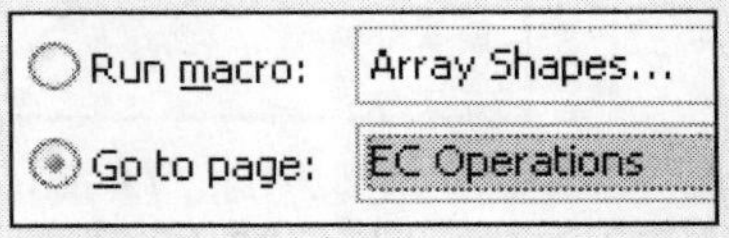 To set a link to the EC Operations page when the Process shape is double-clicked.
Click **OK**	To activate the link and close the dialog box.
4 Double-click the **East Coast Regional Headquarters** shape	To jump to the EC Operations page.
Switch back to the OrgChart page	
Update the drawing	

Hyperlinks

Explanation

Hyperlinks connect a shape or page to a drawing, a document, an Internet address, or a file. To use a shape as an activation point for a hyperlink:

1. Select the shape you want to use as the activation point.
2. Choose Insert, Hyperlinks to open the Hyperlinks dialog box, shown in Exhibit 5-9.
3. In the Address box, enter the Internet address or the path of the file to which you want to link.
4. Click OK.

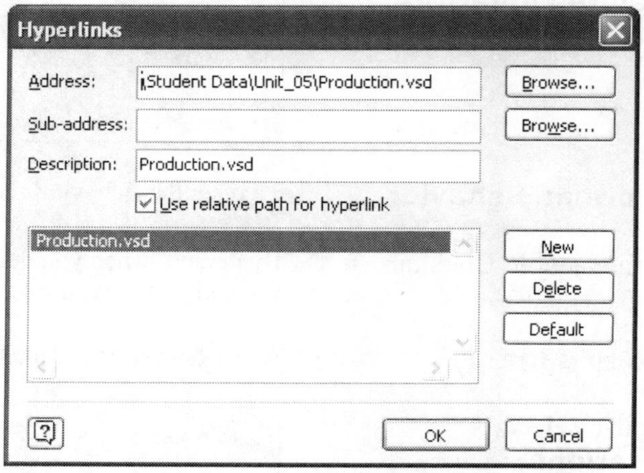

Exhibit 5-9: The Hyperlinks dialog box

Page links

You can also specify a page as a link. To do so, you use the Subaddress field in the Hyperlinks dialog box.

Do it!

C-2: Adding a hyperlink

Here's how	Here's why
1 Select the Westfield Facility shape	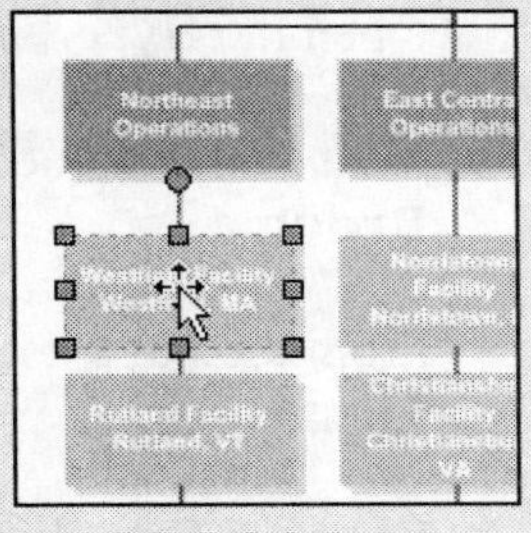 You'll use it as the activation point for a hyperlink.
2 Choose **Insert**, **Hyperlinks…**	To open the Hyperlinks dialog box.
3 Next to the Address box, click **Browse**	
Choose **Local File…**	To open the Link to File dialog box.
Navigate to the current unit folder	In the Student Data folder.
4 Select **WestfieldFloorplan.vsd**	
Click **Open**	To link to the Visio file.
Click **OK**	To create the hyperlink.
Deselect the Westfield Facility shape	Click the blank space of the drawing page.
5 Point to the Westfield Facility shape	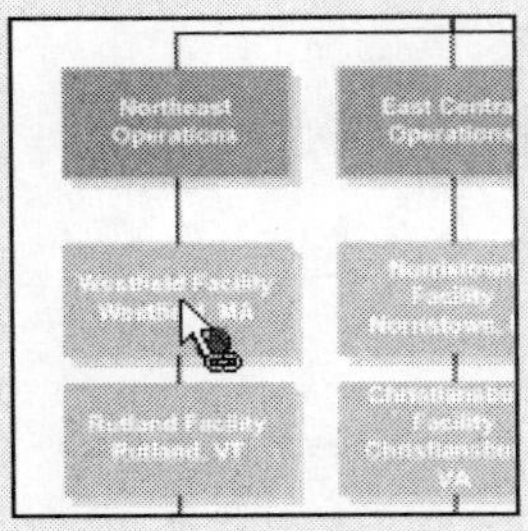 A hyperlink icon appears next to the pointer.
Right-click the shape	To display the shortcut menu.
6 Choose **WestfieldFloorplan.vsd**	To go to the linked drawing. It opens in another window.
7 Choose **File**, **Close**	To close the drawing. Don't save changes if prompted.

8	Verify that the Westfield Facility shape is selected	
	Open the Hyperlinks dialog box	Choose Insert, Hyperlinks.
9	Next to the Subaddress box, click **Browse**	
	From the Page list, select **FirstFloor**	
	From the Zoom list, select **Page**	To zoom to Page view.
	Click **OK**	To create the hyperlink.
	Click **OK**	To close the dialog box.
10	Right-click the Westfield Facility shape	
	Choose **WestfieldFloorplan.vsd**	From the shortcut menu. This time the second page of the drawing is visible.
11	Close the WestfieldFacility drawing	Don't save changes.
	Update the MyOutlanderOrg drawing	

Multiple files and linking

Explanation

It is possible to link multiple files to a single shape. This is helpful if there are several files that are related to one shape in a drawing.

Do it!

EX. click to look at sales or click to look at PDF

C-3: Linking multiple files to a shape

Here's how	Here's why
1 Select the Westfield Facility shape	If necessary.
2 Open the Hyperlinks dialog box	
Click **New**	To add a new link to the shape.
3 Next to the Address box, click **Browse**	
Choose **Local File...**	
Navigate to the current unit folder	If necessary.
4 Select **WestfieldSalesOrg.vsd** and click **Open**	
Click **OK**	To add the link.
5 Right-click the Westfield Facility shape	Both WestfieldFloorplan.vsd and WestfieldSalesOrg.vsd appear on the menu.
Choose **WestfieldSalesOrg.vsd**	
Close the drawing	
6 Update the MyOutlanderOrg drawing	

Linking to other file types

Explanation

In addition to linking drawing files to each other, you can link a drawing to a file of another type, such as an Excel worksheet. This is helpful when you want to keep information about your drawing in another file. You can also designate a specific location that the linked file should display when it opens.

Do it!

C-4: Linking to an Excel file

To go to a certain Sheet! cell/range

Sheet Name! A1:Z27

Sheet Name ! cell or range

EX: Sheet2!A1:Z27

Here's how	Here's why
1 Select the Westfield Facility shape	(If necessary.) You'll link an Excel file that contains Human Resources information for the facility.
2 Open the Hyperlinks dialog box	
Click **New**	To add a new link to the shape.
3 Next to the Address box, click **Browse**	
Choose **Local File...**	
Navigate to the current unit folder	If necessary.
4 From the Save as type list, select **Office Files**	 To see files from Microsoft Office applications.
5 Select **WestfieldHR.xls** and click **Open**	
6 In the Subaddress box, enter **B7**	 To specify cell B7 as the location to go to when the file is opened.
Click **OK**	To add the link.
7 Right-click the Westfield Facility shape	
Open the linked Excel file	From the shortcut menu. The file is listed as WestfieldHR.xls.
8 Observe the file	The file opens with B7 as the active cell.
Close Excel	Choose File, Exit.
9 Update the drawing	

Topic D: Printing diagrams

Explanation

To print diagrams, you use the Print command, which you can issue by choosing File, Print or by clicking the Print Page button on the Standard toolbar. Before you print, you might want to add a header or footer and preview the diagram.

Print Preview

Use Print Preview to see how a page will look before you print it. To open Print Preview, you can choose File, Print Preview or click the Print Preview button on the Standard toolbar, as shown in Exhibit 5-10.

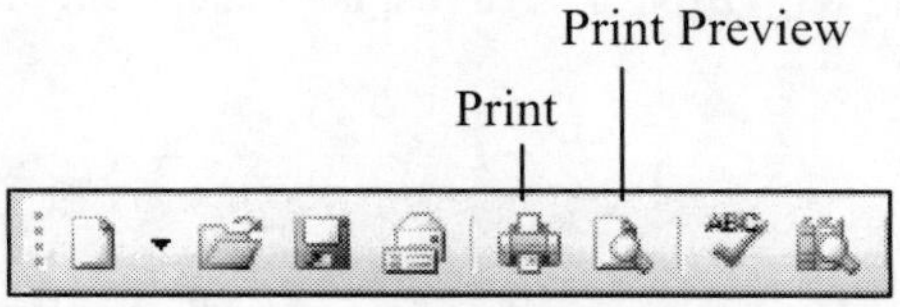

Exhibit 5-10: The Print and Print Preview buttons on the Standard toolbar

The Print Preview window, shown in Exhibit 5-11, shows you how the diagram will look on paper. Use Print Preview to verify that all page components are correctly placed, including the objects, margins, headers, and footers.

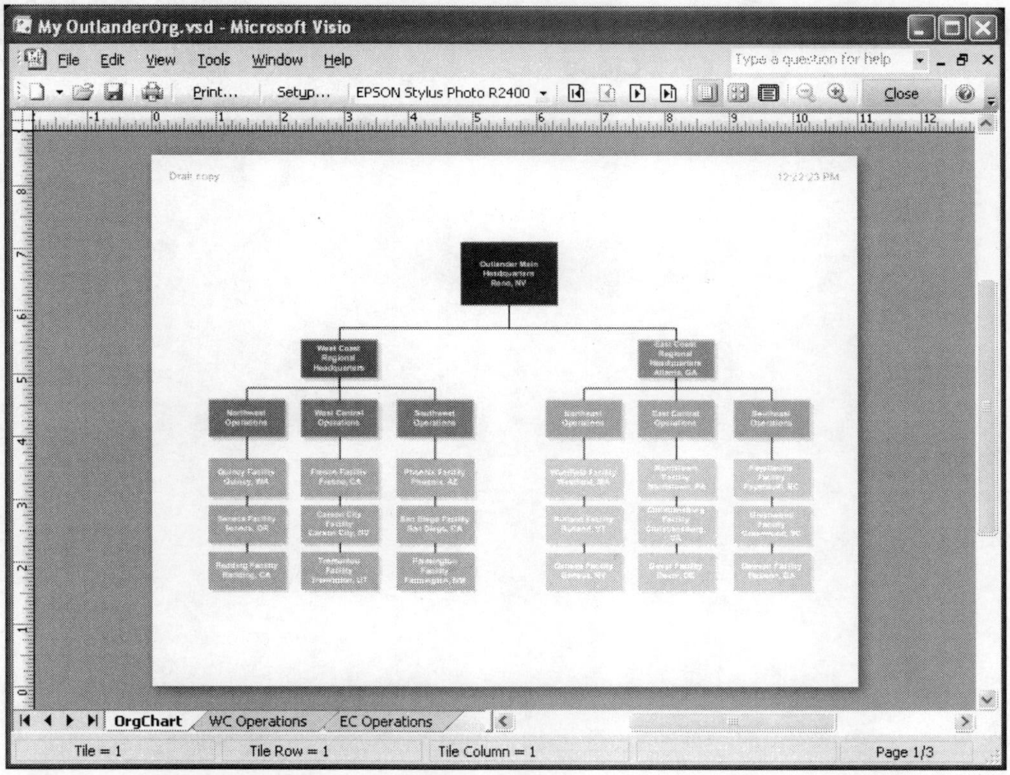

Exhibit 5-11: The Print Preview window

Do it!

D-1: Adding a header in Print Preview

Here's how	Here's why
1 On the Standard toolbar, click	(The Print Preview button.) To open the Print Preview window.
2 Choose **View**, **Header and Footer...**	To open the Header and Footer dialog box.
3 Under Header, in the Left box, enter **Draft copy**	To add the text "Draft copy" to the header.
4 Under Header, from the Right list, select **Current time**	To display the current time in the header.
5 Click **Choose Font**	
Under Color, select **Gray**	To change the font color to gray.
6 Click **OK**	To return to the Header and Footer dialog box.
Click **OK**	To close the Header and Footer dialog box.
7 Observe the preview	The header text and the current time appear in gray at the top of the page.
Click **Close**	To close Print Preview mode.
8 Update the drawing	

Printing

Explanation

After you've previewed your document and confirmed that its content and layout are correct, you are ready to print. You already defined the page setup and margins when you created the file. Now, you can print the diagram by clicking the Print button on the Standard toolbar. If you want to print only one page of a diagram, print multiple copies, or use a printer other than the default printer, use the Print dialog box, shown in Exhibit 5-12. To open the Print dialog box, choose File, Print.

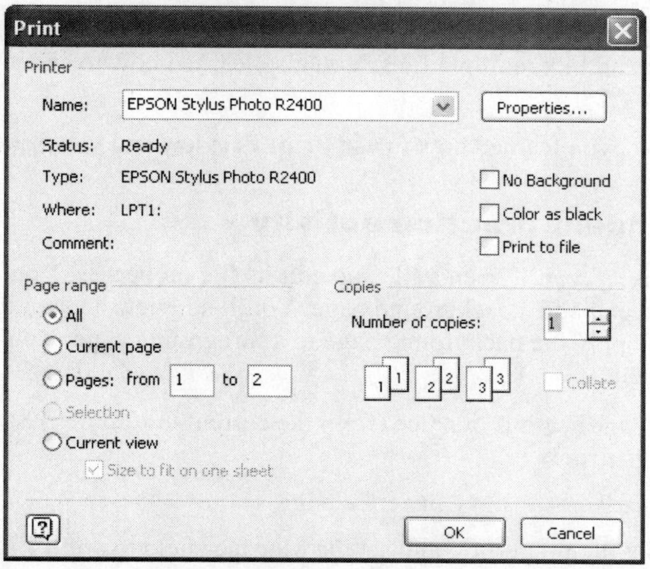

Exhibit 5-12: The Print dialog box

Do it!

D-2: Printing a diagram

Here's how	Here's why
1 Choose **File**, **Print...**	To open the Print dialog box.
2 Observe the Name box	You can change the printer to which the print job is sent.
Observe the Page range options	You can specify the pages you want to print.
Observe the Number of copies box	You can print one or more copies of your drawing by specifying the number in this box.
3 Click **Cancel**	If your computer is connected to a printer and you're directed to do so by your instructor, click OK to print the diagram.
4 Update and close the drawing	

Unit summary: Working with pages

Topic A In this topic, you learned how to define **file properties**, **page size**, and **printer settings** for a file. You also learned how to specify **page properties**.

Topic B In this topic, you learned how to create and edit **background pages**. You learned how to add **fields** and graphics to background pages. You also learned how to apply a background page to a drawing page.

Topic C In this topic, you learned how to create and use **detail pages**. You learned how to add a **hyperlink** and link multiple files. You also learned how to create a link to another file type.

Topic D In this topic, you learned how to use **Print Preview** and you printed a diagram.

Independent practice activity

In this activity, you'll open a file and edit its file properties. You'll change the paper orientation and add a background page. You'll add new content to the background page, and you'll apply the background page to a foreground page. You'll also create hyperlinks.

1. Open Page settings practice (from the current unit folder.) Save the file as **My page settings practice**.
2. Rename Page-1 as **My practice page**.
3. Edit the file properties, and set the Manager field to **John Embury**.
4. Change the paper orientation to Landscape for print settings.
5. Add a new background page and name it **My background page**.
6. Add a blue line at the top and bottom of the background page.
7. Add the name of the file to the lower-left corner, below the blue line, on the background page.
8. Add fields in the format "Page Number of Number of Pages" at the top right, above the blue line, on the background page.
9. Apply My background page settings to My practice page.
10. Insert the picture **OutlanderLogo** in the center of My practice page.
11. Add a Process shape named **Detail Page**.
12. Insert a new page and rename it **Detail_Page**.
13. Create a link from the Detail Page shape to the Detail_Page drawing page.
14. Test the link.
15. On My practice page, create a process shape named **Production**. Insert the hyperlink that opens the Visio file named Production from the current unit folder.
16. Test the link and then close the Production file.
17. Create a Process shape named **Inventory** and add a hyperlink to the Inventory.xls file.
18. Test the link and then close Excel.
19. Update and close the drawing. Don't close Visio.

Review questions

1 In which of the following dialog boxes do you define the page layout?

A Print dialog box

B Format dialog box

C Page Setup dialog box

D File Properties dialog box

2 How many background pages can be applied to a drawing page?

3 What type of information might be contained on a background page?

4 What is the procedure to add a graphic to a background page?

5 What is the procedure to link pages together?

Unit 6

Network and brainstorming diagrams

Unit time: 50 minutes

Complete this unit, and you'll know how to:

A Create network diagrams.

B Create rack diagrams.

C Create brainstorming diagrams.

Topic A: Network diagrams

Explanation

You can use Visio to illustrate complex network layouts for documentation and visualization purposes. A clear and well-documented network diagram is very helpful to a network administrator.

Network shapes

Many of Visio's network diagram shapes are industry-standard *topology shapes*. Topology shapes represent industry configurations such as ring and pipeline topologies used in a network designs. These shapes provide connection points for the device shapes that are arranged according to the layout of the network. Because these are industry-standard shapes, their use in network layouts ensures common understanding.

Topology shapes have square shape handles at their ends and in the middle, as shown in Exhibit 6-1. They also have diamond-shaped connection handles that you can use to connect them to other shapes.

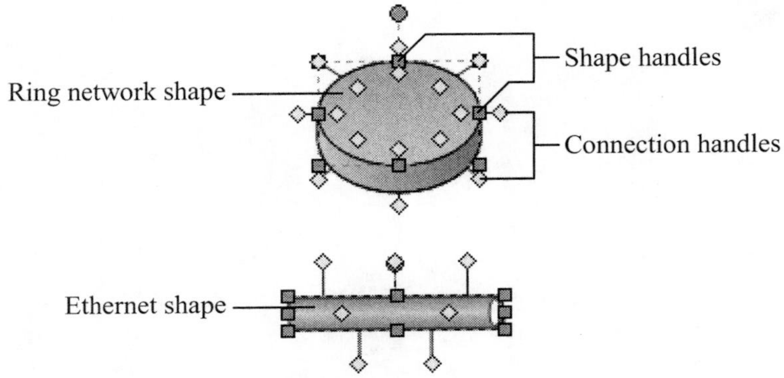

Exhibit 6-1: Examples of topology shapes

Do it!

A-1: Using topology shapes in a network diagram

Here's how	Here's why
1 Choose **File**, **New**, **Network**, **Basic Network Diagram (US units)**	To create a file based on the Basic Network Diagram template. The Network and Peripherals stencil group appears in the Shapes window.
Save the file as **My network diagram**	In the current unit folder.
2 From the Network and Peripherals stencil, drag an Ethernet shape to the center of the page	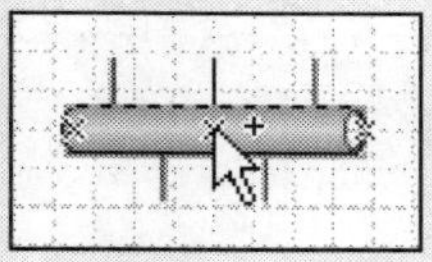
3 From the Zoom list, select **100%**	To zoom in on the shape.
4 On the Standard toolbar, click 	(The AutoConnect button.) To turn off AutoConnect.
5 Point to the center-right shape handle, as shown	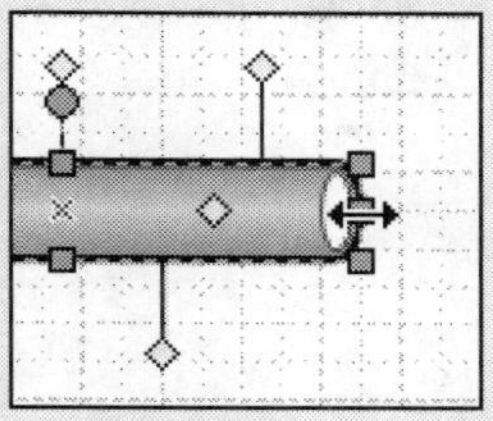 The pointer will become a two-headed arrow.
Resize the shape to approximately 4.5" wide	Use the status bar to determine the size of the shape. You might have to scroll to the right to fully resize the shape.
6 From the Network and Peripherals stencil, drag a Server shape above the top-left connection handle	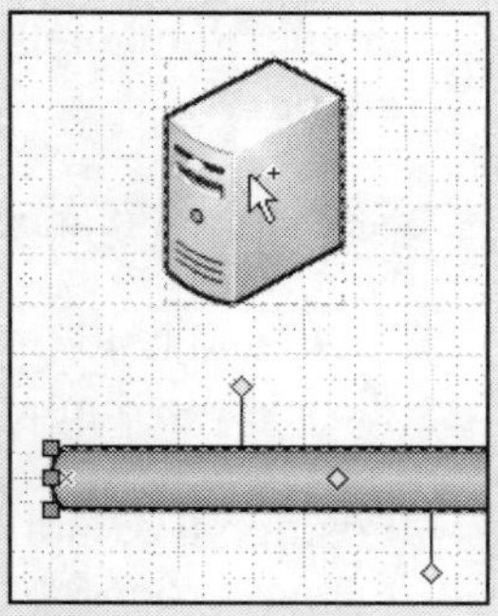 The yellow diamond-shaped handles are connection handles.
7 Type **Finance**	To name the Server shape.
Press ESC	

8 Select the Ethernet shape

Drag the top-left connection handle to the center of the Server shape, as shown

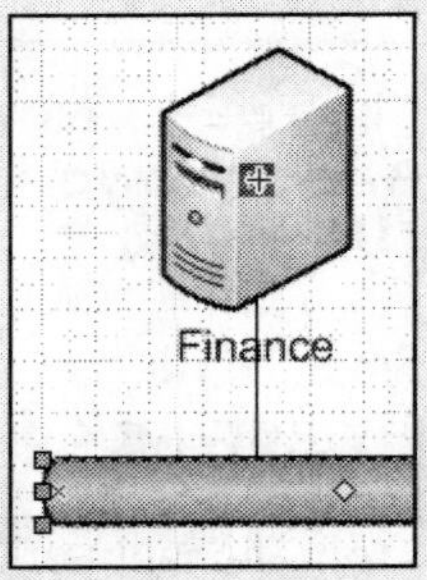

You'll see a red glue handle at the connection point at the center of the Server shape.

9 In the Shapes window, activate the Computers and Monitors stencil

Click the stencil's title bar.

From the stencil, drag a PC shape below the bottom-left connection handle

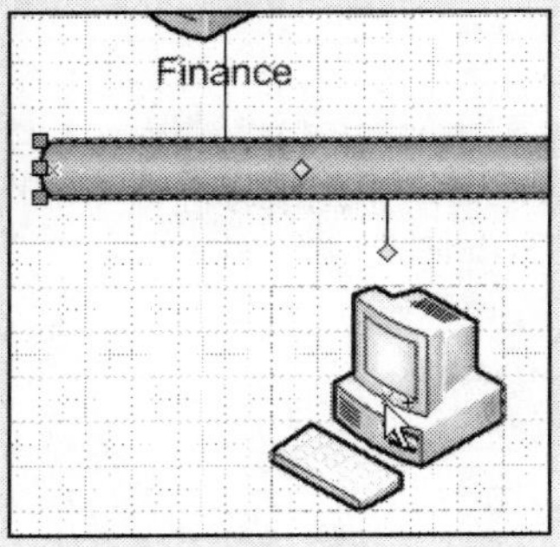

10 Name the PC shape **Computer**

Verify that the shape is selected, type the name, and press Esc.

11 Connect the Ethernet shape to the connection point on the Computer shape

Select the Ethernet shape; then drag the connection handle to the center of the PC shape. Make sure you see the glue handle.

12 Select the Finance server shape

Press and hold CTRL and drag to the right to duplicate the shape

Position the duplicate shape above the next connection handle

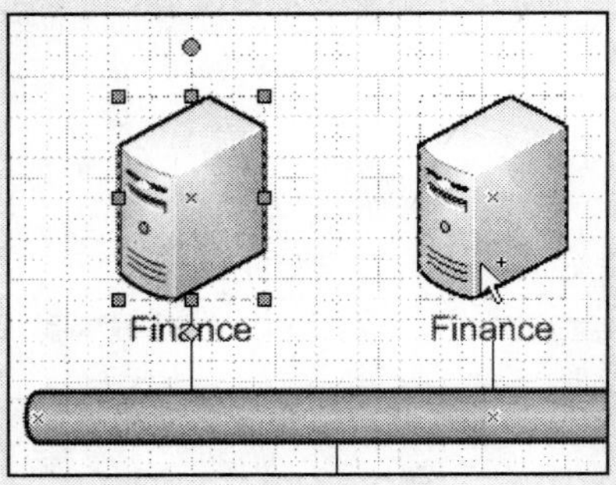

13 Create a third duplicate above the rightmost connection handle	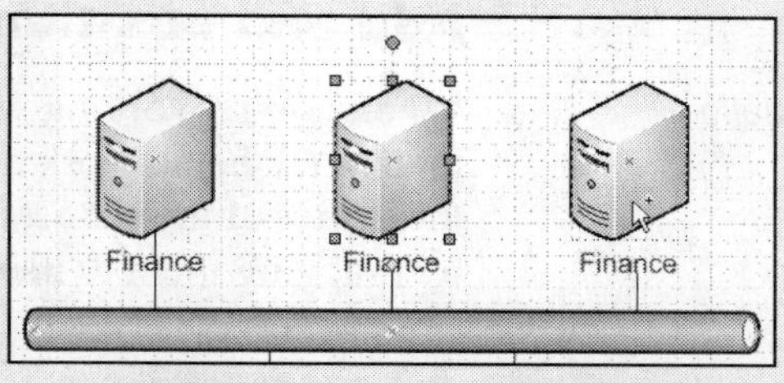
14 Connect the shapes to the Ethernet server shape	Select the Ethernet shape and drag the connection handles to the other shapes.
15 Name the middle Server shape **Marketing**, and the right Server shape **Sales**	Select the shapes and enter the text for each one. Press Esc to exit text mode.
16 Position a duplicate of the PC shape below the rightmost bottom connection handle	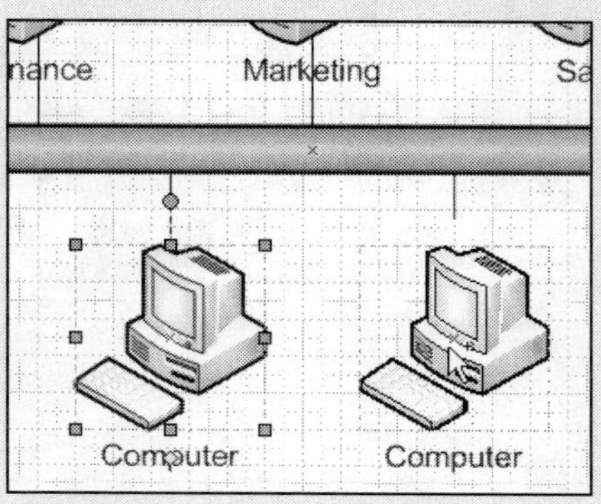
Connect the PC shape to the Ethernet server shape	You do not need to rename the duplicate shape.
17 Update the drawing	

Add and position connection handles

Explanation

When you're working with topology shapes, you can add additional connection handles to expand the network diagram. To do so, drag from the diamond connection handles in the center of the shape, as shown in Exhibit 6-2. You can also move connection handles by dragging them to new locations.

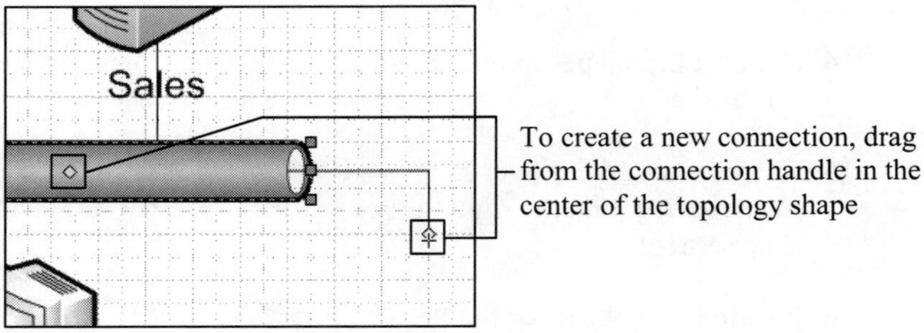

Exhibit 6-2: Creating a new connection handle

Do it!

A-2: Adding a connection handle

Here's how	Here's why
1 Select the Ethernet shape	If necessary.
2 Point to the connection handle on the left side, as shown	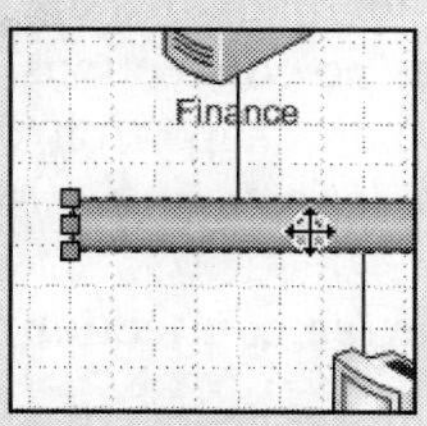
3 Drag the connection handle to the left and down, as shown	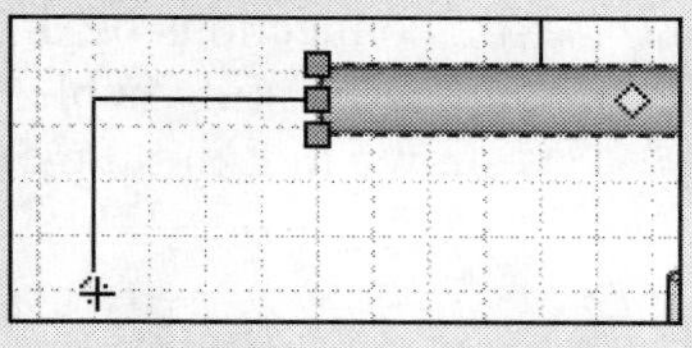 The connection handle appears below the left side of the shape.
4 Switch to the Network and Peripherals stencil	Click the stencil's title bar at the bottom of the Shapes window.
5 Drag a Printer shape below the new connection handle	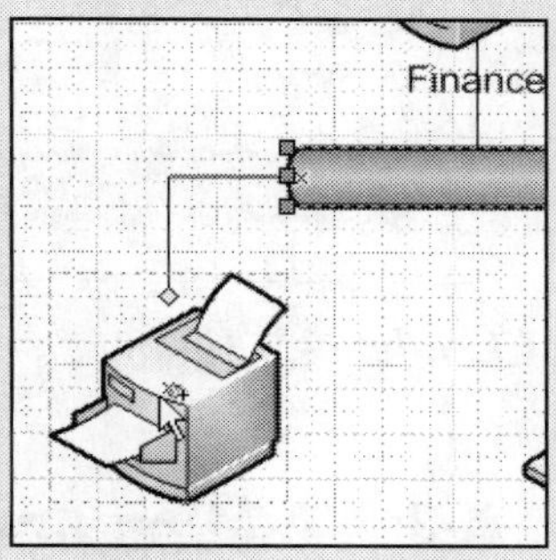
6 Name the Printer shape **Printer 1**	
Connect the Printer shape to the Ethernet shape	Select the Ethernet shape and drag the connection handle to the center of the Printer shape.
7 Update the drawing	

Add and connect topology shapes

Explanation

You can add more topology shapes to a diagram in several ways. You can drag a shape from the stencil, copy and paste a shape, or press the Ctrl key while dragging a shape already on the drawing page. When you create a duplicate of a topology shape, the duplicate maintains the same shape connections as the original. If you want a duplicate that has no connections, then duplicate the shape before using the connection handles or drag a new shape from a stencil. If you add a shape from a stencil, you can often quickly make connections by using the AutoConnect feature.

Hide extra connection handles

Topology shapes will often have connection handles that you don't need. You can hide extra connections by dragging them to the center of the topology shape. The connection handles are still visible when the shape is selected, but the connection lines are hidden, as shown in Exhibit 6-5.

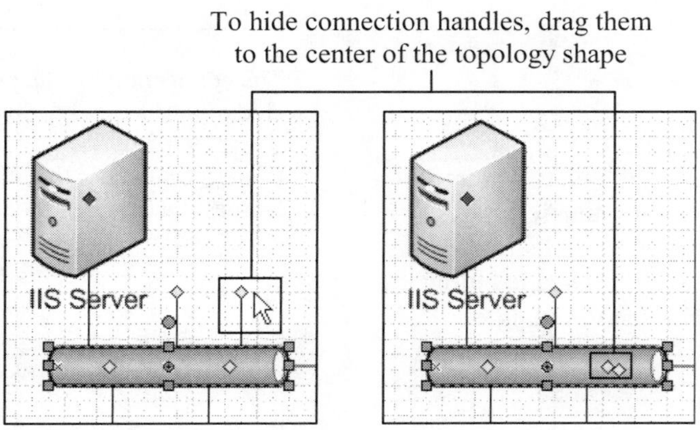

Exhibit 6-3: Hiding an extra connection handle

Do it!

A-3: Adding and connecting topology shapes

Here's how	Here's why
1 Fit the entire page in the work area	From the Zoom list, select Page.
2 Press CTRL + A	To select all the shapes in the drawing.
Position the shapes near the right side of the page	(If necessary.) You'll add another Ethernet shape on the left side of the page and connect it to the existing Ethernet shape. You'll connect the shapes by using AutoConnect. Earlier, you turned off AutoConnect, so you'll turn it back on.
3 On the Standard toolbar, click 	(The AutoConnect button.) To turn on AutoConnect.

4 In the Network and Peripherals stencil, click the Ethernet shape

To make it active.

5 On the drawing page, select the Ethernet shape

AutoConnect handles appear on each side of the shape.

Click the leftmost AutoConnect handle

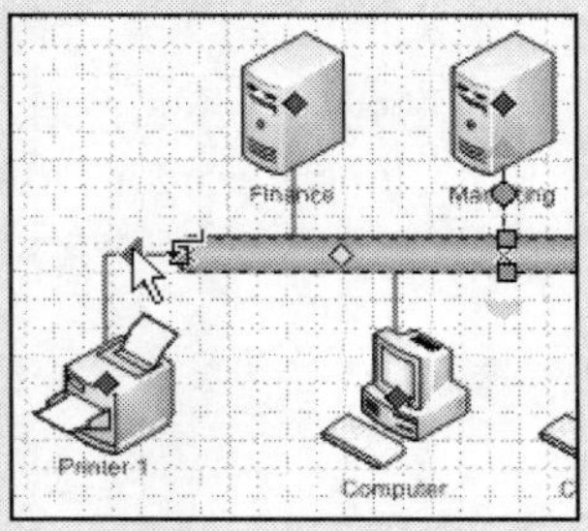

To add a new Ethernet shape to the left of the existing one.

6 Drag the new Ethernet shape toward the left side of the page

(Press Shift as you drag to keep the Ethernet shapes aligned.) The two Ethernet shapes are connected, but no other connections are added.

7 Press and hold CTRL + SHIFT and click the new Ethernet shape

To zoom in on it.

8 Point to the top-right connection handle

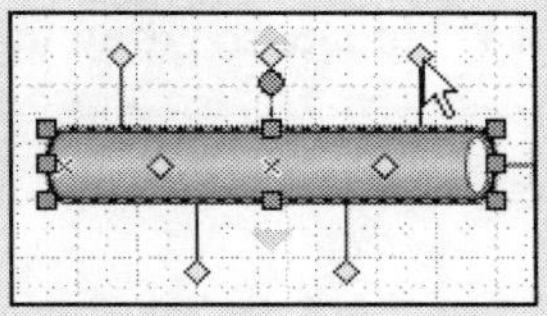

Drag the connection handle to the middle of the Ethernet shape

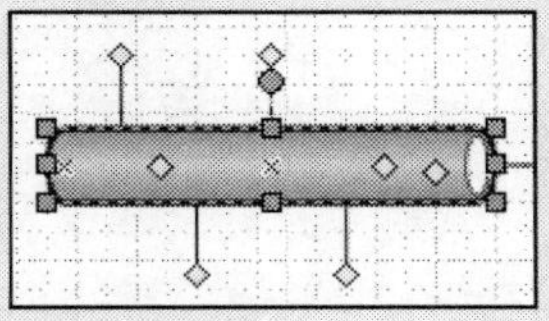

To hide the connection.

9 Hide two more of the connections, similar to the example shown here

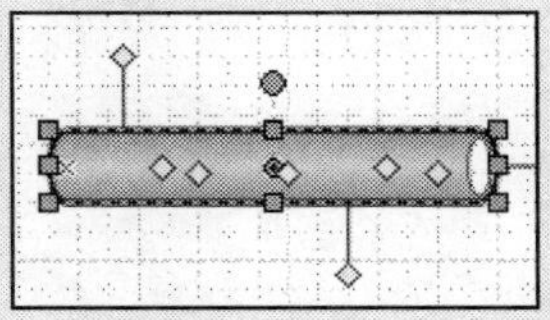

10 From the Network and Peripherals stencil, drag a Router shape below the bottom-right connection handle

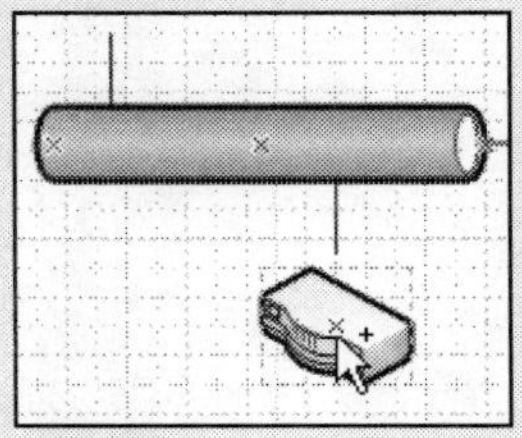

Name the Router shape **Router 1** and connect it to the Ethernet shape

11 Add a Server shape above the top-left connection handle	Either duplicate one of the existing Server shapes, or drag a new one from the stencil.
Name the new server **IIS Server** and connect it to the Ethernet shape	
12 From the Network and Peripherals stencil, drag a Firewall shape between the two Ethernet shapes, as shown	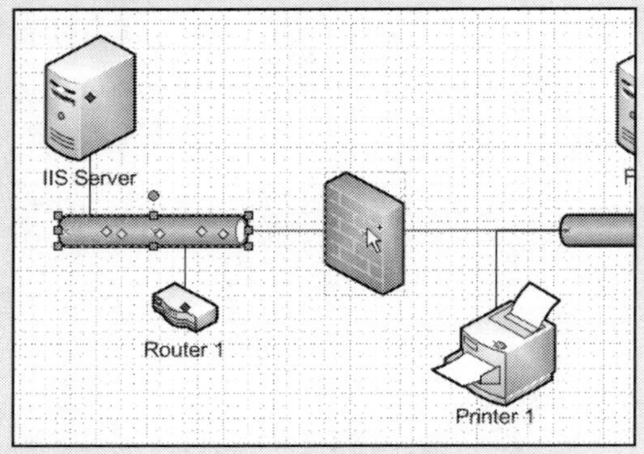 You might have to scroll down in the stencil to find the Firewall shape.
13 View the entire page in the work area	(From the Zoom list, select Page.) To see the entire diagram.
14 Update the drawing	

Move shape text

Explanation

You can use the Text tool to move text blocks. In addition, many shapes provide control handles you can use to move shape text interactively. You can use the yellow control handles on shapes to move the text and improve the readability of your diagram. To move shape text, select the shape whose text you want to move, and then drag the yellow control handle to the new text location, as shown in Exhibit 6-4.

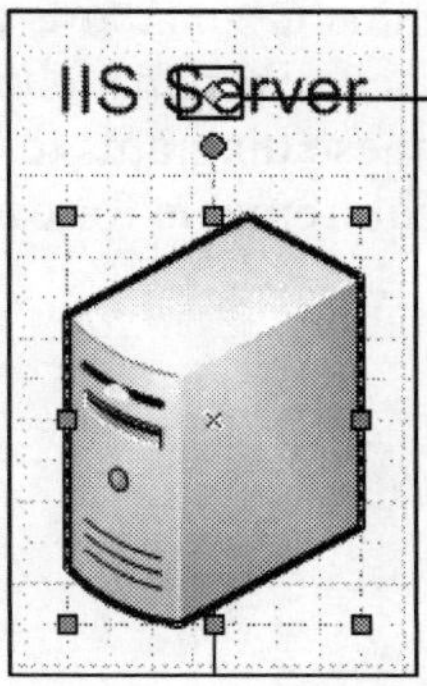

Exhibit 6-4: Using a control handle to move a text block

Do it!

A-4: Moving shape text

Here's how	Here's why
1 Press and hold CTRL + SHIFT and click the IIS Server shape	To zoom in on it.
2 Select the **IIS Server** shape	
Observe the yellow control handle below the text	You'll use it to move the text.
3 Drag the yellow control handle above the shape as shown	 The text related to the shape moves with the control handle.
4 Move the text for the other server shapes	Position the text on the same horizontal line as the IIS Server text block.
5 View the entire drawing in the work area	To preview the results.
6 Update and close the drawing	

Topic B: Rack diagrams

Explanation

You can create diagrams to show the structure of a rack system. The rack diagram template is available in the Network category.

A *rack diagram* is used to design and document a rack system, as shown in Exhibit 6-5. A *rack system* is a collection of computer hardware devices mounted in a steel rack. Visio's network equipment shapes conform to industry standards and are designed to fit together precisely. Network administrators use rack diagrams to understand the configuration of rack equipment. They also use these diagrams to optimize storage space because they can clearly view the space requirements for each type of equipment.

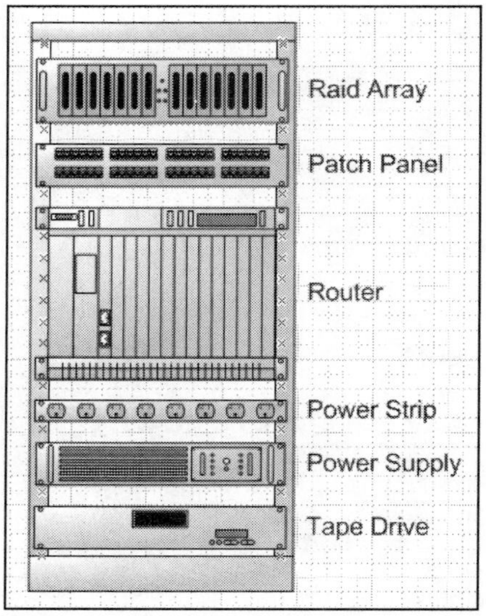

Exhibit 6-5: A rack diagram

Do it!

B-1: Creating a rack diagram

Here's how	Here's why
1 Choose **File**, **New**, **Network**, **Rack Diagram (US units)**	To create a file based on the Rack Diagram template. The Rack-mounted Equipment stencil appears in the Shapes window.
Save the file as **My rack diagram**	In the current unit folder.
2 Drag a Rack shape to the center of the drawing page	To add a Rack shape to the drawing.
3 Right-click the border of the Rack shape	
Choose **Hide U sizes**	To hide the information about the U height for the Rack shape. The U height attribute indicates the height of the rack system.
4 Drag a Tape Drive shape onto the Rack shape, near the bottom	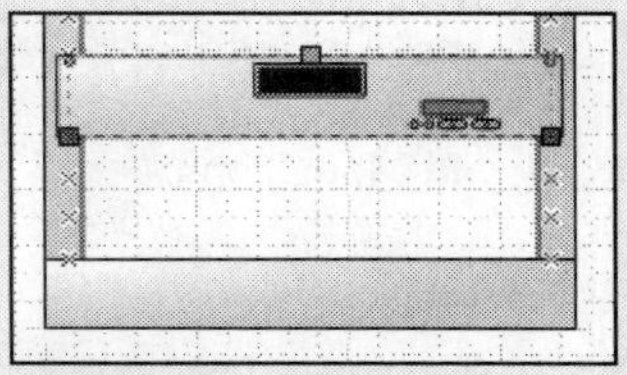 (Refer to Exhibit 6-5 for the locations and sizes of shapes in this activity.) The connection points of the Tape Drive shape are automatically glued to the Rack.
5 Type **Tape Drive**	To name the shape.
Press ESC	
6 Drag a Power supply/UPS shape onto the Rack shape	(Scroll down in the Rack-mounted Equipment stencil.) Place the new shape above the Tape Drive.
7 Type **Power Supply**	
Press ESC	
8 Add the remaining components to the diagram	As shown in Exhibit 6-5.
9 Update and close the drawing	

Topic C: Brainstorming diagrams

Explanation

Brainstorming is a technique used to solve complex problems. Visio provides tools for creating brainstorming diagrams. These tools help you depict a problem and determine its best possible solution.

To Import or Export go to Brainstorming Menu | Import or Export

The *main topic* is the central problem statement or the core heading that forms the basis for planning. For example, to plan resource usage in an organization, the main topic might be the name of the organization. *Topics* are consideration points or factors that you need to discuss to solve the problem. Legend shapes provide additional information about the brainstorming shapes in your diagram, such as priority level, warning, and importance.

When you create a file based on the Brainstorming template, Visio adds the Brainstorming menu to the menu bar. This menu contains commands used to create and manage brainstorming diagrams. The following table describes the commands available on the Brainstorming menu:

Command	Description
Auto-Arrange Topics	Automatically arranges topics in a brainstorming diagram.
Add Main Topic	Inserts a Main Topic shape in a diagram.
Add Sub Topic	Attaches a subtopic for the selected topic.
Add Peer Topic	Inserts a topic at the same level as the selected topic.
Add Multiple Subtopics	Creates several subtopics simultaneously, using the Add Multiple Topics dialog box.
Change Topic Shape	Used to modify the shape of a topic.

Creating brainstorming diagrams

Brainstorming diagrams are used to develop new ideas, solve logical problems, and show relationships between various topics.

Brainstorming diagrams can also help you identify problems and determine their solutions. This type of diagram provides a visual method of understanding a problem. Consider that the management of an organization needs to allocate resources among various departments. You can create a brainstorming diagram that shows all of the departments, similar to the example shown in Exhibit 6-6. Then, you can experiment with allocating resources to find the most appropriate distribution.

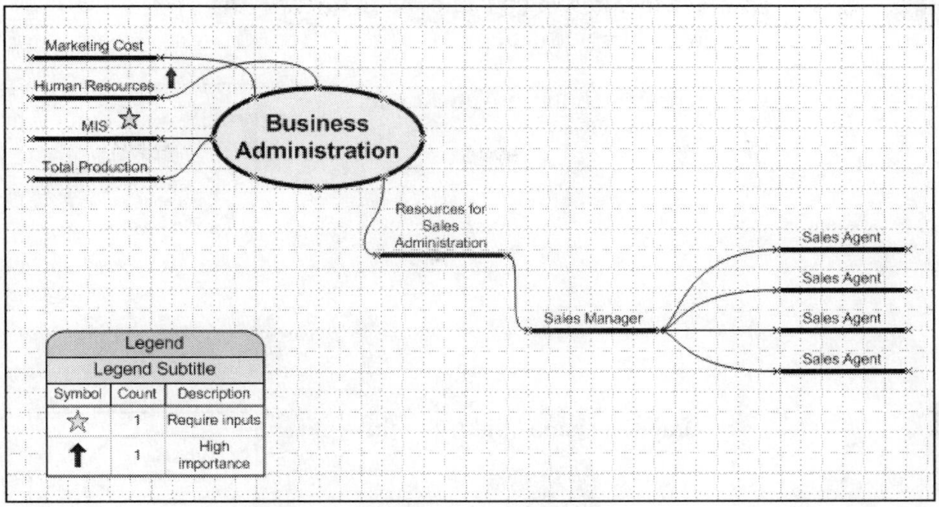

Exhibit 6-6: A brainstorming diagram

Do it!

C-1: Creating a brainstorming diagram

Here's how	Here's why
1 Choose **File**, **New**, **Business**, **Brainstorming Diagram (US units)**	To create a file based on the Brainstorming Diagram template. The Brainstorming Shapes and Legend Shapes stencils appear in the Shapes window. An Outline window is also opened, and the Brainstorming toolbar appears.
2 Close the Outline window	Click the Close button in the lower-left corner.
Dock the Brainstorming toolbar beneath the Formatting toolbar	Drag the toolbar title up until it snaps beneath the Formatting toolbar.
3 Save the document as **My brainstorming diagram**	In the current unit folder.
4 From the Brainstorming Shapes stencil, drag a Main Topic shape onto the drawing page	Refer to Exhibit 6-6 for the locations and sizes of shapes in this activity.
Name the Main Topic shape **Business Administration**	You'll use AutoConnect to add other shapes to the diagram.
5 On the Standard toolbar, activate AutoConnect	If necessary.
6 In the stencil, select the Topic shape	To make it active.

7 On the drawing page, point to the Main Topic shape

AutoConnect handles appear around it.

Click the bottom AutoConnect handle

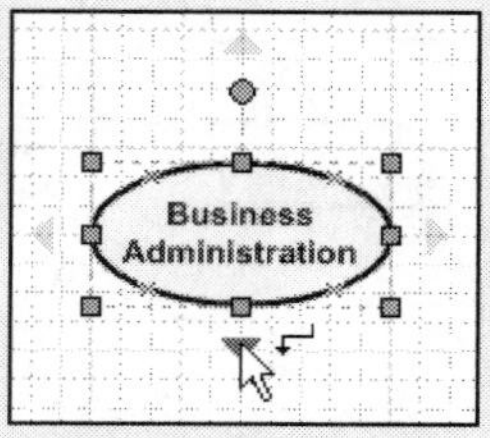

To add the Topic shape below the Main Topic shape.

8 Drag the shape slightly to the right

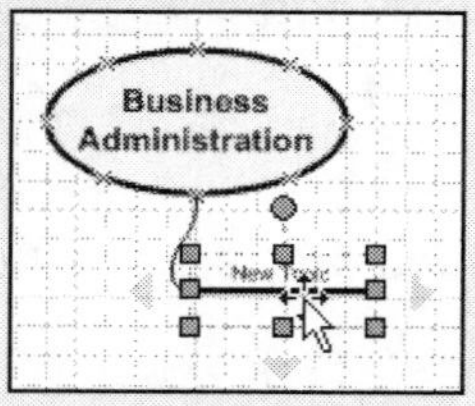

To reverse the direction in which the Topic shape is connected to the Main Topic shape.

9 Name the Topic shape **Resources for Sales Administration**

You'll also add multiple topics to the left of the Business Administration shape.

10 In the stencil, select the Multiple Topic shape

To make it active.

11 Using AutoConnect, link the shape to the left of the Business Administration shape

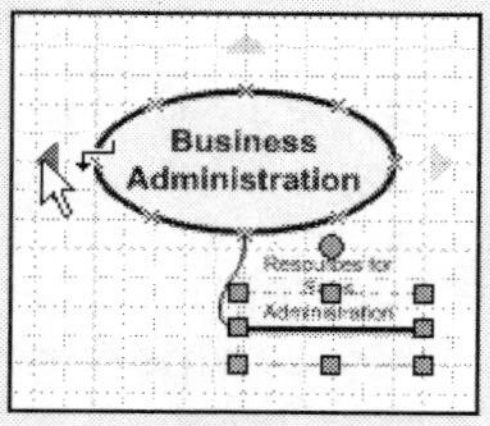

(Point to the Business Administration shape and click the leftmost AutoConnect handle.) The Add Multiple Topics dialog box appears. You'll use it to add subtopics.

12 Type **Marketing Cost**

To name the Topic shape.

Press ENTER

13 Type **Human Resources** and press ENTER

To create another name.

14 Add **MIS** and **Total Production** as the last two subtopics — Type each subtopic name and press Enter after each name.

Click **OK** — To close the dialog box and link the subtopics to the Business Administration shape.

15 Activate the Legend Shapes stencil — (At the bottom of the Shapes window, click the stencil's title bar.) You'll add a legend to the diagram.

16 Press and hold CTRL + SHIFT and click the MIS topic in the Multiple Topic shape — To zoom in on it.

17 Drag a Star shape from the stencil to the top right of the **MIS** topic, as shown

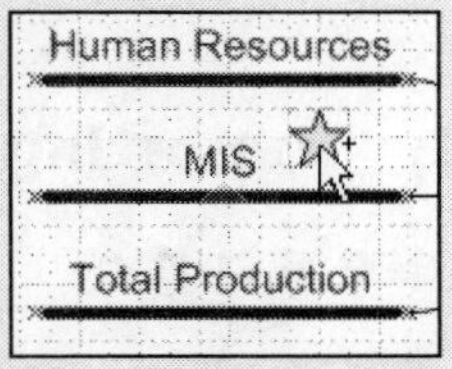

The Star shape indicates that input is required.

18 Press and hold CTRL + SHIFT and right-click the MIS topic — To view the entire page again.

19 Drag a Legend shape to the lower-left corner of the drawing page

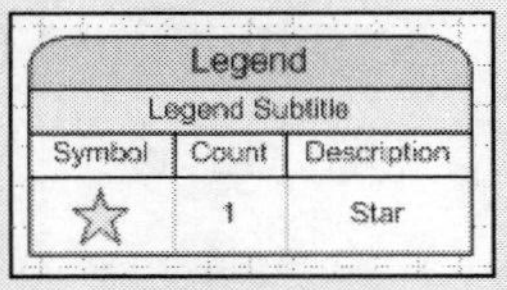

The Legend describes all the Legend shapes added to the drawing. In this case, the Star shape is visible. If you add more Legend shapes to the drawing, each shape description will be added automatically.

20 Press and hold CTRL + SHIFT and click the star description in the legend — To zoom in on it.

Double-click the description **Star** — To select it.

Type **Require inputs** — To change the star's description in the Legend.

21 Deselect the Legend, and view the entire page again — Press and hold Ctrl+Shift, and right-click the page to zoom back out.

22 Create the rest of the brainstorming diagram — As shown in Exhibit 6-6.

23 Update the drawing

Using brainstorming data

Explanation

You can export the data stored in a brainstorming diagram to a Microsoft Word document, a Microsoft Excel workbook, or an XML file. XML is a widely accepted standard for transferring data across applications and platforms. If you need to convert the data from a brainstorming diagram to an XML file format, use the brainstorming export and import tools.

To export a brainstorming diagram to an XML file:

1. Open the brainstorming diagram you want to export.
2. Choose Brainstorming, Export Data, To XML to open the File Save dialog box.
3. Navigate to the location where you want to save the XML file.
4. Click Save. Visio exports the data to the XML file. When it is finished, a message box appears, indicating that the export is complete.
5. Click OK to close the Brainstorming dialog box.

Do it!

C-2: Exporting a brainstorming diagram to an XML file

Here's how	Here's why
1 Choose **Brainstorming**, **Export Data**, **To XML...**	To open the File Save dialog box.
2 Navigate to the current unit folder	If necessary.
Edit the File name box to read **Organization plan**	
Click **Save**	 The Brainstorming message box appears when the export is completed.
Click **OK**	To complete the export process.
3 Update and close the drawing	

Importing XML files

Explanation

Visio provides tools to create brainstorming diagrams by using XML files. Support for XML files in Visio ensures that data can be exchanged between other applications and Visio. The data stored in an XML file is translated into a brainstorming diagram when you import the file.

To import XML data into a brainstorming diagram:

1. Create a drawing based on the Brainstorming Diagram template.
2. Choose Brainstorming, Import Data.
3. Navigate to the location of the XML file you want to import.
4. From the Files of Type list, select XML Files to view the XML files.
5. Select the XML file you want to import, and click Open.

Do it!

C-3: Importing XML data into a brainstorming diagram

Here's how	Here's why
1 Create a file based on the Brainstorming Diagram template	Choose File, New, Business, Brainstorming Diagram (US units).
Save the file as **Import org plan**	In the current unit folder.
Close the Outline window	
2 Choose **Brainstorming**, **Import Data…**	To open the File Open dialog box.
3 From the Files of Type list, select **XML Files**	If necessary.
Navigate to the current unit folder	
4 Select **Organization structure**	
Click **Open**	Visio automatically generates a brainstorming diagram by using the data imported from the XML file, Organization structure.
5 Update and close the drawing	

Unit summary: Network and brainstorming diagrams

Topic A In this topic, you learned how to use network topology shapes to create a basic **network diagram**. You learned how to move control handles to create different connection points and move text blocks connected to shapes.

Topic B In this topic, you learned how to create a **rack diagram** for a rack system in a network. You also learned how to create a **directory service diagram** to show the directory structure of a network.

Topic C In this topic, you learned how to create a **brainstorming diagram**. You also learned how to import data into and export data from a brainstorming diagram.

Independent practice activity

In this activity, you'll create a network diagram. You'll also create a brainstorming diagram and export it to an XML file. Finally, you'll import an XML file into a Visio file.

1. Create a Visio file based on the Basic Network Diagram template. Save the file as **My practice** in the current unit folder.
2. Create a network diagram similar to the example shown in Exhibit 6-7.
3. Update the drawing and close it.
4. Create a Visio file using the Brainstorming Diagram template. Save the file as **My brainstorming practice** in the current unit folder.
5. Add various shapes to the drawing, so it looks similar to the example shown in Exhibit 6-8.
6. Export the brainstorming diagram to an XML file named **My export practice**.
7. Update and close the drawing.
8. Create a Visio file using the Brainstorming Diagram template. Save the file as **My BSD import practice** in the current unit folder.
9. Import the My export practice XML file.
10. Update the topics and legends as shown in Exhibit 6-9.
11. Hide the Brainstorming toolbar.
12. Update and close the drawing. (Don't close Visio.)

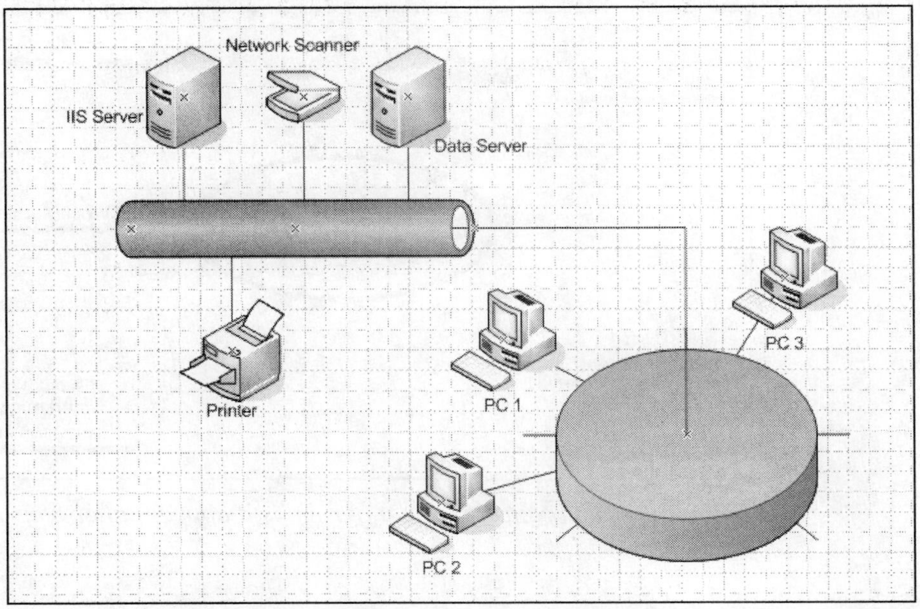

Exhibit 6-7: The network diagram created in Step 2 of the independent practice activity

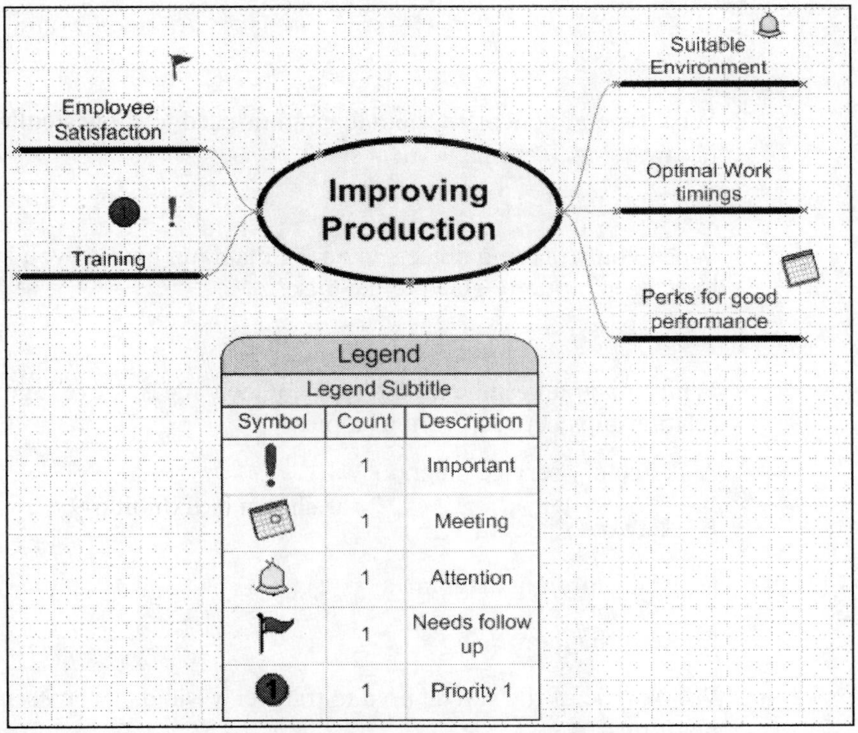

Exhibit 6-8: The brainstorming diagram as it appears after Step 5

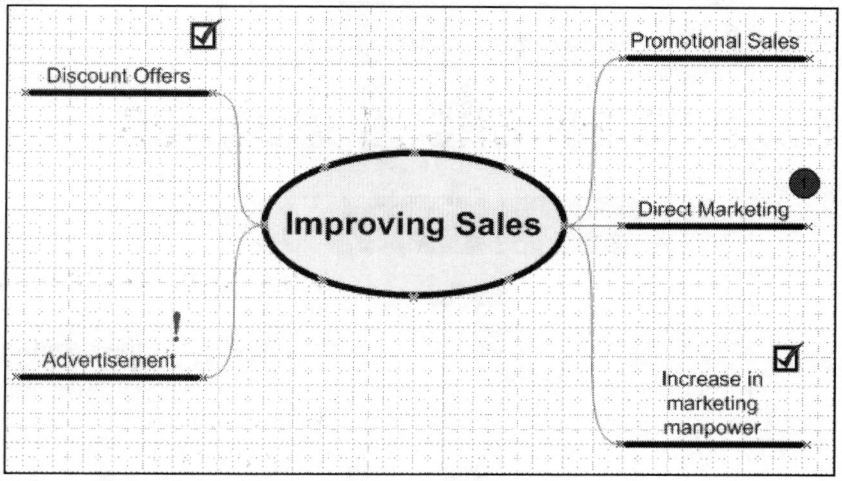

Exhibit 6-9: The brainstorming diagram as it appears after Step 10

Review questions

1 How does Visio make it easy for you to create network diagrams?

2 What type of network system diagram is used to show a collection of various hardware devices in a vertical stack?

3 When you're adding objects to a rack diagram, how do you know when the objects have been properly glued to the rack?

4 Which diagram can be used to develop new ideas, solve logical problems, and show relationships between various topics?

A Directory service diagram

B Network diagram

C Brainstorming diagram

D Rack diagram

5 Which type of file can be used to transfer Visio data across applications and platforms?

A Word document

B Excel worksheet

C Access database

D XML file

Unit 7

Introduction to advanced features

Unit time: 55 minutes

Complete this unit, and you'll know how to:

A Use advanced connection and layout techniques.

B Set custom properties for shapes.

C Create and modify property reports.

Topic A: Advanced layout and connection techniques

Explanation

When creating a diagram, you can add guides to a drawing page to make it easier to position and align shapes precisely. You can create additional connection points on an object as needed, and format a diagram's connectors to clarify a message.

Guides

Guides are nonprinting lines that divide a drawing page into sections to help you accurately place shapes and objects. You can add guides to a drawing by pointing to the horizontal or vertical ruler and then dragging a guide onto the page. You can move them anywhere. You see guides as you work with diagrams, but they do not print.

Glue shapes to guides

Just as you glue shapes to connector lines, you can glue shapes to guides. This is especially helpful when you want all the shapes to be aligned accurately. To glue shapes, you use their selection handles, shown in Exhibit 7-1.

It's best to place guides before placing shapes on a drawing page. If you place guides on a drawing page containing shapes, you'll need to manually reposition the shapes on the guide to glue them.

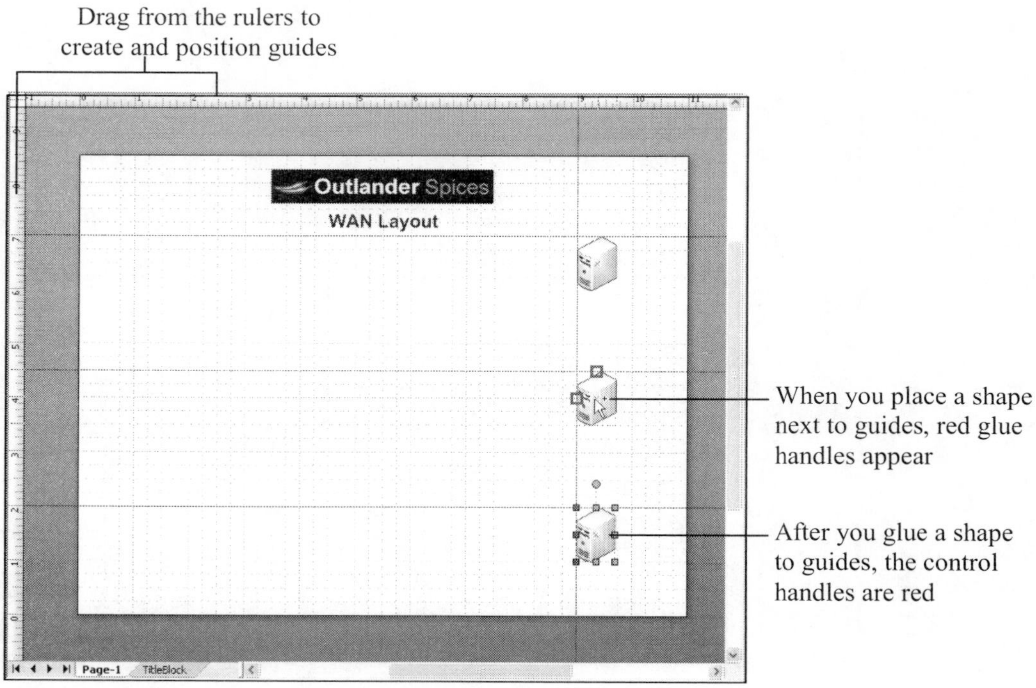

Exhibit 7-1: Adding guides and gluing shapes to them

If you glue shapes to guides, the shapes will move with the guides if you adjust them. To move a guide, drag it to a new location on the page.

Do it!

A-1: Using guides

Here's how	Here's why
1 Open WAN.vsd	From the current unit folder.
2 Save the file as **My WAN**	
Verify that the Pointer tool is selected	If necessary.
3 Point to the vertical ruler	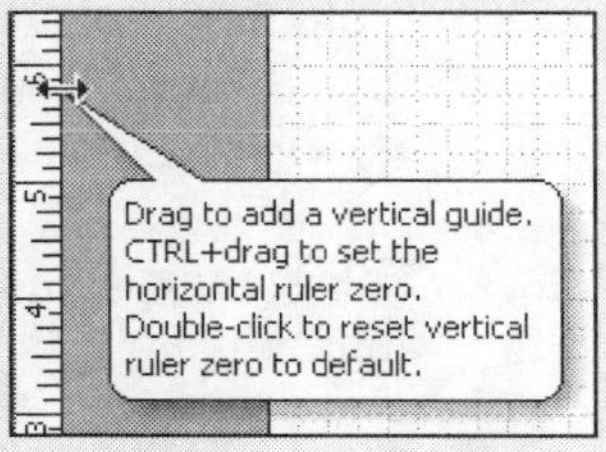 The pointer changes to a double-headed arrow.
Drag to the right and place a guide at the 9" mark on the horizontal ruler	Watch the horizontal ruler as you drag to place the guide.
4 Point to the horizontal ruler	
Drag a horizontal guide to the 7" mark on the vertical ruler	To create a horizontal guide on the page.
5 Add two more horizontal guides at the 2" and 4.5" marks	There should be three horizontal guides and one vertical guide on the drawing page.
6 From the Network and Peripherals stencil, drag a Server shape onto the page	
7 Place the shape at the intersection of the top horizontal guide and the vertical guide until two red squares appear, as shown	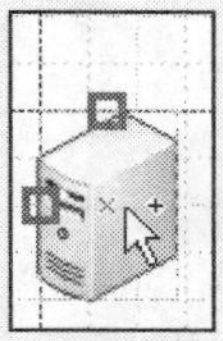 The red squares indicate that the shape will be glued to both guides.
When the red squares are visible, release the mouse button	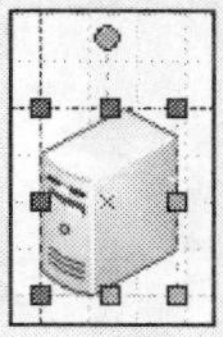 The control handles on the left side and top of the shape are red, indicating that the shape is glued to the guides.

- Click and drag rulers on the page;
drag shapes on to page and connect w/ guides until turns red.
- Moves guides. Shapes should move w/guide if connected correctly.

TIP
hoose Edit | Select by Type.
o remove guides. Deselect ll checkboxes except guide.

8 Add two more Server shapes to the drawing and position them as shown in Exhibit 7-1	
9 Click the vertical guide	The guide turns green, indicating that it is selected.
Drag the guide to 8.5"	(On the horizontal ruler.) The shapes move with the guide.
10 From the Network and Peripherals stencil, add a Router shape to the drawing page	Do not glue the shape to any guides yet.
Enlarge the Router shape to approximately 1" wide	Drag one of the corner shape handles to make the shape larger. Use the status bar to set the size.
11 Glue the Router shape to the top horizontal guide, approximately 4" to the left of the top Server shape	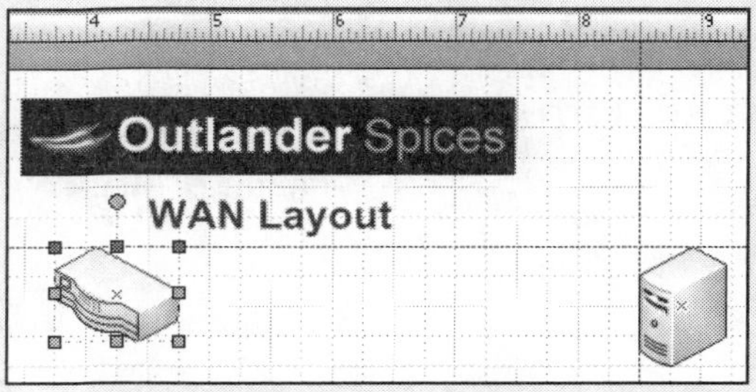
12 Create two duplicates of the Router shape	
Place the duplicates as shown	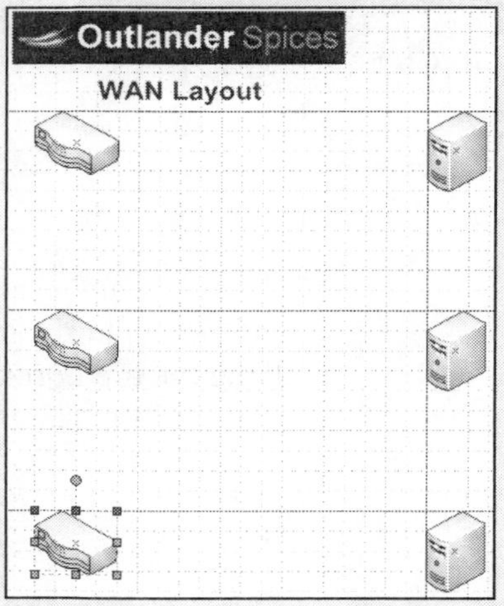

13 Name the top Server shape **Communication Server**	(You'll need to press Enter as you type the text to position it on two lines.) You'll move the text block to the right of the shape.
Move the shape text to the right of the shape, as shown	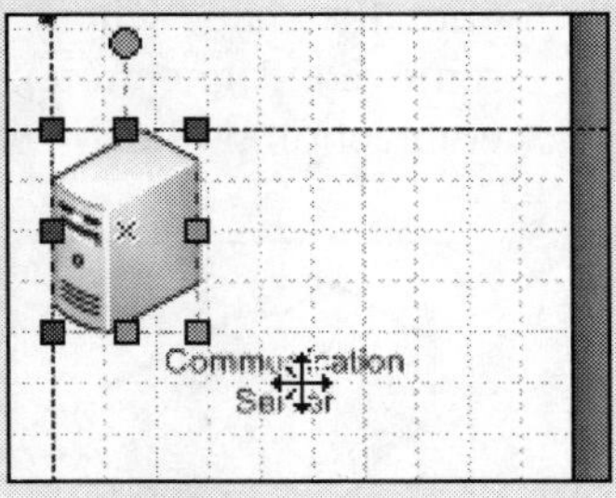 Drag the yellow control handle to move the text.
14 Name the middle Server shape **Server 1 Apple Talk**	
Align the shape text similarly to the previous shape	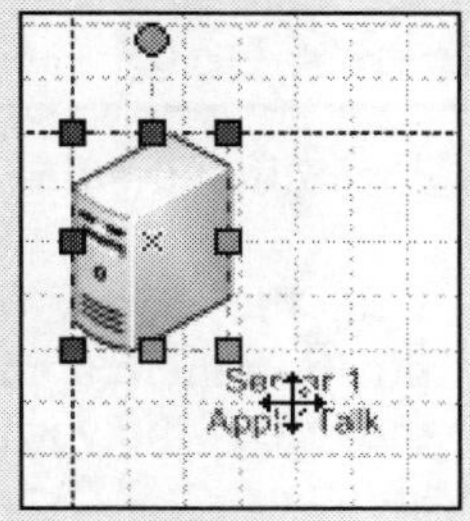
15 Name the bottom Server shape **Server 2 IPX Only**	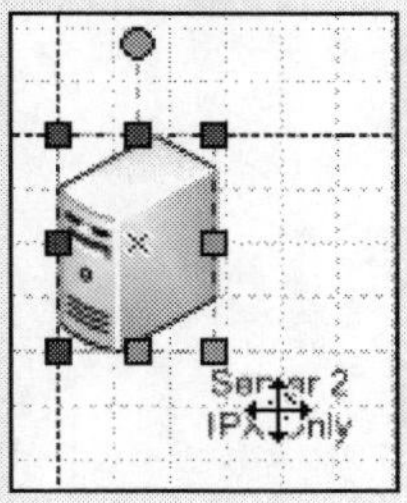 Move the shape text after you've entered it.
Drag the top horizontal guide down by 0.5"	Both shapes glued to this guide move as well.
16 Choose **View**, **Guides**	To hide the guides. Though they are no longer visible, the guides remain on the drawing page.
Make the guides visible again	Choose View, Guides.
17 Update the drawing	

New connection points

Explanation

Most shapes have only one connection point on each side. If you need additional connection points, use the Connection Point tool on the Standard toolbar. To add points, click the shape where you want to add the connection point, as shown in Exhibit 7-2. To remove a connection point, click it to select it and then press Delete. You can move connection points by dragging them with the Connection Point tool.

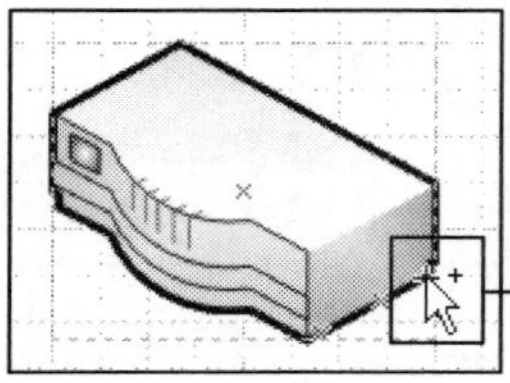

To add a connection point, press and hold Ctrl, and click where you want the point to be added to the shape

Exhibit 7-2: Adding connection points to a shape

Do it!

A-2: Adding connection points

	Here's how	Here's why
1	Ctrl+click the three router shapes	To select them.
	Drag the shapes to the left and position them approximately 1" to the left of the vertical guide, as shown	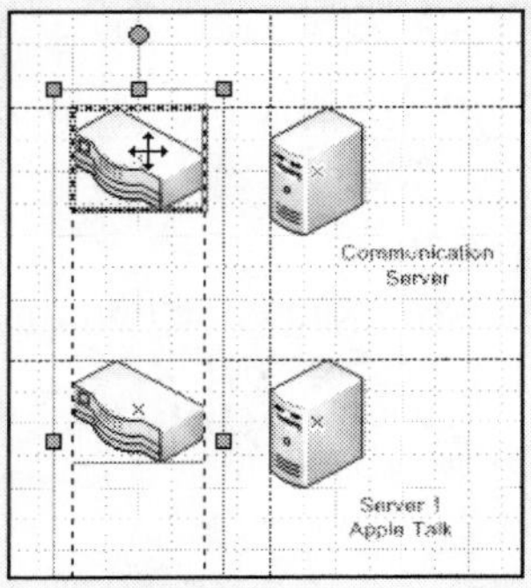
2	From the Computers and Monitors stencil, add three PC shapes to the drawing page	
	Place the shapes on the top horizontal guide as shown	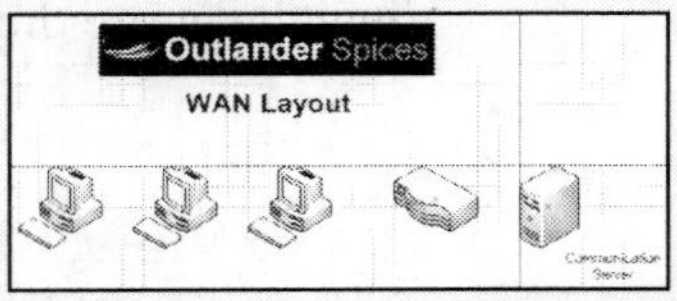
3	Press and hold CTRL + SHIFT and click the top Router shape	To zoom in on it.
4	Release CTRL + SHIFT and click the shape	To select it.

5	On the Standard toolbar, expand the Connector Tool list, as shown	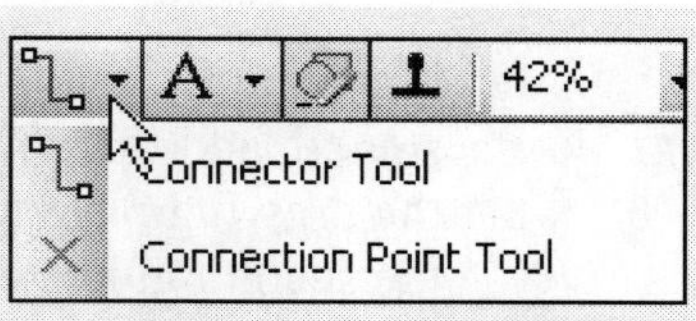
	Select the Connection Point Tool	You'll add new connection points to the shapes.
6	Press and hold CTRL	
	Point to the edges of the Router shape	A plus sign (+) appears in the upper-right corner of the pointer.
	Click the bottom-right part of the shape, as shown	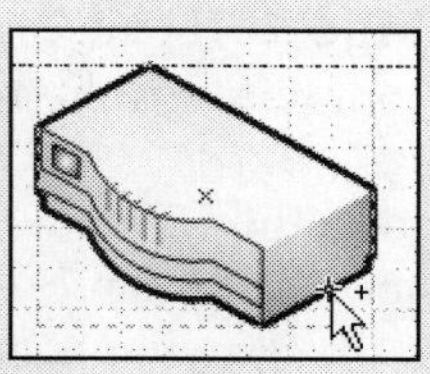 To add a new connection point.
	Release CTRL	
7	Add two more connection points to the router	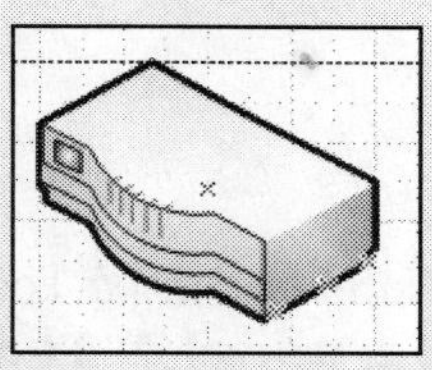 (Add them along the bottom edge, on each side of the existing connection point.) Remember to hold Ctrl as you click to add the connections.
	Add the same connection points to the other two Router shapes	You'll need to select each shape before you can add connection points to it.
8	Select the Pointer tool	
	View the entire drawing page	From the Zoom list, select Page.
9	Name the three PC shapes **PC 1**, **PC 2**, and **PC 3**, from left to right, respectively	
10	Name the three Router shapes **Router 1**, **Router 2**, and **Router 3**, from top to bottom, respectively	

11 From the Computers and Monitors stencil, add three iMac shapes to the drawing page, gluing them to the second guide, as shown

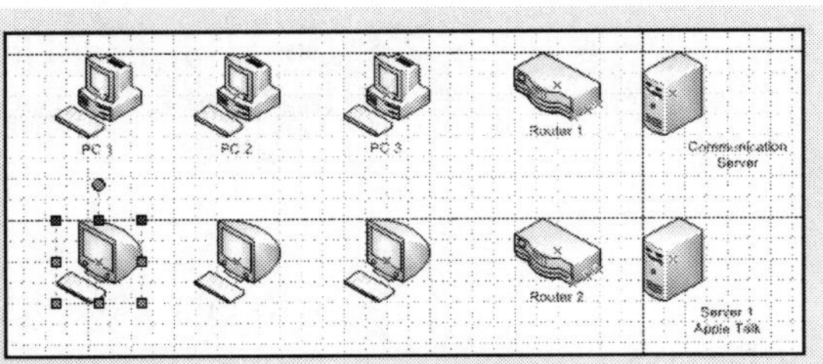

Use the PC shapes to help place the iMac shapes on the middle guide.

Name the three iMac shapes **iMac 1**, **iMac 2**, and **iMac 3**, from left to right, respectively

12 From the Computers and Monitors stencil, add three Terminal shapes to the drawing page, gluing them to the third guide, as shown

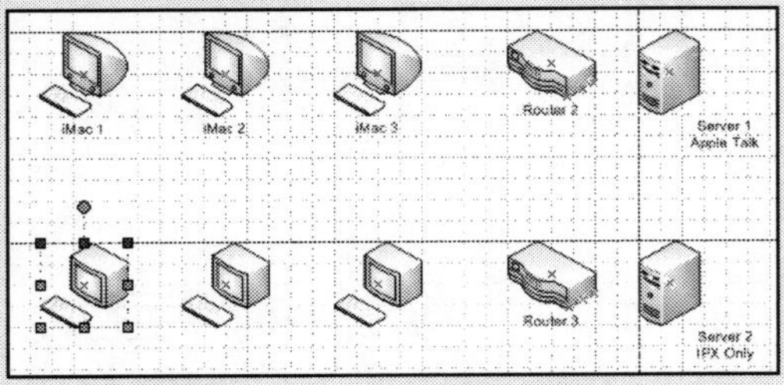

Use the iMac shapes to help place the Terminal shapes on the bottom guide.

Name the three Terminal shapes **Terminal 1**, **Terminal 2**, and **Terminal 3**, from left to right, respectively

13 Update the drawing

Select by Type

Explanation

Sometimes you might want to select similar objects and shapes. For example, you might be working on a complex drawing and need to select multiple objects of the same type for editing. To do this, you can use the Select by Type dialog box, shown in Exhibit 7-3. To open the dialog box, choose Edit, Select by Type. You can use the dialog box to select shapes, groups, guides, and other drawing-page objects.

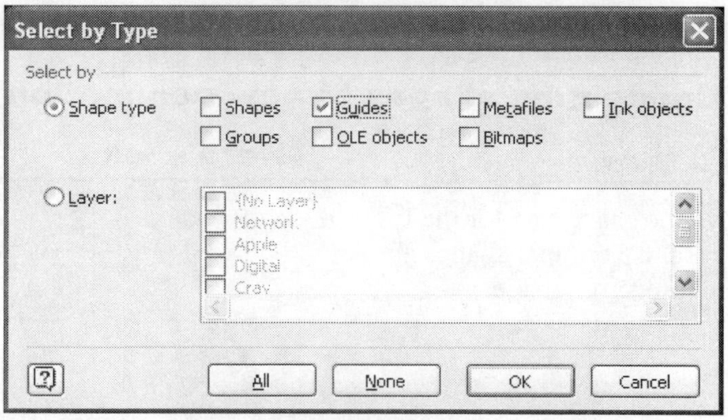

Exhibit 7-3: The Select by Type dialog box

Do it!

A-3: Selecting objects by type

Here's how	Here's why
1 Choose **Edit**, **Select by Type…**	To open the Select by Type dialog box. By default, all shape types are selected.
2 Click **None**	To clear the check boxes next to the Shape types.
3 Next to the Shape type, check **Guides**	
4 Click **OK**	To select only the guides.
5 Press DELETE	To delete the guides from the drawing page.
Update the drawing	

Shape connections

Explanation

You connect shapes to new connection points by using the same techniques you would use to connect unaltered shapes. However, if you want to precisely position the connections, you can use the Connector tool on the Standard toolbar to draw the connections manually. AutoConnecting the shapes can produce erratic results. Also, if you've already positioned shapes in a drawing, using the Connector tool can produce better results. The connectors are not dynamic, but that's okay as long as the shapes won't need to be moved much.

Do it!

A-4: Connecting shapes to new connection points

Here's how	Here's why
1 Move the shape text for the PC, iMac, and Terminal shapes above their respective shapes	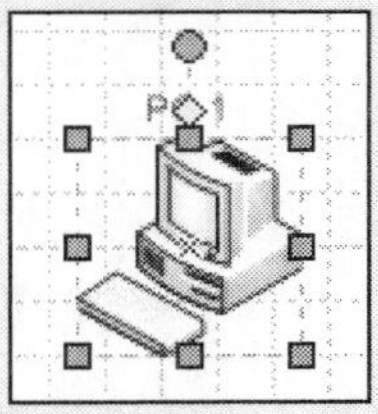 Drag the yellow shape text handles to the top-center shape handle.
2 On the Standard toolbar, from the Connection Point Tool list, select the Connector tool	
3 Point to the center of the Communication Server shape, as shown	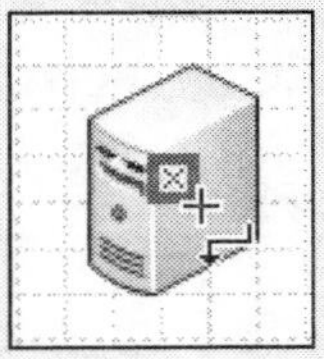 The connection point in the center has a red box around it, indicating that the connection will be glued to it.
Drag to the left, to the connection point in the center of the Router 1 shape	To connect the two shapes. The connector has green control handles you can use to adjust it.
4 Using the control handles, adjust the shape of the connector, as shown	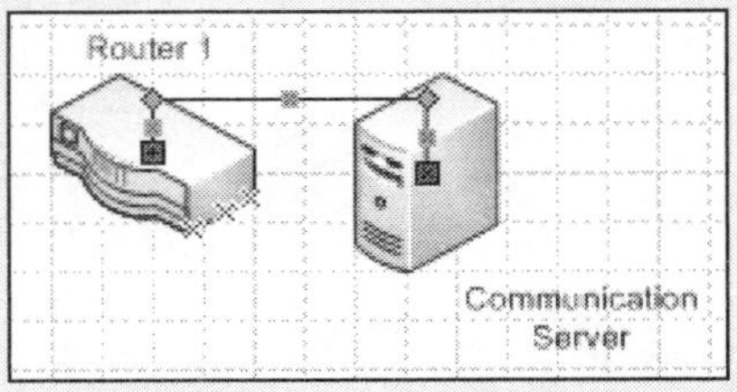
5 Connect the other Server shapes to their respective Router shapes	

6 Connect the PC 3 shape to the leftmost connection point on the Router 1 shape

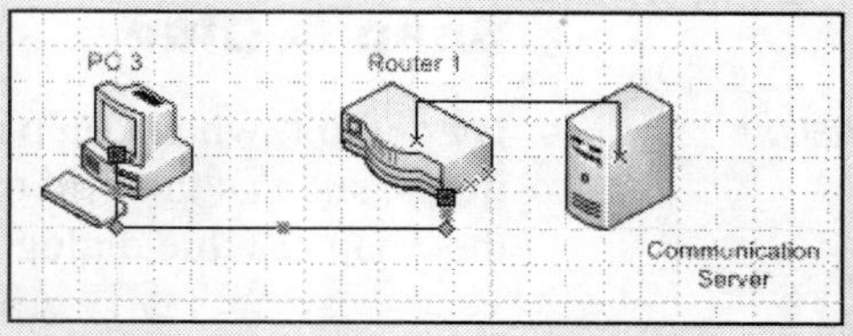

You might have to adjust the connector after you draw it.

7 Connect the PC 2 shape to the middle connection point on the Router 1 shape

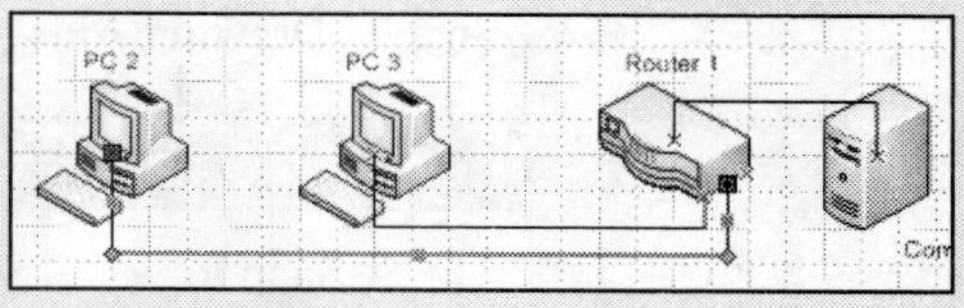

8 Connect the PC 1 shape to the rightmost connection point on the Router 1 shape

The three PC shapes are now connected to Router 1.

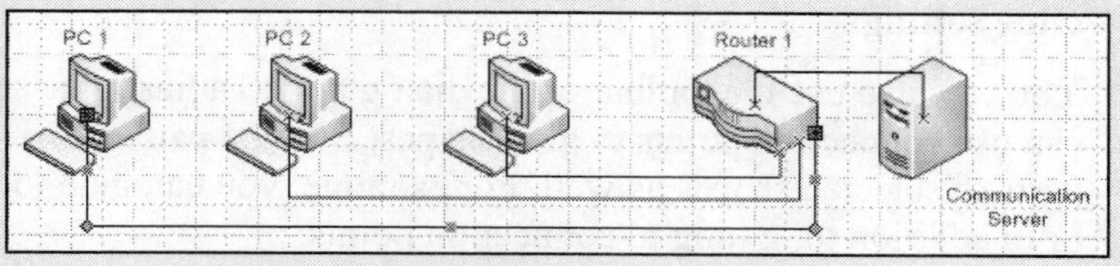

9 Repeat the process for the iMac and Terminal shapes

Connect the shapes to the Router shape in the same row.

10 Update the drawing

Snap & Glue

Explanation

By default, when you position and adjust objects in a drawing, they snap to different items, such as the grid or ruler subdivisions. To adjust the way items snap, you can use the Snap & Glue dialog box or the Snap & Glue toolbar, shown in Exhibit 7-4.

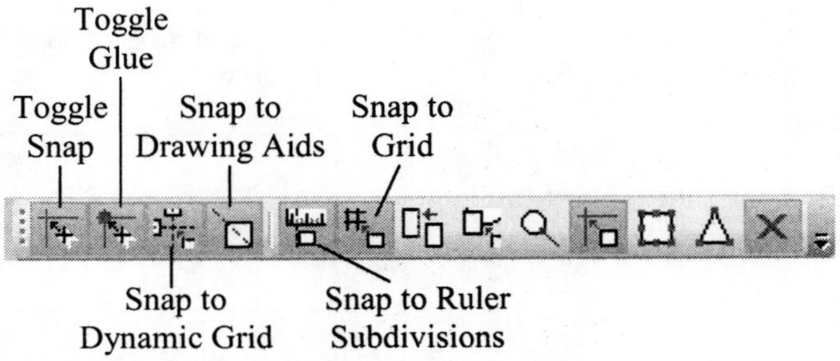

Exhibit 7-4: The Snap & Glue toolbar

Glue settings

You can also use the toolbar or the dialog box to adjust glue settings. By default, you can use connection points to glue shapes. But you can modify glue settings to use other parts of selected shapes as well. For example, you can glue to shape handles instead of, or in addition to, gluing to connection points.

Do it!

A-5: Changing Snap & Glue settings

Here's how	Here's why
1 Press and hold CTRL + SHIFT and click the Router 1 shape	To zoom in on it.
2 Select the connector between the Router 1 shape and the Communication Server shape	
Using the center connector control handle, drag the line up and down	As you drag, the connector snaps to the grid increments.
3 Right-click anywhere on a toolbar and choose **Snap & Glue**	To display the Snap & Glue toolbar.
4 On the toolbar, click	(The Snap to Grid button.) To turn off the Snap to Grid option.
Drag the connector line up and down again	It still seems to snap in increments. The connector is still snapping to the ruler increments.
5 On the Snap & Glue toolbar, click	The Snap to Ruler Subdivisions button.
Drag the connector line up and down again	Now the line seems to move freely, although it still snaps when it crosses its original location.
6 On the toolbar, click	The Toggle Snap button.
Drag the connector line up and down again	Now the line moves freely, even when it crosses its point of origin.
7 View the entire drawing page again	From the Zoom list, select Page.
8 Update the drawing	

Topic B: Custom properties

Explanation

You might want to track information associated with your drawing. For example, you might want to store information about a server, such as its manufacturer, CPU speed, hard drive space, and IP address. You can do so by using custom properties. *Custom properties* are data fields that store information about shapes.

To define custom properties for a shape:

1. Select the shape you want to define. If you want to define a custom property for a shape that you'll reuse in several drawings, select the master shape on the stencil.
2. Right-click the shape and choose Properties to open the Shape Data panel, shown in Exhibit 7-5.
3. In the appropriate data fields, enter the information you want to track.
4. To add information for another shape, select the shape and then enter the information in the panel.
5. Click the small "x" in the corner to close the panel, if necessary.

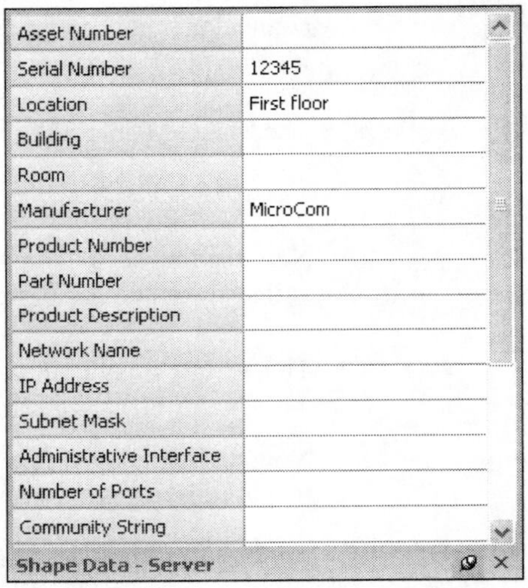

Exhibit 7-5: The Shape Data panel

Do it!

B-1: Adding custom properties to shapes

Here's how	Here's why
1 Right-click the Communication Server shape and choose **Properties**	To open the Shape Data panel. The panel is small at the bottom of the work area, so you'll expand it.
2 Point to the top edge of the panel	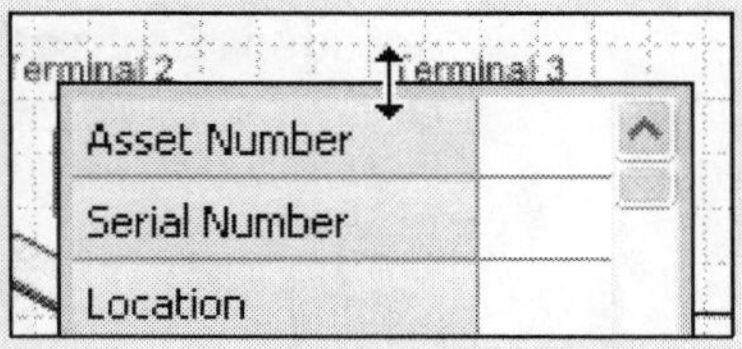 Until the pointer becomes a double-headed arrow.
Drag up	To increase the height of the panel.
3 Using the same technique, increase the width of the panel	(Point to the right edge of the panel and drag to the right.) You'll add information about the Communication Server shape.
4 In the Manufacturer box, enter **MicroCom**	To record the name of the manufacturer.
In the Serial Number box, enter **12345**	To record the server's serial number.
5 In the Location box, enter **First floor**	To record the server's location.
In the Department box, enter **Communications**	(You might have to scroll down in the list to see the category.) To record the department to which the server belongs. You'll add information about the other server shapes. First, you'll move the panel so that you can see the shapes better.
6 Point to the Shape Data panel's title bar	 Until the pointer becomes a four-headed arrow.
Slowly drag to the left until the panel docks to the left side of the work area	

7	Select the Server 1 Apple Talk shape	
	In the Shape Data panel, specify the following properties: Manufacturer: **Apple** Serial Number: **33456** Location: **Second floor** Department: **IS**	Open the Custom Properties dialog box and enter the data.
8	Select the Server 2 IPX Only shape	
	Specify the following information: Manufacturer: **Dell** Serial Number: **77865** Location: **First floor** Department: **IS**	
9	Update the drawing	

User-defined custom properties

Explanation

All shapes have a predefined set of fields for entering custom properties. However, you might want to store information that isn't defined in the default set, such as hard drive size or CPU speed. You can create one or more user-defined custom properties for the data fields you need. If you have more than one property, you have a *property set.* Custom properties can be applied to multiple shapes. You can create a new property set or modify an existing set.

To create a property set:

1 Right-click in the Shape Data panel and choose Shape Data Sets to open the Shape Data Sets panel, shown in Exhibit 7-6.

2 Click Add to open the Add Shape Data Set window.

3 Enter a descriptive name for the property set, verify that "Create a new set" is selected, and click OK.

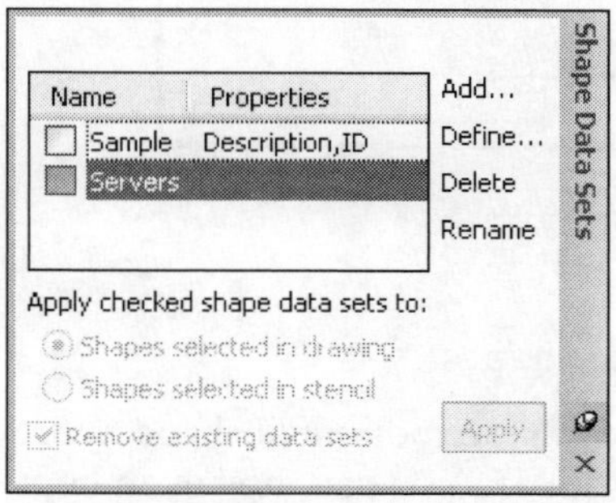

Exhibit 7-6: The Shape Data Sets panel

To add custom properties to a property set:

1 In the Shape Data Sets panel, select the property set you want to define custom properties for.

2 Click Define to open the Define Shape Data dialog box, shown in Exhibit 7-7.

3 Specify the type of information you want for the property.

4 Click New to add the property and reset the dialog box.

5 Using the same technique, add any other properties you want for the set.

6 When you are finished, click OK to close the dialog box.

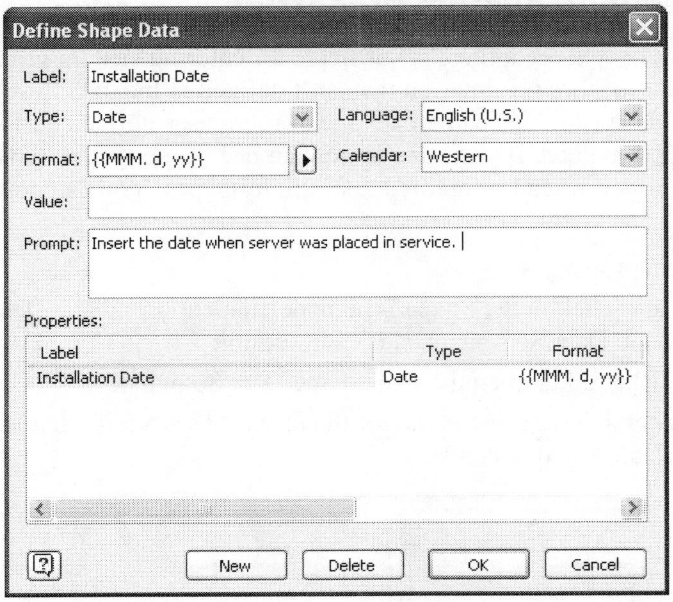

Exhibit 7-7: The Define Shape Data dialog box

Custom properties for individual shapes

When you create custom properties for an individual shape, those properties will be associated with only the specified shape. You can, however, copy the properties for an individual shape into a custom property set if you want to use them for other shapes.

Do it!

B-2: Creating custom property sets

Here's how	Here's why
1 Right-click in the Shape Data panel and choose **Shape Data Sets…**	To open the Shape Data Sets window.
2 In the Shape Data Sets window, click **Add…**	To open the Add Shape Data Set dialog box.
In the Name box, enter **Servers**	To name the property set.
Select **Create a new set**	(If necessary.) You can create a new set or use an existing set.
Click **OK**	To close the dialog box.
3 In the Shape Data Sets window, click **Define…**	To open the Define Shape Data dialog box.
4 In the Label box, enter **Installation Date**	
From the Type list, select **Date**	
From the Format list, select **Oct. 3, 93**	To set the date format.
In the Prompt box, enter **Insert the date when server was placed into service.**	
5 Click **New**	You'll add another custom property to the set.
6 Enter the following information for the new property: Label: **Storage** Type: **Number** Format: **Whole number (3)** Prompt: **Insert the storage capacity in gigabytes.**	To define the property's data.
7 Click **OK**	To close the dialog box.
8 Update the drawing	

Using custom properties

Explanation

After creating a custom property set, you can apply the properties to the shapes in your drawing. The new property set will be added to the existing property set for the shape.

To apply a custom property set to a shape:

1 Select the shape to which you want to apply the custom property set.
2 In the Shape Data Sets panel, check each property set you want to add to the selected shape.
3 Select whether to apply the checked property set(s) to shapes selected in the drawing or to shapes selected in the stencil, as shown in Exhibit 7-8.
4 If you want to remove a property set, check "Remove existing data sets."
5 Click Apply.

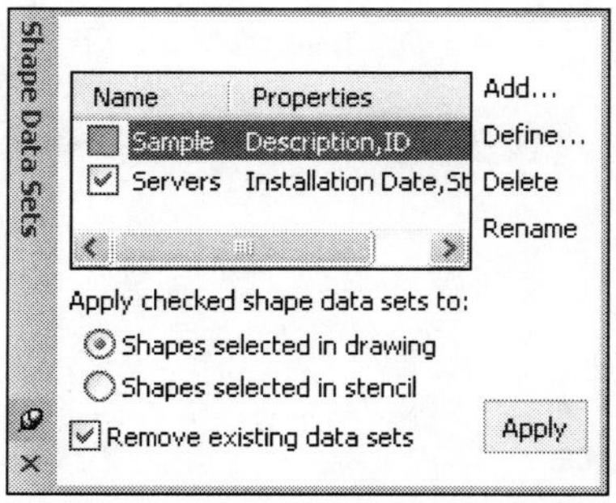

Exhibit 7-8: Applying a custom property set by using the Shape Data Sets panel

Do it!

B-3: Applying user-defined custom properties

Here's how	Here's why
1 In the Shape Data Sets panel, check **Servers**	
2 Under "Apply checked shape data sets to," verify that "Shapes selected in drawing" is selected	
3 Dock the Shape Data Sets panel to the upper-left side of the work area	Drag the panel's title bar to move the panel. You might have to reduce the height of the Shape Data panel to be able to dock the Shape Data Sets panel in the upper-left corner.
4 Select the Communication Server shape	
In the Shape Data Sets window, click **Apply**	
5 In the Shape Data panel, scroll to the bottom of the list	The new custom properties, Installation Date and Storage, have been added at the bottom of the list.
6 Click the Installation Date box	To make the property active. A small button appears on the right side.
7 Click as shown	 To display a calendar.
Select a date from the calendar	
8 In the Storage box, enter **39**	You'll add the custom properties to the other two server shapes.
9 Ctrl+click the Server 1 Apple Talk and Server 2 IPX Only shapes	Click the Server 1 Apple Talk shape; then press Ctrl and click the Server 2 IPX Only shape.
In the Shape Data Sets window, click **Apply**	
10 Enter values for the Storage and Installation Date properties for the other two servers	Enter different values. (You'll need to select each of the server shapes individually.)
11 Close the Shape Data Sets and Shape Data panels	
12 Update the drawing	

Topic C: Reporting

Explanation

You can include the data from custom properties and statistical data in a drawing report. You can also modify a report, sort data, format report shapes, and update a report with modified data.

The Report Definition Wizard

To create a report, you use the Report Definition Wizard, which guides you through the steps for creating a report. As you create a report, you define the information that will be included and the layout for displaying and sorting the data.

TIP Highlight all shapes if running reports for shapes selected.

To run the Report Definition Wizard:

1 Choose Data, Reports to open the Reports dialog box, shown in Exhibit 7-9.
2 Click New to open the Report Definition Wizard, shown in Exhibit 7-10.
3 Make the selections you want on each page of the wizard, and click Next to continue to the next page.
4 When you are finished, click Finish to close the wizard.

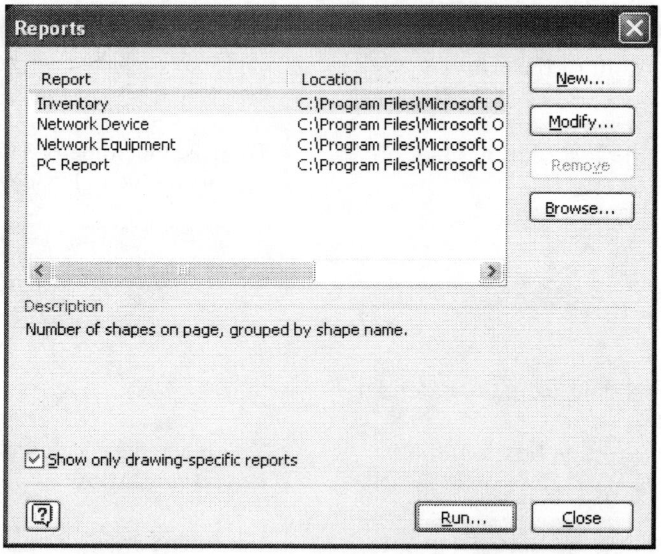

Exhibit 7-9: The Reports dialog box

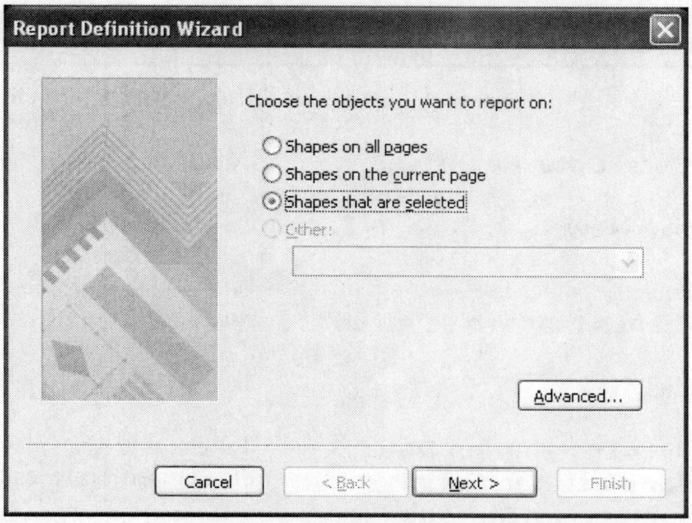

Exhibit 7-10: The first page of the Reports Definition Wizard

Do it!

C-1: Creating a report

Here's how	Here's why
1 Select all three server shapes	Hold down Ctrl and click each shape.
2 Choose **Data**, **Reports...**	To open the Reports dialog box.
3 Click **New**	To start the Report Definition Wizard.
Select **Shapes that are selected**	To run a report that includes all shapes on the page.
Click **Next**	To move to the next page of the wizard.
4 Check **Installation Date**, **Manufacturer**, **Serial Number**, and **Storage**	To select the data to be included in the report. (The properties are in alphabetical order.)
Click **Next**	
5 Under Report Title, enter **Server storage capacity**	To specify a title for the report.
6 Click **Sort...**	You'll define sorting options for the report.
Under Column order, select **Storage**	
Click **Move Up** three times	To move the Storage column to the top of the list. The columns will be arranged from left to right in the order of the list.
7 Under Row order, from the first Sort by list, select **Storage**	To sort the rows by storage capacity in ascending order.
Click **OK**	To return to the wizard.
8 Click **Next**	You'll specify where the report will be saved.
Under Name, enter **Server storage**	
Verify that "Save in this drawing" is selected	To save the report as part of the drawing.
9 Click **Finish**	To complete the report definition and return to the Reports dialog box.

Running reports

Explanation

After you've defined a report, you run it to see the results. You can also run one of the default reports included with Visio to see the data. To run a report:

1. If necessary, open the Reports dialog box. (Choose Data, Reports.)
2. In the list, select the report you want to run.
3. Click Run to open the Run Report dialog box, shown in Exhibit 7-11.
4. From the list, select the format you want for the report. In order to add the report as a Visio shape within a Visio drawing, you must have Microsoft Excel installed on your computer.
5. Select whether you want to create a copy of the report or specify a link to the report.
6. Click OK.

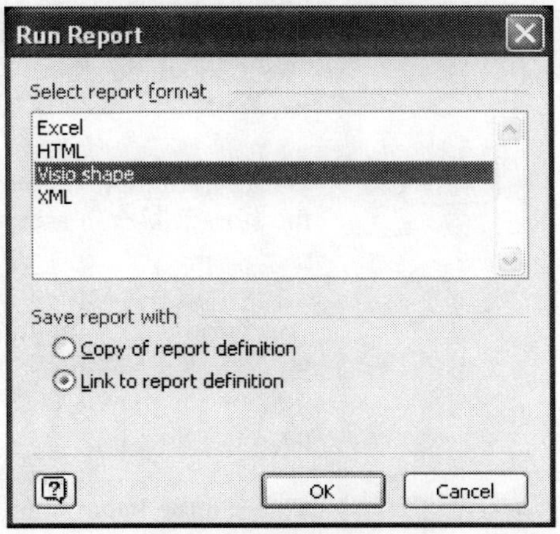

Exhibit 7-11: The Run Report dialog box

Do it!

C-2: Running a report

Here's how	Here's why
1 In the Reports dialog box, select **Server storage**	If necessary.
Click **Run**	To open the Run Report dialog box.
2 Select **Visio shape**	To insert the report as a Visio shape.
Verify that "Link to report definition" is selected	To maintain a link between the report and the output shape.
3 Click **OK**	To close the Report dialog box and run the report.
Observe the drawing page	The Visio table shape is placed on the drawing page.
4 Press and hold CTRL + SHIFT and click the table	To zoom in on it. The information is sorted by the storage size in ascending order.
	The report overlaps some of the shapes, so you'll move it to the top of the drawing. Before you do, you'll remove the logo and drawing title that are visible via the TitleBlock background page.
5 Choose **File**, **Page Setup...**	To open the Page Setup dialog box.
6 Activate the Page Properties tab	
From the Background list, select **None**	To remove the TitleBlock background page.
7 Click **OK**	To close the dialog box. Now the logo and page title are no longer visible.
8 Position the Visio Table Report shape at the top of the page	So that it doesn't overlap any shapes.
9 Update the drawing	

Report updates

Explanation

You might need to update a report for a variety of reasons, such as changes in property values or the addition of new shapes to a drawing. The process for updating a report will depend on the modifications made. If you've added new shapes or a new property, you'll need to modify the report before running it again.

Linked reports

If you link a report to a shape containing property data, then when you run the report, you can update any property data that has changed. To do so, right-click the report and choose Update Report.

Do it!

C-3: Updating a report

Here's how	Here's why
1 Select the Server 2 IPX Only shape and open the Shape Data panel	Right-click the shape and choose Properties.
2 Change the storage value to **45**	
Close the Shape Data window	You'll now update the report to reflect the change.
3 Select the Visio Table Report shape	
4 Ctrl+click the three Server shapes	To add them to the selection. You should have the Visio Table Report shape and the three Server shapes selected.
5 Right-click the Visio Table Report shape and choose **Update Report…**	The Update Report dialog box appears.
6 In the Report list, verify that Server storage is selected	
7 Click **Run…**	The report is updated to reflect the change.
8 Update the drawing	

Modifying a Visio Table Report shape

Explanation

Sometimes you might want to format a Visio Table Report shape with colors other than the default light blue and yellow shading in the cells. A Visio Table Report shape is actually an embedded Excel worksheet. You can format it by double-clicking the shape. When you do, the Excel chart becomes active and Visio changes to show basic Excel menu options, as shown in Exhibit 7-12. To format a cell, you must first select it by clicking it. If you want to apply formatting to multiple cells, press and hold Shift while selecting each cell and then apply the desired formatting. When you are finished, press Esc to return to Visio menus.

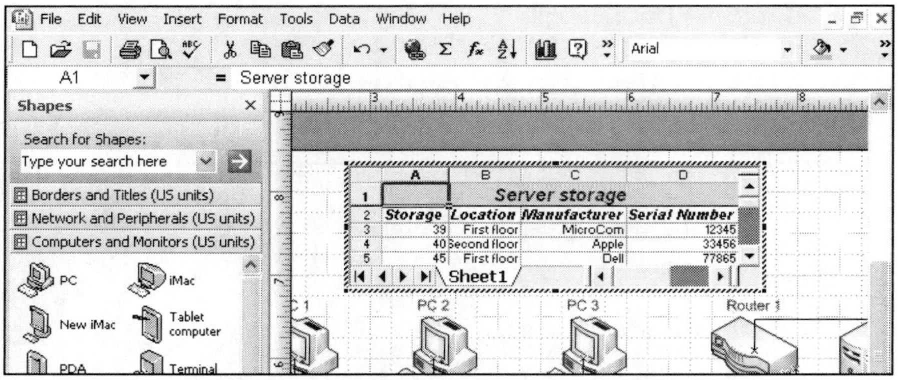

Exhibit 7-12: An embedded Excel worksheet

Do it!

C-4: Formatting a Visio Table Report shape

Here's how	Here's why
1 Double-click the Visio Table Report shape	To switch to the Excel worksheet.
2 Select the title cell	
3 On the Standard toolbar, expand the Fill Color list and select a light green color	To change the color of the cell.
4 Press ESC	To revert to the Visio Table Report shape.
Update and close the drawing	

Unit summary: Introduction to advanced features

Topic A In this topic, you learned how to use **guides** to align and glue shapes. You also learned how to add connection points to a shape and toggle **Snap & Glue** options.

Topic B In this topic, you learned how to add **custom properties** to shapes. You also learned how to create and apply **custom property sets**.

Topic C In this topic, you learned how to create and run **reports** on the custom properties of shapes. You also learned how to format a report object and update a report.

Independent practice activity

In this activity, you'll add guides to a Visio file and add and connect shapes. You'll also add custom property data to shapes and create a custom property set.

1. Open WAN practice (from the current unit folder). Save the file as **My WAN practice**.
2. Add a vertical guide at the 8" mark on the horizontal ruler, and add two horizontal guides at the 3" and 6" marks on the vertical ruler.
3. Drag a Server shape, Router shape, Printer shape, and three Desktop PC shapes to the drawing page, and position them as shown in Exhibit 7-13.
4. Move the text blocks for the PC shapes and the Router shape above the shapes. Move the Server shape text to the right side of the shape.
5. Connect the right side and the top of the Server shape to the corresponding sides of the Printer and Router shapes.
6. Increase the size of the Router shape and add two connection points to the bottom of it. Adjust the connection between the Server and Router shapes, if necessary.
7. Connect the three PC shapes to the Router shape.
8. Drag the horizontal guide at the 6" mark on the vertical ruler down to 5".
9. Add custom property data to each of the PC shapes as follows:
   - Manufacturer: **Dell**
   - Location: **Seattle**
   - Department: **Support**
10. Create a custom property set called **Install data**. (*Hint:* In the Shape Data dialog box, click Define.)
11. Add a different installation date for each PC shape. (*Hint:* From the shape's shortcut menu, choose Properties.)
12. Run a report that displays the <Master Name> and Installation data for the three PC shapes. Sort the report by installation date in ascending order. (*Hint:* Modify the existing Inventory report.)
13. Update and close the drawing.
14. Close Visio.

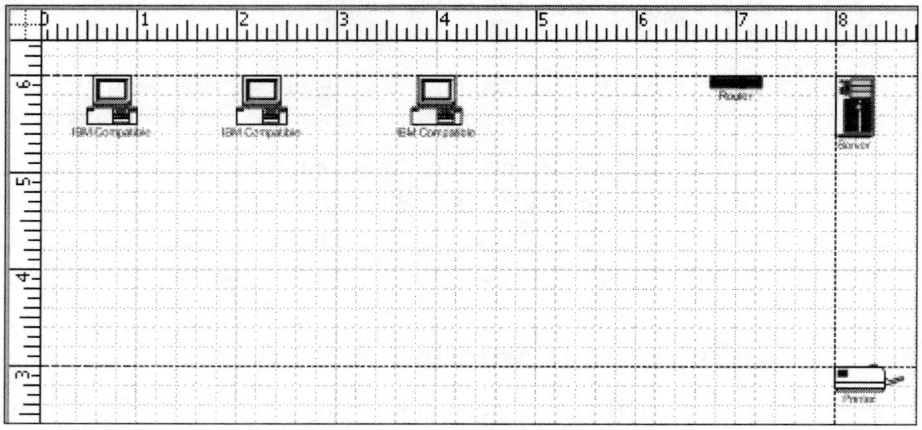

Exhibit 7-13: The My WAN network practice file after Step 3 of the independent practice activity

Review questions

1 How do you add a guide?

2 After shapes have been glued to a guide, what happens when the guide is moved?

3 How do you add connection points to a shape?

4 What is a custom property?

5 What is the procedure for defining custom properties for a shape?

6 What is the Report Definition Wizard?

Course summary

This summary contains information to help you bring the course to a successful conclusion. Using this information, you will be able to:

A Use the summary text to reinforce what you've learned in class.

B Determine the next courses in this series (if any), as well as any other resources that might help you continue to learn about Visio Professional 2007.

Topic A: Course summary

Use the following summary text to reinforce what you've learned in class.

Unit summaries

Unit 1

In this unit, you learned how to start Visio and create a file. You examined the Visio work environment and learned how to use Visio Help. You also learned how to open a Visio file and navigate in a drawing. Then, you learned how to open **stencils**. You also learned how to move stencils in the Shapes window and **float** stencils in the drawing area. Then, you learned about **selecting**, **moving**, **scaling**, and **resizing** objects. Finally, you learned how to save and close a file and close Visio.

Unit 2

In this unit, you learned how to use the **drawing tools** to create and reshape objects. Then, you learned how to use the Freeform tool, create **compound lines**, and duplicate objects. Finally, you learned how to **align**, **distribute**, **group**, and **rotate** objects.

Unit 3

In this unit, you learned how to plan a basic **flowchart**. Then, you learned how to place and link shapes by using AutoConnect. You also learned how to add text and add **text blocks** to shapes. Finally, you learned how to create and modify an **organization chart**.

Unit 4

In this unit, you learned how to format text by using color and styles. You also learned how to increase the size of text and how to use the **Text dialog box** to apply various formats simultaneously. Then, you learned how to format text blocks, change their margins, apply a background color, align and indent text, set line spacing, and add bullets. You also learned how to format shapes and lines by adding **drop shadows** and **fill patterns**. You learned how to use the Format Painter to copy formatting. Finally, you learned how to change **line patterns** and use the **Line dialog box** to simultaneously apply multiple formats.

Unit 5

In this unit, you learned how to define **file properties**, **page size**, and **printer settings** for a file. Next, you learned how to create, edit, and apply **background pages**. You also learned how to add **fields** and **graphics** to background pages, and how to create and use **detail pages**. You learned how to add a **hyperlink** and link multiple files. You also learned how to create a **link** to a file of another type. Finally, you learned how to use Print Preview and print a diagram.

Unit 6

In this unit, you learned how to use **network topology shapes** to create a basic **network diagram**. You learned how to move **control handles** to create different connection points and move text blocks connected to shapes. Then, you learned how to create a **rack diagram**. Finally, you learned how to create a **brainstorming diagram** and how to import data into and export data from a brainstorming diagram.

Unit 7

In this unit, you learned how to use **guides** to align and glue shapes. You also learned how to add new **connection points** to a shape and how to use the **Snap & Glue** features. Next, you learned how to add **custom properties** to shapes and how to create and apply **custom property sets.** You learned how to create and run **reports** on the custom properties of shapes. Finally, you learned how to format a report object and update a report.

Topic B: Continued learning after class

It is impossible to learn to use any software effectively in a single day. To get the most out of this class, you should begin working with Microsoft Visio Professional 2007 to perform real tasks as soon as possible. We also offer resources for continued learning.

Next courses in this series

This is the first course in this series. The next course in this series is:

- *Visio Professional 2007: Advanced*

Other resources

For more information, visit www.axzopress.com.

Visio Professional 2007: Basic

Quick reference

Button	Shortcut keys	Function
	CTRL + O	Opens the Open dialog box.
	CTRL + 1	Activates the Pointer tool, used to select objects on the drawing page.
	CTRL + Z	Undoes the last action.
	CTRL + ↓	Redoes the last action.
	CTRL + S	Saves a file.
	CTRL + 8	Activates the Rectangle tool.
	CTRL + 9	Activates the Ellipse tool.
	CTRL + 6	Activates the Line tool.
	CTRL + 7	Activates the Arc tool.
	CTRL + 5	Activates the Freeform tool.
	CTRL + 4	Activates the Pencil tool, used to draw lines and arcs.
		Activates the Rotate tool.
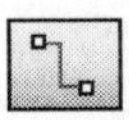	CTRL + 3	Activates the Connector tool.
		Connects selected shapes.
	CTRL + 2	Activates the Text tool.

Button	Shortcut keys	Function
		Increases the font size of selected text.
		Decreases the font size of selected text.
		Applies a color to selected text.
	CTRL + B	Makes selected text bold.
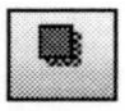		Applies a drop shadow to the selected shape.
		Applies a fill color to the selected shape.
		Applies a fill pattern to the selected shape.
		Copies the formatting from one object to another object.
		Applies a color to the selected line.
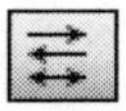		Applies an end style to a line.
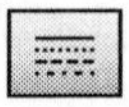		Applies a line pattern.
		Applies a line width.
		Displays a Print Preview of the drawing.
		Arranges all subtopics automatically.
		Adds a main topic to the drawing.
		Adds multiple subtopics to a topic.
		Adds a peer topic.
		Adds a subtopic to a topic.
		Centers shapes on the drawing page.
		Aligns shapes with the top of the drawing page.

Button	Shortcut keys	Function
		Aligns shapes with the bottom of the drawing page.
		Aligns shapes.
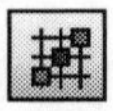		Distributes the selected shapes uniformly.
		Configures the layout of shapes on the drawing page.
		Moves a shape in front of other shapes.
		Sends a shape behind other shapes.
		Creates a bulleted list of items.
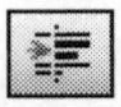		Increases the indent setting.
		Decreases the indent setting.
		Increases space between paragraphs.
		Decreases space between paragraphs.
	CTRL + X	Cuts the selected text or shape.
	CTRL + C	Creates a copy of the selected text or shape.
	CTRL + V	Pastes the last object(s) you cut or copied.
	DELETE	Deletes the selected text or shape.
		Creates rounded corners for a shape.
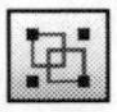		Groups a set of shapes.
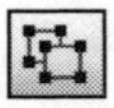		Ungroups the shapes in a group.
		Applies transparency settings.
		Rotates an object horizontally.

Button	Shortcut keys	Function
		Rotates an object vertically.
		Rotates an object to the left.
		Rotates an object to the right.
		Rotates text.
		Opens the Diagram gallery in a new window.
		Opens the Drawing Explorer window.
	CTRL + F	Searches in a shape or text.
	F5	Sets the drawing-page size to full screen.
	CTRL + K	Adds a hyperlink to a shape or text.
	CTRL + P	Prints a drawing.
		Magnifies a drawing page.
		Displays a Shape stencil.
	F1	Opens Visio Help.
	CTRL + D	Duplicates the selected shape.
	CTRL + F1	Opens the task pane.
	F3	Opens the Fill dialog box.
	F6	Browses through different stencils opened in the Shapes pane.
	F7	Activates the spelling checker.

Glossary

Background page
The type of Visio page you use to display elements—such as page numbers and borders—that you want to repeat on multiple pages in a drawing.

Bitmap
An image composed of dots, created with pixels.

Brainstorming
A problem-solving technique in which people try to generate a wide variety of ideas or solutions (without initially judging their suitability).

Brainstorming diagrams
Diagrams used to develop ideas, solve logical problems, and show relationships between various topics.

Center of rotation
The point that you rotate objects around, using rotate handles.

Compound line
A line that consists of multiple line segments.

Connection points
Small blue x's that appear along the sides of a shape. Connection points provide a fast way to connect the shapes in a diagram.

Control handles
Components that appear on a shape when it is selected and that are used to modify the shape.

Custom properties
Data fields that store information about shapes. You define these data fields by using the Custom Properties dialog box.

Distribute Shapes
A tool that is used to space all selected objects an equal distance from either their centers or their edges.

Docked
The status of a stencil or toolbar that remains in a fixed location.

Eccentricity handles
Controls that appear at the ends of a dotted line that runs through a round control handle. Eccentricity handles are used to refine the curvature of a line or arc.

Fields
Placeholders that can contain details about a drawing file, such as its file name and location.

File properties
Information about a file, such as its location, creation date, author, and subject.

Fill pattern
A color or pattern added to the background of a shape.

Floating
The state of a stencil or toolbar when you can move it anywhere in the work area and resize it as needed.

Footer
Text that appears at the bottom of each page. Headers and footers are placed on background pages.

Foreground pages
The type of Visio page on which you create drawings.

Format Painter tool
A tool used to copy formatting from one shape to another.

Formatting
The process of changing the appearance of elements, such as by changing colors, adding shadows, changing line properties, and changing the font and size of text.

Gesture recognition
The feature by which the Freeform tool creates exactly what you draw as you move the mouse pointer, similar to the way you draw with a pencil and paper.

Gluing
Securing shapes together so that when one of them is moved, the connections remain intact.

Grid
A series of horizontal and vertical lines, similar to graph paper, in the drawing area. Grids can help you place shapes more accurately.

Grouping
Holding multiple objects together so that they act as one.

Guides
Nonprinting lines that divide a drawing page into sections to help you accurately place shapes and objects.

Header

Text that appears at the top of each page. Headers and footers are placed on background pages.

Hyperlinks

Items used to connect a shape or page to a drawing, a document, an Internet address, or a file.

Layout

A setting that defines the way in which shapes are arranged.

Master shapes

The basic building blocks of any Visio diagram or drawing.

Object

Another term for "shape."

Open shape

A one-dimensional shape that has a begin point (a green box with an "x") and an endpoint (a green box with a "+"). Lines, arcs, and curved lines are examples of open shapes.

Organization chart

A diagram used to show superior-subordinate relationships, reporting hierarchies, and inter-department links within an organization.

Page orientation

A setting that defines whether a page will print in portrait orientation (8.5"×11") or landscape orientation (11"×8.5").

Page tabs

Controls that appear at the bottom of the drawing area and that you can use to navigate in a drawing with multiple pages.

Panning

Moving the page freely in any direction, without using the scrollbars.

Pixel

The smallest unit of display of a color on a monitor.

Property set

A collection of properties.

Rack diagram

A diagram used to design and document a rack system.

Rack system

A collection of various hardware devices—such as patch panels, routers, and power supplies—used in a computer network system.

Reference shape

The first object you select in a selection net. The thick pink border identifies it as the first shape selected in the group.

Resizing

Changing a shape's height and/or width.

Resolution

The level of detail provided by a monitor or in an image or drawing. On screen, resolution is defined by the number of pixels per square inch. The more pixels per inch an image has, the greater its resolution.

Scaling

Changing the height and width of a shape while maintaining the height-to-width proportions.

ScreenTip

Information that appears when you point to a button on a toolbar or a shape on a stencil.

Selection box

A box that appears around an object when it is selected.

Selection handles

Eight solid-colored squares that appear on the selection box. You can resize an object by dragging a selection handle.

Selection marquee

A temporary boundary created by dragging the pointer around multiple objects. When you release the mouse button, a selection box appears around all of the objects, and all of the objects are selected.

Shapes window

A window that displays the stencils associated with the selected template.

Snap

A feature that improves the accuracy of placing objects and shapes by making them align with the grid lines and rulers.

Stencil

A collection of shapes that are related to a drawing type or template. Stencils have the file-name extension .vss.

Template

A file that provides a starting point for a drawing; the template contains the basic elements needed to create an illustration. Templates have the file-name extension .vst.

Text block

(1) A container for text. (2) A shape component that is used to label or define a shape.

Text style

A set of predefined formats that you can apply by selecting the set from the Text Style list.

Topology shapes

Shapes that represent common configurations, such as ring and star topologies, used in creating a network structure. These shapes provide connection points for the device shapes that are arranged according to the layout of the network.

Vector-based illustrations

Drawings composed of mathematically computed lines. Unlike bitmap images, vector-based images are not resolution-dependent.

Vertex point

A line component that is added where a line changes direction, anchoring one segment and beginning another segment in any direction.

Work area

The window where you create drawings in Visio. The work area is divided into two main sections: the Shapes window and the drawing page.

XML

A widely accepted standard for transferring data across applications and platforms.

Index

N

O

P

R

S

T

V

W

X

Z